ISLAMIC ART AND LITERATURE

Islamic Art and Literature

Oleg Grabar
Cynthia Robinson
EDITORS

Markus Wiener Publishers
Princeton

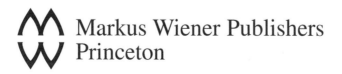

Cover illustration: "Young Portuguese," 1634, Riżā ʿAbbāsī, Gift of Robert H. Tannahill in memory of Dr. Wilhelm R. Valentiner. Photograph courtesy of the Detroit Institute of Arts.

Reprinted from *Princeton Papers: Interdisciplinary Journal of Middle Eastern Studies,* Volume VIII.

For information write to: Markus Wiener Publishers
231 Nassau Street, Princeton, NJ 08542

Book Design: Cheryl Mirkin, CMF Graphic Design
Cover Design: Maria Madonna Davidoff

Library of Congress Cataloging-in-Publication Data

Islamic art and Arabic literature: textuality and visuality in the Islamic world/
Oleg Grabar and Cynthia Robinson, editors.
Includes bibliographical references.
ISBN 1-55876-232-9 (alk. paper)
ISBN 1-55876-233-7 (pbk.)
1. Arts, Islamic. 2. Art and literature—Islamic countries.
I. Grabar, Oleg. II. Robinson, Cynthia.
NX688.A5 I84 2000
700'.917'671—dc21 00-047721

Markus Wiener Publishers books are printed in the United States of America on acid-free paper, and meet the guidelines for permanence and durability of the committee on production guidelines for book longevity of the council on library resources.

Dedicated to the
memory of

Charles Issawi

Contents

Acknowledgments

Thanks to the British Library; the Detroit Institute of Arts; the Metropolitan Museum of Art; the Department of Rare Books and Special Collections, Princeton University Library; the Topkapı Palace Museum; and the Vatican Library for permission to reproduce images from their collections.

Prologue

Over the last decade or so, scholarship in Islamic visual culture has witnessed an increasing awareness of (and, possibly, competence in handling) written sources in its consideration of the relationships between the textual and visual worlds in the Medieval and early modern periods. Likewise, scholars of Arabic and Persian literature have become aware of the comparative and interpretive possibilities contained in visual sources. The next few years should see the publication of monographs, some by contributors to this volume, which will perhaps make this field of comparative investigation solidly present in the larger context of Middle East Studies; nevertheless, it would seem fair to say that, as far as existing and available literature is concerned, separation between visual and textual fields of inquiry remains prevalent. With the six essays in this volume, we hope to address—but hardly to resolve—a variety of issues posed by comparative text-and-image studies in the broadly defined context of the Islamic world. Three essays have been written by art historians and three by specialists in Arabic and Persian literature; the result is a collaborative model which is envisioned largely as a springboard for other such efforts within the field of Islamic studies. In the fields of "Western" Medieval and early modern cultures, a significant body of literature already exists in which visual and textual interactions are probed against the backdrop of a larger interest in questions of aural, textual, visual, and general cultural "literacy" which has now been several decades in the making;[1] in contrast, such comparative and broadly based studies on material from the Islamic world (as well as the more specific and detailed studies of *minutiae*, of individual artifacts, which take into account all of the cultural dimensions of those artifacts, necessary for larger pictures to come clearly into focus) are almost completely lacking. Before comparisons of cultural literacy—involving balanced considerations of both text and image—and its expressions in Arabic- and Persian-speaking contexts with the more fully-studied Latinate and Romance-speaking worlds may be undertaken, much groundwork remains to be done on the Islamic side of things. While this volume cannot hope to compensate for that imbalance, it can perhaps spark interest or debate on these issues among Islamicists, which will eventually lead to further research. It is hoped as well that our contributions might prove of interest to specialists in "western" cultures of the Medieval and early modern periods. Dialogue based on specifics rather than generalities between these two traditionally separate fields of study is needed, amid today's academic and larger cultural complexities, as never before; Islamicists must work to provide a basis for these comparative forays both as broad and as nuanced as those which exist for the study of western European cultures.

Both of the essays which comprise Section One address texts which, while unillustrated, engage the listener's or reader's powers of visualization in very direct ways; through better understanding of these processes of linguistically-induced "mental vision," we may gain new insights into the ways in which word and image in illustrated texts make use of, react to, or go against the grain of, these programs of "textual images." Michael Cooperson, in a consideration of classical Arabic biographies, points out that, although these texts are never illustrated, many biographers claim to provide the reader, through the evocative powers of language, with a powerful (indeed, almost physically "present") mental image of their subjects, a claim supported by the reactions of readers who declare that, as a result of the text's powers of description, they were able to visualize, or to imagine, these subjects almost as though they stood before them. Julie Scott Meisami turns to a relationship with a longer scholarly history—that of the building both described and, in a sense, created and imagined in panegyric poems about architecture, dedicated to a ruler and performed before an assembled public. Meisami specifically contrasts the *quṣūriyyāt*'s[2] generalities with the *mathnavī*,[3] focusing particularly on the "realness" of the imaginary places evoked by the latter through a surprisingly specific architectural and descriptive vocabulary, leading to provocative questions concerning these texts' possible influence on viewers' "perceptions" and interpretations of the architectural spaces described therein.[4] Her approach also cautions against the inappropriate application of texts to visual (or architectural) contexts where no such juxtaposition is culturally warranted.

Section Two is composed of two essays which re-examine specific instances and precise contexts in which texts and images clearly intended to form part of one cultural product have been studied separately; the processes and evocations of mental visualization probed in Section One might be kept in mind as cases of words and their accompanying illustrations are considered. Although the visual and textual components of these products may, and probably did, function independently, these functions would always reach their conclusions in the form of audience reception, an audience whose members would be, even as they experienced the textual element, conscious of the presence and meanings of the visual, and vice versa. Jerome W. Clinton revisits the traditionally accepted distinction between illustration and painting in Persian miniatures through a consideration of Ferdowsi's use of linguistic metaphor to evoke images of events narrated or described in the mind of the reader. He then addresses the possible mediating function exercised by these metaphors between written text and image, and their potential to inform a reader's or listener's experience of a text. The only illustrated Arabic manuscript to have survived from almost nine centuries of Arabic-speaking and Muslim presence in the Iberian peninsula is the subject of Cynthia Robinson's contribution. Robinson's essay brings the text and images of the *Ḥadīth Bayāḍ wa Riyāḍ* (Vat. Ar. Ris. 368) back together in order to place them into the context of oral performance and instruction in "courtly" behaviour. She also sketches paths for further investigation of this text's importance by focusing on its place in a Mediterranean context which also includes "courtly" literature and culture from Latinate-Romance spheres.

Both contributors to Section Three expand the scope of investigation beyond interactions between word and image to include the object of which these two elements form part. David Roxburgh's essay, through a consideration of non-narrative illuminations within the context of the overall and highly conscious structuring of page, encourages us to re-examine our privileging of text-image relationships with narrative content over considerations of the book as a whole. Roxburgh focuses on the book as an integral cultural product which exists and functions at levels and in manners independent of those elucidated by the narrative-image-text relationships more familiar to scholarship. Sussan Babaie's paper examines (and reconsiders traditional approaches to) narrative possibilities to be found in the "reading" of Persian single-sheet paintings, whose earliest production is to be assigned to the sixteenth century. She argues that meaning in such works of art operates in a mental world of shared literary and pictorial allusions both performative and newly democratized; her research also suggests intriguing parallels between Safavid visual and literary culture and the newly self-conscious importance of the image and its author in the context of the (European) "Renaissance."

Again, we hope that this collection of essays will encourage further inquiry along the paths we have taken, or along others parallel to them. We would desire that these and future close readings of word and image from within the context of the Islamic world might provide the basis for a broader and deeper understanding of that world's Medieval and early modern culture[s] so that, eventually, the differences between the "Islamic" world's use and understanding of words and pictures and those which prevailed in the "West" might be more clearly understood, perhaps nuanced, or even revealed to be not differences, but similarities.

Cynthia Robinson
Institute for Advanced Study
Princeton, New Jersey

Notes

1. Among the many publications which might be cited in this context are those by Brian Stock, fundamental to the establishment of the theoretical framework within which text-image studies on "western" medieval material have been carried out; Brian Stock, *The implications of literacy: written language and models of interpretation in the eleventh and twelfth centuries* (Princeton, N.J.: Princeton University Press, 1983) and, more recently, *Augustine the reader: meditation, self-knowledge, and the ethics of interpretation* (Cambridge, Mass.: Harvard University Press, 1996). Also instrumental, and published at approximately the same moment as Stock's seminal work on literacy, were Jesse M. Gellrich's *The Idea of the Book in the Middle Ages: language theory, mythology, and fiction* (Ithaca, NY: Cornell University Press, 1985), and Stephen G. Nichols' *Romanesque signs: early medieval narrative and iconography* (New Haven: Yale University Press, 1983); Nichols has recently turned his attention to the "whole book" as a physical as well as an intellectual artifact (*The Whole Book: cultural perspectives on the medieval miscellany*, eds., Stephen G. Nichols and Siegfried Wenzel [Ann Arbor: University of Michigan Press, 1996]), mapping out a direction of inquiry which, as Roxburgh points out in his contribution to this volume, is a productive one for the consideration of "Islamic" material as well. Roxburgh's forthcoming monograph will address "whole book" issues in the context of Persian albums; in the essay in the present volume, he also remarks that the margins and the wider world of the page (cf. Michael Camille's seminal *Image on the Edge: the margins of medieval art* [Cambridge, Mass.: Harvard University Press, 1992]) represent all but *terra incognita*, and certainly *terra un-explorata*, for students of Islamic visual culture. Likewise needed are close and contextual readings of individual illustrated works which give equal time, attention, and expertise to word and image, and which view them as an integral product rather than casual and accidental occupants of the same sheets of paper or parchment; examples, again, might be found in the work of western medievalists; see Jeffrey Hamburger's *The Rothschild Canticles: art and mysticism in Flanders and the Rhineland circa 1300* (New Haven: Yale University Press, 1990), or Camille's *Mirror in Parchment: the Luttrell Psalter and the making of medieval England* (Chicago: University of Chicago Press, 1998); in the secular spheres of culture, among many excellent studies, one might look to Sandra Hindman's *Sealed in Parchment: rereadings of knighthood in the illuminated manuscripts of Chrétien de Troyes* (Chicago: University of Chicago Press, 1994), or to the several recent considerations of the *Roman de la Rose*, salient among them being *Rethinking The Romance of the Rose:*

text, image, reception, eds., Kevin Brownlee and Sylvia Huot (Philadelphia: University of Pennsylvania Press, 1992). Key bodies of Arabic and Persian illustrated texts require such balanced study; the fact that Oleg Grabar's *The Illustrations of the Maqamat* (Chicago: University of Chicago Press, 1984), has not been followed by the sort of close readings to which the Chrétien corpus is being subjected is indicative. Potentially helpful might be such publications as the two-volume set recently edited by Keith Busby and Alison Stones *Les Manuscrits de Chrétien de Troyes* (Amsterdam and Atlanta, GA: Rodopi, 1993), in which an entire corpus of related texts and images, along with invaluable bibliography, is made available for convenient study. The approach would fruitfully be applied to the *Maqāmāt* and the *Shahnameh* bodies of texts, for example; CD-Rom editions, which greatly facilitate such research as is needed, and such as those which are available for most large bodies of "western" Medieval texts, are also to be desired; likewise, more facsimiles along the lines of Sheila S. Blair's *A Compendium of Chronicles: Rashid al-Din's illustrated history of the world* (London: Nour Foundation in association with Oxford University Press, 1995) would be immensely useful. Grabar and Blair's *Epic Images and Contemporary History: the illustrations of the great Mongol Shahnama* (Chicago: University of Chicago Press, 1980), indeed, represents a valuable rarity; the most recent work to address the *Maqāmāt* illustrations (Shirley Guthrie, *Arab social life in the Middle Ages: an illustrated study* [London: Saqi Books, 1995]) barely takes the texts into consideration at all.

2. Although it appears frequently in modern criticism and scholarship, the term is not one used in the classification of poetic compositions by medieval Arabic-speaking poets or critics. The literal translation would be "poems about palaces"; medieval critics generally include such compositions in the larger category of *waṣf* or "descriptive" poetry. Such compositions are, more often than not, panegyric in purpose.

3. A Persian verse form (used for narrative) with double rhymes (similar in many ways to the heroic couplet).

4. Such connections between buildings and the texts performed in them are also examined at length for an eleventh-century Andalusī context in Cynthia Robinson, *In Praise of Song: The Making of Courtly Culture in al-Andalus and Provence, 1005–1134 A.D.* (forthcoming; Brill, 2002).

Seeing Things: Why Pictures in Texts?

OLEG GRABAR

A standard task of the historian of art, primarily of medieval art, is to explain the presence of illustrations and of ornamental devices of all sorts in the midst of texts with an independent coherence of their own and with a long tradition of philological investigation. The query is not peculiar to students of Islamic art. It is in fact from the study of Antique and Late Antique objects and Christian religious manuscripts of the Middle Ages that emerged most of the theoretical apparatus dealing with images in books. This scholarship was symbolized, for many decades, by the scholarly achievements of Kurt Weitzmann at Princeton University and, in a different way using sophisticated tools for the preservation and dissemination of information, the Index of Christian Art, also at Princeton University. A set of principles was developed about the ways in which images or illuminations reflected (or did not reflect) the texts which surrounded them. The assumption throughout was that the latter set the stage for the former, either by providing narrative or symbolic content for images or by offering spaces for ornament. The visually perceived vocabulary of forms actually used for images and ornament, on the other hand, derived from many sources and could have, and often did, a history of its own, independent of its adaptation to any one manuscript. Once adapted, however, the same motifs were copied and transformed, giving, thereby, rise to families of images and of ornaments and to a taxonomy of the corresponding vocabulary. A third component, which exists next to text and image, has only recently been acknowledged and recognized. It is the very fact of the book or album itself, that is to say the very object in which most remaining images from Muslim lands are found.[1] Two processes of investigation have been applied to the book or album. One is codicology, which explores the technical components and the make-up of the book. The other one is contextual study, which led to studies of patronage, taste, esthetic or ideological purposes, and to consideration of responses by viewers and collectors.

This methodologically sensible schema of three key components in the discussion of the art of decorating books and of putting albums together can be applied to any artistic culture, especially those with books commonly used for private or public purposes. Yet, its application to the study of Islamic art takes several unexpected turns and yields results of interest to other fields of research as well. This is so for three reasons, all of which are reflected, directly or indirectly, in the essays which follow. The first of these reasons is that the source of inspiration for the overwhelming majority of images and for decoration was secular, as opposed to Christianity or Buddhism where religious topics predominated in the arts. Persian and, to a smaller degree, Arabic prose or poetic literature rather than scriptures or comparable texts dominate as inspiration for illustration. The princely court, rather than the mosque or the *madrasa,* was the main sponsor of images and there are signs, in the thirteenth and sixteenth centuries, of the emergence of an urban art market with illustrated books or single images made, so to speak, on speculation, in the expectation of a buyer. The importance of secular sources and of a courtly patronage is that other procedures and other principles for the making and judgement of art prevailed than were at work in religious art. For instance, the automatic copying of older models, while existing no doubt, was not required by the nature and social function of the text. Innovation and variety could be praiseworthy and, even if traditions often predominated, their significance was not that of religious and pious works, where the maintenance of traditions simply reflects more or less immutable liturgical practices or symbolic references. Matters are far more complicated with secular images, for which a much wider range of possible explanations can be envisaged. Persian painting, most particularly, can easily serve, if much needed comparative work is carried out in the future, to illuminate our understanding of secular art in many other parts of the world, most specifically Europe.

The second reason for the originality of the Islamic examples of illustrated books is that there has occurred in them a fascinating osmosis or exchange between texts and images. Next to the well-known and obvious inspiration of images by texts, we encounter texts, poetical ones in particular, that evoke images. At times they may very well have been inspired by visual memories of some sort, and they can even become like pictures in the ways in which they affect the viewer or the listener; they compel mental images of settings for events and even of the events themselves. Books like anthologies have their parallel in albums with images. Without losing their original significance, texts were often reinterpreted according to new ideological, social, or individual needs, or else in order to meet a new taste. So were images, even though we are less able today to understand the different ways in which images were enjoyed over the centuries, except in the few instances where the transformation of an old image into a new one can be demonstrated. As a result of these parallel transformations, the physical character and the composition of the container for text and image, i.e., the book or album, became affected by its contents. It is, in other words, possible to posit that the relationship between text and image which operated in Islamic art was more varied and more complicated than that which obtained elsewhere. Why this was so still needs investigation, but one reason may well be that a uniquely rich combination of people, from courtly patrons to street vendors and buyers, and activities, from the manufacture of paper to fancy binding and to the use of books for social and political gifts, affected and even controlled the making and use of illustrated volumes.

And the third reason justifying the special consideration of texts and images in Islamic art is that the usual dimensions of books, restricted by the standards of manufacture used for quires and sheets of paper, determined the sizes of paintings. As a result, even when, in the sixteenth century (and probably already earlier), independent paintings appeared as a genre, they preserved the size of miniatures and the formal or esthetic values of book illustrations. At least so it seems at first glance. Matters are in reality more complicated, because these drawings became a fascinating example of a genre in which viewers required the vehicle of the book or of a book-like album in order to feel and enjoy paintings which actually expressed different values and fulfilled different expectations from those of illustrations found in a book. It is as though the social and personal practice of books imposed an automatic and expected format for the perception of images. It becomes reasonable, then, to seek in the infinite details of the latter the meanings which, in other artistic traditions like the western European one, often appeared magnified into huge canvases.

Thus it is that the very nature of the Persian or Arabic, medieval or pre-modern, images in literature and in art leads to questions and problems which are of significance in two different ways. One is that it can contribute to our understanding of the cultures of the Islamic world itself which created and presumably enjoyed, or at the very least, appreciated these paintings. The other one enhances our understanding of the art of representation itself, the infinitely complex ways in which images were made to interact with texts, whether present or implied, or with an audience of readers and viewers. The essays of this volume are but a few illustrations of the wealth of material works of Islamic art which can help historians of all arts as well as all those who try to understand the ways of Islamic culture over the centuries. The acknowledgment of differences can be illuminating for all those who became conscious of them.

Oleg Grabar

Note

1. I am not taking into consideration mural paintings which have been very poorly preserved, although often referred to in written sources. At times connected with the art of book illustration, the art of mural painting forms, at this stage of research and theoretical thinking, a different topic altogether.

I.

IMAGINING SPACE AND THE SPACES OF IMAGINATION

Images Without Illustrations: The Visual Imagination in Classical Arabic Biography

MICHAEL COOPERSON

Les auteurs arabes anciens n'ont pas de visage. Pour des raisons religieuses, la peinture et les arts de la représentation en général avaient mauvaise presse. On ne confiait pas son corps à la toile, on ne se livrait pas au miroir des couleurs; aussi est-il rigourousement impossible d'*imaginer* les hommes d'autrefois. Certains le regrettent aujourd'hui et s'efforcent, d'après de rares informations livresques, de tracer des portraits approximatifs. Le modèle étant absent, la représentation est, bien sûr, aléatoire.

—Abdelfattah Kilito, *L'Auteur et ses doubles*, 59.

In the genealogy room, the yearning for kinship is audible. Dozens of people sit hunched over whirring microfilm viewers.

The 1870 census is the first in which African Americans are listed by name, not number....

Three hours later, the scrawled penmanship of one census taker changes into the elegant script of another, and Lavinia Emanuel scrolls into view.

My great-great-great-grandmother was about 40 years old in 1870, the census recorded, and she could read and write.

I envy the census taker. I want to talk to Lavinia too, to ask questions about her life, about plantation life and freedom, about her mother and father, about Jerry Dial.

Through tears, as though I'll be able to feel her, I run my fingertips over the black lines on the screen.

—Lisa Richardson, "Going Back to Find Lavinia," A12.

Classical Arabic biographies, whether individual or collective, lack illustrations.[1] It is therefore surprising to find references to the notion that readers and listeners were supposed to visualize the persons they were reading or hearing about. According to the fourth/tenth-century geographer and historian al-Masʿūdī, the caliph al-Qāhir one day summoned Muḥammad b. ʿAlī, a courtier well-versed in history, and demanded to hear biographies of the Abbasid caliphs. The courtier dutifully described the "character and disposition" of all the dynasts from al-Manṣūr down to al-Mutawakkil. At the end of the recitation, al-Qāhir declared: "I have heeded your words, and it is as if I have seen the people you have described, and gazed upon them as you spoke."[2] This response is striking, particularly because Muḥammad b. ʿAlī had described the policies and personalities of the Abbasids, not their physical appearance. Evidently, however, a description of "character and disposition" was supposed to produce a visual image in the caliph's mind. Centuries later, the biographer al-Subkī declared that his colleagues should possess "a good imagination" (*ḥusn al-taṣawwur*), an endowment which would enable them to reconstruct their subject's life and circumstances.[3] Although the historian need not supply a physical description of the subject, the technique by which he invokes and orders the past is, etymologically at least, visual in its essence.

In al-Ṣafadī's *Wāfī bi 'l-wafayāt*, a massive collection that represents the culmination of the classical tradition, the project of imagining the subject of biography finds fullest expression. In his introduction, al-Ṣafadī describes the effect of reading about the great personages of the past:

> The reader familiar with tales of people now dead, with the feats of those plunged into the cavern of extinction never to emerge, with the lore of those who scaled the heights of power, and with the virtues of those whom Providence has delivered

> from the stranglehold of adversity, feels that he has known such men in their own time. He seems to join them on their pillowed thrones and lean companionably with them on their cushioned couches. He gazes at their faces—some framed in hoods, others lambent under helmets—seeing in the evil ones the demonic spark, and in the good ones that virtue which places them in company of angels. He seems to share with them the best pressings of aged wine in an age where time no longer presses, and to behold them as in their battles they breathe the sweet scent of swordplay in the shadows of tall and blood-stained lances. It is as if all that company were of his own age and time; as if those who grieve him were his enemies, and those who give him pleasure, his friends.[4]

This passage invokes the Qur'ānic account of Paradise according to which the blessed will recline "on couches, looking around; you will see in their faces the glow of plenty" (83:23–24, 35; cf. 18:31, 36:56, 76:13). In the hereafter, all those who have ever lived will be present at the same time (a notion reflected also in the recurrent stories about Hadith scholars—collectors of reports about the Prophet—who, upon entering Paradise, seek out the Prophet to ask whether a particular report is authentic). Because each soul will be assigned its proper place in the Garden or the Fire, one need only look at a person to determine his "character and disposition." The blessed will exude a healthy glow, while the damned will bear the marks of their torment. Until that day comes, however, one can only imagine what it will be like, an act of visualization which biography (in al-Ṣafadī's view, at any rate) is designed to promote.

In keeping with this metaphorical understanding of vision as the perception of virtue or its opposite, al-Ṣafadī is no more forthcoming than any other biographer about the actual appearance of most of his subjects. His ideal reader is concerned with the virtues and vices of historical figures, not their physical appearance. Even so, it is impossible to imagine seeing the dead without seeing their bodies and clothing as well. The Qur'ān reports that the blessed will wear silk (22:23, 35:33, 76:12), and al-Ṣafadī himself imagines that they will also continue to wear their characteristic garb ("hoods" and "helmets"). More detailed descriptions occur in reports of dreams, the narration of which was a commonplace of biography. In posthumous visions, the blessed are often dressed in shimmering white or green. Some boast crowns, jewel-encrusted slippers and even wings, all by way of reward for their noble actions while on earth. (Rarely do the damned appear in dreams; apparently dreamers preferred to err on the side of charity in their reports.) Given such visions of the heavenly reward, the appearance and character of historical figures were not entirely insignificant in that these attributes would determine, to some undefined extent, the appearance of the resurrected dead in the afterlife.

Even on this side of the grave, the physical appearance of certain historical figures assumed particular importance in view of the necessity or desirability of emulating their conduct in every way possible. The characteristic object of emulation in this regard is of course the Prophet Muḥammad, whose habits of dress, hygiene, and grooming are thoroughly documented in the Hadith. But such accounts are not confined to the enumeration of precedent (*sunna*). Rather, certain reports were transmitted, to all appearances, for the sake of those believers who wished to have a picture of the Prophet in their minds. One such report is ascribed to Anas b. Malik, who described him as "of medium height, neither tall nor short; with a bright complexion, neither pallid nor reddish; with hair neither short and curly, nor lank."[5] This tentative account appears to have served as the basis for more positive descriptions, such as the one ascribed to the Prophet's cousin and son-in-law, ʿAlī b. Abī Ṭālib:

> [Muḥammad] was neither tall and lanky, nor short and stunted. He was of a middling height. His hair was neither short and curly, nor lank; but wavy and flowing. His face was neither thin nor plump, but rounded. His complexion was creamy white, and his eyes large and deeply black, with long lashes. He was big-boned, with wide shoulders. His body was hairless except for his chest, and his hands and feet were thick. When he walked, he would stride as if descending a slope; and when he turned to face someone, he would turn with his whole body and look at him straight on.[6]

ʿAlī's "thick description" is practically an illustration in prose, and indeed served as the basis for works in the visual arts. Strikingly, however, such works were not paintings of Muḥammad,[7] but rather calligraphic renderings of the description itself. In the Ottoman period, calligraphers framed ʿAlī's verbal portrait (*hilye*) of the Prophet amid Qurʾānic verses and decorative motifs rendered in ink, colors, and gold.[8]

Elaborate descriptions like ʿAlī's tend to defamiliarize their object: that is, to compel attention to previously unremarked detail and so create the impression that one is experiencing the object for the first time. In classical Arabic biography, some of the most detailed descriptions of persons turn up in reports by narrators who are meeting those persons for the first time, often without knowing their identity. An unusually long example is the report attributed to ʿAbd Allāh b. Masʿūd, who met the Prophet before becoming a Muslim.

> The first I knew of the Prophet was when I came to Mecca, either with some uncles of mine or with some other people from my tribe, to buy some things. We were looking for perfume, and they sent us to al-ʿAbbās b. ʿAbd al-Muṭṭalib, whom we found sitting by [the well of] Zamzam. We sat down with him, and as we were there, a man came through the Ṣafā gate. He was light-skinned with a ruddy complexion, and had curly hair falling halfway over his ears. He walked holding his head high. He had a small, hooked nose; dark eyes, flashing teeth, fine hair on his chest, stubby hands and feet, and a dense beard. He was wearing two white robes, and looked like the moon on a dark night. On his right walked a good-looking boy, adolescent or a little older, and behind them followed a woman concealed by her clothing. He made his way to the [Black] Stone and kissed it. Then the boy kissed it, and the woman; then they walked around [the Kaʿba] seven times. After that he turned to the corner, lifted his hands, and said 'God is great,' and the woman followed suit. He knelt for a time, then lifted his head, held his position for a moment, and then prostrated himself, with the woman and the boy following him.
>
> This was something new to us; we had never seen such a thing in Mecca. We turned to ʿAbbās and asked, "Is this religious

> practice [*dīn*] a new thing among you, or is it something we just didn't know about before?"
>
> He said, "Oh, of course! You wouldn't know about this!"
>
> "That's right, we don't."
>
> He said: "That's my nephew, Muḥammad b. ʿAbd Allāh, and the boy is ʿAlī son of Ibn Abī Ṭālib, and the woman is Khadīja bt. Khuwaylid, [Muḥammad's] wife; and by God, we know of no one on the face of the earth who worships God with that *dīn* except those three!"[9]

According to Ibn ʿAsākir, certain transmitters condemned this report and disputed its authenticity. Strictly speaking, it is the testimony of a pagan: only later did its narrator become a Muslim and a Companion of the Prophet. Moreover, the report's rapt attention to external detail arguably distracts from what is really important about Muḥammad, namely, his prophetic message. Even more disturbing, perhaps, was the implication that one could *see* the Prophet without *recognizing* him as such.

After the Prophet, a good many figures were also deemed worthy of emulation, or at least of antiquarian curiosity. These included Companions, imams, caliphs, and celebrated scholars and ascetics, biographies of whom often contain descriptions of their demeanor and surroundings. Minimally, we find a brief account of physical appearance. The caliph al-Maʾmūn, for example, was "light-complexioned with a yellowish cast, with large eyes and a long, fine beard streaked with grey; he was narrow in the forehead, with a mole on one cheek."[10] Other reports offer more detail about such matters as clothing and even state of mind, like the following account of a meeting with the Hadith scholar Ibn Ḥanbal:

> I entered the anteroom and there he was sitting on the dirt floor. The dye in his hair had run, and I could see the white roots of his hair. He was wearing a small and soiled *karāmīs* waist-wrapper and a coarse shirt with dirt on the shoulder and sweat-stains on the collar. I asked him a question about scrupulosity and the acquisition of merit. No sooner had I asked the question than I saw his face fall and assume a sorrowful expression, as if he

were disgusted with, and sorry for, himself, so much so that it pained me to watch him. As we were leaving, I said to someone who was with me, "Some days he seems so dissatisfied with himself."[11]

This report has the narrator flatly declare his impression of the subject. More commonly, however, narrators merely describe their subject and his or her environment, leaving their audience to draw the appropriate conclusions. "I went in to see Rābiʿa," says an eyewitness quoted in a biography of the Basran renunciant. "She was aged and ancient, eighty years old, like a tottering waterskin. In her room I saw a reed mat and a Persian clothes-stand made of cane, standing two cubits high and blocking off most of the room with its bulk. Often she had there a mat, a large jar, a jug, and a woolen mat where she slept and prayed. On the clothes-stand lay her shroud."[12] Like a miniature portrait, this description frames the subject in an architectural space that includes furniture. Beyond filling space, however, the items in Rābiʿa's house serve as emblems of her pious austerity and her awareness of mortality. Other descriptions, finally, invoke impressions a painted portrait could not, including sensations of smell and sound. A slave woman reports of the Twelver Shiite Imam ʿAlī al-Riḍā, for example, that he perfumed himself with incense of Indian sandalwood, rose-water, and musk; and that "no one could raise his voice in his house, no matter what; everyone would always speak in a low voice."[13]

Such verbal portraits are remarkably dispassionate, reporting even the grittiest details of physical appearance, dress, and material culture. Even so, they are—except sometimes in the case of the caliphs—essentially laudatory, revealing as they do the subject's piety and indifference to the trappings of the world. Only occasionally do we encounter a description that fulfills al-Ṣafadī's promise that we should "see in the evil ones the demonic spark," and even then the description tends to mockery rather than moral outrage. Among the most famous examples of such mockery in classical Arabic prose literature is Ibn Zaydūn's letter to Ibn ʿAbdūs, his rival for the hand of Wallāda. Assuming the voice of Wallāda, Ibn Zaydūn offers Ibn ʿAbdūs his impression of him:

> You stoop like one ignobly born, with bushy mustache all unshorn. You stretch your neck like an imbecile; you're crude of speech, and by nature vile. You never listen, and your replies are crude; your physique is repellent, and your visits rude. Demons whisper in your head; your breath is foul, and your virtue dead. When you speak, you stammer and stutter; or mumble and mutter; should you explain, you addle the brain; and your laughter comes straight from the gutter.[14]

Similar is al-Tawḥīdī's devastating portrait of al-Ṣāḥib b. ʿAbbād, whom he depicts as a pompous and overbearing windbag. "When he recited poetry," one passage runs, "his neck would twist, his eyes would bulge, and his shoulders would writhe; he would sway and wriggle like a man smitten by demons."[15] More vivid than these verbal portraits, if less satisfyingly historical, is al-Azdī's description of Abū al-Qāsim al-Baghdādī. Abū al-Qāsim, a long-winded parasite and drunkard, is the hero of al-Azdī's description of Buyid-period Baghdad. He is introduced in a passage of rhymed prose that combines visual detail with an assessment of character:

> He was an old man with a white beard that shone against the redness of his face, and practically dripped unwatered wine. His eyes shone like green glass and glittered as if revolving in quicksilver. He was a howling, growling, bellowing boor; a sponger, a tippler, and a man of letters wondrous strange. Refined and polite, yet carousing by night, he was fulsome in his praise and scurrilous in his abuse. He was by turns elegant, genteel, and convivial, or arrogant, lewd, and trivial; pridefully invidious, and amiably perfidious. He was a night-talker, a gambler, a pederast, and a catamite; an obnoxious, sarcastic, back-biting scandalmonger; and a tale-bearing, fault-finding, foul-mouthed, and riotously drunken gossip. He was pious and ascetical, impulsive and heretical; a blazon and a blemish; a duplicitous, hard-boiled, and hard-bitten scoundrel; a pimp and a panderer as inscrutable as a coffered scroll bolted inside a battlement. Sealed in amber and wrapped in green silk, he stank like the mud of a fish-market, and reeked like a tannery...[16]

With its rhetorical exuberance, this description abandons the sober enumeration of concrete detail in favor of the manneristic elaboration characteristic of *waṣf* or descriptive poetry. *Waṣf*, along with its cognate genres of *munāẓara* (disputation) and *al-maḥāsin wa 'l-aḍdād* (virtues and vices), relies heavily on visual imagery, but does not seek to create a portrait of a particular individual. Rather, it strives to coin striking metaphors for the appearance of some object (e.g., the rose or the narcissus) or type of person (e.g., beautiful woman or boy) already familiar to the audience.[17] In similar fashion, Abū al-Qāsim is presented as an archetype, that is, "an exemplar of the manners and morals" of the Baghdadis "and a composite image (*ṣūra*) that subsumes all they have in common."[18]

At this point, we have left the confines of biography proper and broached the genre of the *maqāma*, a genre most famously and lavishly illustrated despite its relative lack of concrete descriptions of persons.[19] Even so, it is noteworthy that al-Azdī claims to have modeled Abū al-Qāsim on a man of his acquaintance. And, despite its tendency toward mannerism, al-Azdī's *Ḥikāya* contains plentiful examples of concrete visual imagery applied to the description of persons (and a good deal else, including food, riding beasts, and furniture). A man wearing a large turban is compared to "a porter with a bundle on his head" and "a quince topped off with a soup tureen"; another man is likened to "a painting on an outhouse door" (the appearance of which, alas, is not divulged).[20] Abū al-Qāsim's doggerel depiction of a lute-player (produced, says the text, after a good look at the man) calls to mind any of the numerous portraits of musicians in classical Islamic art:

> I like him, sir, he's a worthy man,
> Who loves his plate of meat;
> He bolts his wine down by the jug,
> And favors pudding for a sweet.
> His elegant mustachios
> Curl like sparrow's wings;
> And when his dinner's tucked away,
> He takes up his lute and sings.[21]

Finally, Abū al-Qāsim's head-to-toe description of a typical Baghdadi singer is detailed enough to serve as a painter's model. According to the description, she wears a flowing transparent gown, green pantaloons tied with a silken drawstring, a headdress wrapped in four folds around a gilded cap studded with emeralds and rubies, a necklace of amber, and sandals crafted out of a thousand dinars' worth of beads. With her maids carrying her costumes and lifting her train, she enters the room and stands "like one astonished by her own silky flesh, ample girth, voluptuous legs, and jiggling rump." When she moves, she does so "like a startled gazelle, with her neck extended, as if she had been surprised by a hunter."[22]

Having glanced at some examples of verbal illustration and visual imagery in classical Arabic literature, we might conclude by asking why biography in particular never adopted pictoral illustrations (at least, not of the persons treated in the entries). In one sense, of course, the question is moot. It is impossible to make a conclusive argument about something whose absence was apparently never perceived as a lack. In another sense, however, picking up the problem from the wrong end can suggest new insights into the nature of biography on the one hand and illustration on the other. Certainly one might answer the question by citing the familiar Hadith prohibiting the depiction of living things. However, this stricture was so often violated that—even though it may apply in this particular case, most biographers being Hadith scholars of one sort or another —it cannot serve as a convincing explanation for the absence of biographical illustration.

A more persuasive argument might refer to the nature of biographical writing itself. Biography, like history, consisted of *akhbār musnada*, i.e., reports narrated by ostensible eyewitnesses and transmitted in an unbroken chain of authorities ending with the compiler. Within biographical entries, the reports—each one a scrap of testimony about a single event as experienced by the narrator and then recollected in tranquillity—would be arrayed, sometimes in a particular order but more usually not, to form a composite image of the subject. A painting of a historical figure could not fit into this notion of portraiture, since the painter could not have seen the subject. Even if the painting had been made from life, there was no protocol for authenticating and transmitting such evidence. In theory, an artist could reconstruct his subject's appearance from the verbal portrait or from other sources, as the illustrators of the *maqāmāt* must have done. In the case of biography, however, it seems that such a reconstruction was the reader's (or auditor's) job.

According to comments by several biographers, audiences were supposed to visualize the persons they encountered in books. In certain cases, however, this appears to have meant visualizing them as they would appear in the afterlife, where the blessed and the damned will gaze upon one another and perceive immediately the moral standing of their fellow souls. Given the awe-inspiring nature, not to mention the inevitability, of this event, it may have seemed unnecessary if not blasphemous to anticipate it by a crude visual approximation. Those who needed to see the dead could do so by other means, namely, evidentiary dreams, in which the recently deceased appear in all their heavenly finery and report on their fate. In other cases, the information that was most important—the subject's asceticism, poverty, or prepossessing appearance—could be effectively communicated using verbal rather than pictoral *ekphrasis*. When verbal description became exceedingly dense, as in *waṣf* poetry and in certain fictional compositions, the language itself became the focus of aesthetic delectation, while the object was relegated to a pretext.

The transformation of the descriptive text into an object of contemplation in itself is most strikingly exemplified by the *ṣifat al-Rasūl* or verbal portrait of the Prophet, which figures as the centerpiece of the Ottoman-period calligraphic panels. In effect, the viewer of the *hilye* stands before a portrait of the Prophet, suitably framed and ornamented. But the object at the center of her gaze is a block of text containing a detailed description of the Prophet's physical appearance. On the basis of this text, the beholder can construct the portrait for herself. Indeed, the text is so vivid that is is practically impossible for her to read it without seeing Muḥammad in her mind's eye. It is doubtless too much to assume that all biographical texts were supposed to work this way: far too many of them are merely cursory listings of genealogies, death dates, and books composed (though even laconic entries can stir powerful emotions under certain conditions, as Richardson's report, quoted at the head of this essay, demonstrates). Yet the metaphor of the *hilye*, in conjunction with the explicitly visual language of classical Arabic biography, provides sufficient justification to accept the biographers' invitation to reconstruct for ourselves the image of persons whose appearance is irretrievably lost—especially in cases when the biographers evidently expended a good deal of effort to preserve the memory of what their subjects looked like. If nothing else, such mental exercises may instill a more active appreciation of texts whose illustrations come ready-made.

Notes

1. The famous paintings of the Greek physician Dioscorides appear in manuscripts of his *Materia medica* but not his biographies (see C. E. Dubler, "Diyusḳuridīs," and references cited). Another ostensible exception, the seventh/thirteenth-century illustrated *Kitāb al-aghānī*, is not really an exception at all. Five of the frontispieces depict a stylized ruler, and the sixth a group of courtly women. Although the ruler has been identified with an actual thirteenth-century figure, he, like the women, does not represent any of the persons named in the biographical entries. Johnson thus concludes that "the themes of the miniatures do not relate to the subject matter of the volume in which each is found" (Johnson, *Study*, 6); though others have proposed that the themes may have been "suggested by the story that follows" (Ettinghausen, *Arab Painting*, 63).
2. Masʿūdī, *Murūj*, 5: 211–14. This and all subsequent translations are mine.
3. Subkī, *Ṭabaqāt*, 2: 22-25.
4. Ṣafadī, *Wāfī*, 1: 4.
5. Bukhārī, *Ṣaḥīḥ*, 5:29 (*kitāb al-manāqib*, *bāb* 24, Hadith 27).
6. From a *hilye* executed by Hasan Rıza Efendi (1849–1920), illustrated, described, and translated in Zakariya, *Music for the Eyes*, 15. The translation above is mine.
7. For an unusual painting of the Prophet, see Farès, "Une miniature nouvelle."
8. See Zakariya, *Music*.
9. Ibn ʿAsākir, *Taʾrīkh*, 39: 19–21.
10. Khaṭīb, *Taʾrīkh Baghdād*, 10: 182 (no. 5330).
11. Ibn al-Jawzī, *Manāqib*, 209.
12. Ibn al-Jawzī, *Ṣifat al-ṣafwa*, 4: 17.
13. Ibn Bābawayh, *ʿUyūn akhbār al-Riḍā*, 2: 179.
14. Ibn Nubāta, *Sarḥ*, 6.
15. Tawḥīdī, *Mathālib al-wazīrayn*, 73.
16. Tawḥīdī, *Risāla* [= al-Azdī, *Ḥikāya*], 47–50.

17. See further Saden, "*Waṣf*," and Heinrichs, "Rose versus Narcissus."

18. Tawḥīdī, *Risāla* [= al-Azdī, *Ḥikāya*], 42–43.

19. A *maqāma* is a composition in rhymed prose commonly featuring an eloquent beggar and a gullible narrator. See further Grabar, *Illustrations*; Guthrie, *Arab Social Life*.

20. Tawḥīdī, *Risāla* [= al-Azdī, *Ḥikāya*], 62.

21. Ibid., 68.

22. Ibid., 197–98. The full description is much longer (pp. 189–205), but most of it is manneristic rather than concretely descriptive.

Works Cited

Bukhārī, al-. *Ṣaḥīḥ*. Ed. M. T. ʿUwayḍa. 8 vols. Cairo: Lajnat Iḥyāʾ Kutub al-Sunna, 1393/1973.

Dubler, C. E. "Diyusḳuridīs." *Encyclopaedia of Islam*. New edition. Leiden: E. J. Brill, 1958–in progress. Vol. II, 349–50.

Ettinghausen, Richard. *Arab Painting*. New York: Rizzoli, 1977.

Farès, B. "Une miniature nouvelle de l'école de Bagdad datée 614 H. figurante le prophète Muhammad." *Bulletin de l'Institut d'Égypte* 28 (1947), 259–62.

Grabar, Oleg. *The Illustrations of the Maqamat*. Chicago, 1984.

Guthrie, Shirley. *Arab Social Life in the Middle Ages: An Illustrated Study*. London: Saqi, 1995.

Heinrichs, Wolfhart. "Rose versus Narcissus. Observations on an Arabic Literary Debate." In G. J. Reinink and H. L. J. Vanstiphout, eds. *Dispute Poems and Dialogues in the Ancient and Medieval Near East*. Leuven, 1991.

Ibn ʿAsākir, *Taʾrīkh madīnat Dimashq*. Ed. S. al-Shihābī and M. al-Ṭarābīshī. 47 vols. Damascus: Majmaʿ al-Lughah al-ʿArabīyah, 1981–1997.

Ibn Bābawayh al-Qummī. *ʿUyūn akhbār al-Riḍā*. Ed. Mahdī al-Ḥusaynī al-Lājavardī. Qum: Dār al-ʿIlm, 1377/1957-1958.

Ibn al-Jawzī, Abū al-Faraj. *Manāqib al-imām Aḥmad Ibn Ḥanbal*. 2nd. ed. Beirut: al-Khānjī wa-Ḥamdān, n.d.

Ibn al-Jawzī, Abū al-Faraj. *Ṣifat al-ṣafwa*. 2 vols. Hyderabad: Dāʾirat al-Maʿārif al-ʿUthmānīya, 1936-38.

Ibn Nubāta. *Sarḥ al-ʿuyūn fī sharḥ risālat Ibn Zaydūn*. Ed. Muḥammad Abū al-Faḍl Ibrāhīm. Cairo: Dār al-Fikr al-ʿArabī, 1383/1964.

Johnson, Elizabeth. "A Study of the Miniatures of an Illustrated Kitab al-Aghani: Their Relation to Contemporary Seljuk Painting and to Central Asian Traditions." Ph.D. dissertation, University of California Los Angeles, 1975.

Khaṭīb al-Baghdādī, al-. *Ta'rīkh Baghdād, aw Madīnat al-Salām*. Ed. Muṣṭafā ʿAbd al-Qādir ʿAṭā. 24 vols. Beirut: Dār al-Kutub al-ʿIlmīya, 1417/1997.

Kilito, Abdelfattah. *L'Auteur et ses doubles*. Paris: Éditions du Seuil, 1985.

Masʿūdī, al-. *Murūj al-dhahab wa-maʿādin al-jawhar*. Ed. Charles Pellat. 5 vols. Manshūrāt al-Jāmiʿa al-Lubnānīya, 1974.

Richardson, Lisa. "Going Back to Find Lavinia." *Los Angeles Times*, Sunday, January 16, 2000, A1, A12-13.

Saden, J. "*Waṣf*." In Julie Scott Meisami and Paul Starkey, eds. *Encyclopedia of Arabic Literature*. 2 vols. London: Routledge, 1998, 2: 806-807.

Ṣafadī, Khalīl b. Aybak al-. *Al-Wāfī bi 'l-wafayāt*. Ed. Helmut Ritter et al. 22 vols. to date. Istanbul: Deutsche Morgenlandische Gesellschaft, 1931-in progress (since 1962, Wiesbaden: Franz Steiner).

Subkī, Tāj al-Dīn al-. *Ṭabaqāt al-shāfiʿīya al-kubrā*. Ed. Maḥmūd al-Ṭanāḥī and ʿAbd al-Fattāḥ al-Ḥulw. 10 vols. Cairo: ʿĪsā al-Bābī al-Ḥalabī, 1964–76.

Tawḥīdī, Abū Ḥayyān al-. *Mathālib al-wazīrayn*. Ed. Ibrāhīm al-Kīlānī. Damascus: Dār al-Fikr, 1961.

Tawḥīdī, Abū Ḥayyān al-. [attr.]. *Al-Risāla al-Baghdādīya* [= Abū al-Muṭahhar al- Azdī, *Ḥikāyat Abī al-Qāsim al-Baghdādī*]. Ed. ʿAbbūd al-Shālijī. Beirut: Dār al-Kutub, 1400/1980.

Zakariya, Mohamed. *Music for the Eyes: An Introduction to Islamic and Ottoman Calligraphy*. Published in conjunction with the exhibition "Letters in Gold: Ottoman Calligraphy from the Sakıp Sabancı Collection, Istanbul." Los Angeles County Museum of Art, 1998.

Palaces and Paradises: Palace Description in Medieval Persian Poetry

JULIE SCOTT MEISAMI

The palace, or palace-complex, is a potent and visible symbol of its builder's power, wealth, and status. So, indeed, is any building, public or private: one may think—to take only one example—of Maḥmūd of Ghazna's Friday mosque in Ghaznīn, much of it built with spoils brought back from Maḥmūd's Indian campaigns (see Bombaci 1964, and cf. Grabar 1978: 65–66). In the realm of secular building, the palace holds a special place as a nexus of power which joins the human and the cosmic; and the palace-complex becomes, both for its builders and (perhaps especially) for those who praise it, a symbol of something beyond the merely material.

This is clearly seen in the Arabic palace-poems generated by the Samarran building project, especially under the Caliph al-Mutawakkil (232–47/847–61)—a project unique in its extent, its planning, and its self-containment, which was celebrated, in particular, by al-Buḥturī (d. 284/897). (On the Samarran palace-poems see Meisami 2001.) While there appears to be no equivalent, either in Arabic or in early Persian poetry, of that sustained outpouring of poems on Samarra (with the partial exception of Arabic poetry in the West, which both celebrated and elegized the palaces and gardens of al-Andalus), there are enough early Persian poetic descriptions of palaces to be of more than casual interest.

Despite its obvious value, this poetry has not yet been properly studied (cf. Grabar 1993: 100, n. 14) What follows must be viewed as a preliminary effort to explore what it offers by way of testimony both to the place of palaces in the poetic imagination and to the potential importance of poetic texts for an art historian. Here I will be concerned only with lyric poetry, and specifically with the panegyric *qaṣīda*; and my primary focus will be (for reasons which will become apparent) on the poetry composed at the Ghaznavid court in the first half of the 5th/11th century.

One can read palace descriptions as examples of poetic *ekphrasis*, laden with symbolic meaning, or as sources of evidence for a material culture whose physical remains have largely vanished. I hope that by presenting both the material and the symbolic aspects of the poems, we may be able to "see" both the palaces and what they meant. For we can no longer see the palaces themselves; palaces seldom survived the princes (or the dynasties) that built them, and fell to ruin far faster than did buildings with a religious or commemorative purpose—mosques, *madrasa*s, mausolea—which were more regularly maintained. It is with such buildings that archaeological and art-historical studies have been mainly concerned. "Islamic architectural history has been dominated by religious monuments," notes Gülru Necipoğlu, not only because few palaces have survived, but because of "the traditional view that the visual and material culture of the Muslim world was *primarily* shaped by religion." As Necipoğlu further observes, "the stereotyping of Islamic architecture... [has encouraged] the taxonomic classification of building types according to formal, chronological and geographical criteria," to the exclusion of other, more contingent factors, and the tendency has been to consider "Islamic" buildings in isolation from their human context (1993: 3, emphasis added; cf. Blair 1998: 68, who defines the "distinctive types of Islamic buildings" as "mosques, madrasas and minarets").[1]

Art-historical studies have in general relied chiefly on archaeological evidence; textual evidence plays a decidedly secondary role. Historical texts may be used for purposes of dating or as sources of descriptions, which are often quoted out of context or, in fact, incorrectly;[2] less often are they consulted for insights into (for example) the motivation behind a particular building.[3] Poetic texts are even less often utilized, despite their potential value.[4]

Let us turn now to some poetic texts, drawn chiefly from the panegyric *qaṣīda*. In panegyric, description (*vaṣf*)—of palaces, gardens, landscapes and so on—most often functions as an introduction to the larger praise-poem. Descriptions of palaces and palace-complexes (and, especially, of their gardens) both demonstrate and figure the power and magnificence of the *mamdūḥ*, the ruler or other patron who is praised. A common occasion for such descriptions is the celebration of the palace's completion; but they may also be generated by an event taking place within the palace: a feast, a wedding, or the like. The earliest surviving palace descriptions appear to date from the early Ghaznavid period, and specifically from the reign of Maḥmūd of Ghazna (338–421/998–1030).[5] Both Maḥmūd himself, and the Ghaznavid nobles and officials, were energetic builders;[6] and Maḥmūd's court poets described various palaces built by the ruler and by other princes and officials.[7] Of these buildings, only the ruins of the palace-complex of Lashgarī Bāzār near Bust (about which we will hear more in what follows) survive.[8]

Let us begin with an example. In a *qaṣīda* addressed to the Amīr Abū Yaʿqūb Yūsuf ibn Sabuktigīn (d. 422/1031), Maḥmūd's younger brother and governor of Khurasan, the Ghaznavid panegyrist Farrukhī Sīstānī (d. after 422/1032–3) celebrates both the birth of a son to the Amīr and his installation in his new palace (1932: 130–32). In the exordium the poet, asked by his "beloved" if his weary state is due to the hardships he has endured on his recent journeys, replies that it is not his travels that have made him thin and wasted, but separation from the Amīr's court. After congratulating the Amīr on his son's birth, he continues:

> In joy and pleasure the Amīr has settled in his new palace,
> from whence ascend to Venus the flute's lamenting strains.

"What sort of palace?" he asks, and proceeds to describe it. It is "a palace like the dome of the pyramids [*kākhī chu gunbad-i haramān*]," covered from top to bottom with inscriptions in gold, "like a Koran." It has four vaulted porticoes (*ṣuffa*), each of which opens upon a different scene: one towards the garden, one towards the mountain slope (*rāgh*), one towards the "sea" (*baḥr*; presumably, a river is meant), and one towards dry land (*barr*). The palace's walls have been whitened with camphor and polished with rosewater; "Turkish jade" (*yashm-i Turkī*) and marble have been employed in its construction.[9] In its wall-paintings cornelian (*ʿaqīq*) has been used instead of vermillion; in its columns there are pearls instead of plaster. Its ceiling is made of white balsam-wood and red sandal; in its earth (or floor? *khāk*) are black musk and fresh amber.

> The palace
> Is lofty as the Amīr's judgement, and strong as his aspiration;
> brilliant as his nature, and worthy as his words.

It is so tall that from its tower one can steal the Pleiades from the heavens, and see Alexander's Wall from its roof. Its walls are so lofty that the astronomer cannot reckon the number of battlements (*kangura*) upon its towers. Below the palace is a garden "like that of Paradise," in which there are "a thousand kinds of brave forms and images." Varicolored tulips make it resemble the (Buddhist) temples of Farkhār; the gliding cypresses on its borders make it seem like Kashmar.[10] Nightingales sing on the cypress branches "like lovers at dawn, tried by separation." Sweet marjoram, "like the curling locks of beauties," grows in the garden's streams; it is bordered by wild thyme, like down on the cheeks of handsome youths.

> The heavens feel shamed by this palace and this garden;
> O lord, (may you) enjoy this palace and this garden!

This palace—or palace-complex, with buildings and gardens, all of which are intimately connected—is not merely a reflection of Paradise but its rival: its builder has created an earthly Paradise which is the envy of the heavenly Garden itself. Its loftiness is praised (spaciousness and light are other qualities often mentioned in the poetry);[11] the precious materials used in its construction and decoration are noted; and the palace is identified with its builder, whose qualities and virtues it both mirrors and embodies.

Can we "see" this palace? Farrukhī's description is concrete in some details, tantalizingly vague in others. We know that the palace is built on what art-historians would call the "four-*īwān*" plan, with four vaulted porticoes (*ṣuffa*), each opening onto a different scene.[12] But those scenes —garden and mountainside (*bāgh u rāgh*), "sea" and land (*baḥr u barr*) —also symbolize its inclusivity: the palace-complex is a perfect microcosm. Similarly inclusive are the references to the palace's ceiling and its floor (that is, its uppermost and lowermost parts); and the white balsam and red sandal of the former, the musk and amber of the latter, embody a contrast in colors which may be said to stand for the whole spectrum. But while the ceiling's materials may be taken literally, are the "musk and amber" real, or do they figure the palace's opulence and its pleasant atmosphere?[13]

For Farrukhī's audience such vagueness would not have been a problem: they were present in the palace, and would no doubt have appreciated references to its distinctive features. For us, however, it is difficult to "see" either building or garden, not least because the palace is not described as a unit, while the garden's features are (as is typical of garden descriptions) aligned both with sacred places of the past (the Buddhist temples of Farkhār; the sacred cypress of Kashmar), and with the beauties of the courtly love song (who may be identified with the pages, cup-bearers, and others attendant on the courtly feast).

Farrukhī's older contemporary, Maḥmūd's poet-laureate (*malik al-shuʿarā*) ʿUnṣurī (d. after 422/1031–2), dedicated 54 lines of an 80-line *qaṣīda* to the palace-complex built by Maḥmūd's vizier, Ḥasan ibn Aḥmad Maymandī, in his home-town of Maymand (1944: 66–70).[14] The poem begins:

> *bahār-zīnat bāghī na bāgh bal-ki bahār*
> *Bahār-khāna-yi mishkūy u mishk-būy bahār*
> A spring-adorned garden; no garden, but a temple:
> a pavilion, an idol-temple, and musk-perfumed spring.[15]

ʿUnṣurī moves between palace (or garden-pavilion, which I take to be the sense of *mishkūy*),[16] garden, and palace proper; and it is sometimes difficult to tell whether he is describing pavilion, palace, garden, or all at the same time. Its colorful images are the painter's model-book; the fragrance of its earth is the perfumer's bill of lading. Its perfumes make it a Tibet (a source of musk) to those who breathe them; the freshness and verdancy of its earth make it seem, to those who see it, a Farkhār.

> From its pictures, sight becomes a world of images,
> were you to look closely towards its wall.

A variant has *ashjār*, "trees," for *dīvār*, "wall," which suggests that some copyist also had difficulty in deciding whether it was the garden or the palace being referred to. For the moment we will assume it is the palace (or the pavilion), as the poet describes what are either wall-paintings (the reading I favor) or trees. Like a meadow, one painting (tree?) contains a lion; another, like the magical trees of the island of Vāqvāq, bears human faces as fruit. One, like a rhinoceros (*karg*), carries an elephant impaled on its horn (or branch, *shākh*; this seems to have been a popular subject for wall-painting); another, like a citadel (*arg*), has a fortress (*ḥiṣār*) raised high:

> Fortresses filled with sky-blue images;
> not Iram, but each, separately, like Iram.
> Like a dome whose covering is Mānī's *Artang*;[17]
> like the Kaʿba whose garment is a royal brocade.

Now we move to the garden, where the nightingale sings as if "it had a harp in its mouth and a *mizmār* in its throat." [18] Near the end of the lengthy description which follows,[19] the poet states,

> You'd think all was the pages of Euclid,
> whose forms give work to the geometers.

The garden is "no sphere" but, like the sphere, is the center of light; "it is a star," but a moving star (i.e., a planet); and, like the Milky Way, a stream runs through it,

> Clear as the scholar's judgement, pure as the gnostic's soul,
> fluent as fine poetry, swift-flowing as the true faith....

Finally, ʿUnṣurī turns to the palace itself: "Should you seek to describe its great dome [*khum*]," he states, "its description would require the most excellent of your poetry; for upon it fancy has set crenellated towers [*shuruf*] established on nobility [*sharaf*], like the lofty aspirations of kings."[20]

> The heavens were the model for its great arch [*ṭāq*],
> and fate (itself) designed its lofty dome.
> Its inscriptions are beautiful, its bricks exceedingly fair;
> its pictures are pure perfection, its fragrances glorious.

(ʿUnṣurī's "bricks" [*khisht*] perhaps refer to the palace's ornamental brickwork.) Now the poet takes us on a "guided tour" of the palace, beginning with its "camphor room" (*kāfūr-khāna*),[21] which is bright as "sunrise at the day's beginning" and white as Moses' miracle-working hand, or as "the face of those destined for Paradise on Judgement Day." The ornamental bands (*tirāz*) on its walls are like the golden embroidery (*tirāz*) which adorns the robes of kings.[22]

Next we enter the picture-gallery (*khāna-yi nigāristān*), whose "brilliant cupola (is) like the cup of Kaykhusraw;"[23] in it, "the twelve [houses of the zodiac] and the seven [planets] travel and rotate," suggesting that the gallery's dome was adorned with astrological images. (On examples of such decoration, and on the persistence of the literary identification of palace domes with the Dome of Heaven, see Bloom 1993.)

> Like idol-temples, its arches [*ṭāq*] (are) filled with pictures,
> blooming like roses, flawless as the hearts of the pious.
> The brilliance of their moonlike faces ever shows forth roses;
> the curls of their black locks ever scatter pitch....

The paintings "are not embroidered fabrics [*vashy*], yet all (wear) embroidered robes;" they are "not a gold mine, but all of purest gold, not a silver mine, but all of silver-work."[24]

> Therein is limned—with auspicious portent and felicitous star—
> the lord, feasting and fighting, upon the throne, and in the hunt.
> Hunting for lofty fortune; fighting the rage of foes;
> demonstrating everlasting affluence at the feast....[25]

The poet then turns to "the dome of the upper chamber [*gunbad-i farvār-khāna*],"[26] whose limned words become splendid and lustrous [*farr-dār*] through the Koran" (i.e., it is decorated with Koranic verses), and describes the (Kufic?) script of its inscriptions:

> It is like the curls of idols, plaited together,
> its knots in the middle, its curls on the edges:
> One curl, and more than a thousand knots upon it;

one knot, and more than a thousand curls upon it.
And if you look from the private chamber towards the garden,
it will appear, to your eyes, the hue of chrysolite [*zabarjad*]....
Such is the garden of our lord in Maymand,
who is the steward of the world and the lord of noble men.

These two poems provide us with a basic repertoire of typical components of palace-descriptions: dome(s) (*khum*, *gunbad*); vaults or arches (*ṭāq*);[27] the *ruvāq* (an arched portico or stoa).[28] The bowl or drum (*khum*) of the *ayvān* of Maḥmūd's palace at Bust (Lashgarī Bāzār) is higher than that of Saturn (ʿUnṣurī 1944: 107, and see also 30); that of the palace of the Ghaznavid official Bū Sahl Ḥamdavī surpasses the famed Īwān Kisrā (Farrukhī 1932: 402). Each of the four *ṣuffa*s of Amīr Yūsuf's palace opens upon a different scene; the *ṣuffa* of Maḥmūd's palace of Bāgh-i Naw in Ghazna opens towards the *manẓar*, the belvedere from which one can survey the garden, and is adorned with paintings of the ruler feasting and in battle (ibid.: 55; cf. Digby 1967: 51). Poets also speak of the palace's walls, parapets, battlements, and towers (*burj*, *burūj*), and crenellations (*shuruf*). The towers of Maḥmūd's palace at Bust are elevated like the Moon in Cancer (ʿUnṣurī 1944: 107); the tower of one of Amīr Yūsuf's palaces has atop it not a parapet (*kangura*), but a "golden helmet" (Farrukhī 1932: 133)—presumably, a gilded cupola.

This poem (ibid.: 133–34) is worth looking at more closely, especially as it speaks of multiple palaces (*kākh-hā*) "at the door" of the prince's residence (*ba-dar-i khāna*), each "beautiful as the garden in spring" and "radiant as the moon before daybreak," each containing "an entire sphere," or "a whole blooming spring," each "like a bride who adorns her face, and dons gold-threaded brocades over her gown."[29]

Especially that palace which has been built at his gate:
that is no palace, but a heaven, filled with suns and moons.
In place of latticed windows [*panjara*], around it is a silver coat of mail;[30]
in place of a parapet, its tower wears a golden helmet.
It is a feasting place [*bazm-gāh*], but when you look at it from

afar,
it looks like a battlefield [*razmgāh*], from so many swords and shields.
Its awnings [*sāyabān-hā*] are lowered, and beneath them, the palace
is like a Sīmurgh which has cast its feathers at its feet.[31]

Inside the palace the prince's servants are busy and active: "One has dirhams in his hand, one dinars; one holds wild roses, one a wine-cup." Behind each lattice [*panjara*] are placed vessels filled with coins and sugar to be scattered at the wedding (cf. O'Kane 1993: 252, on a later illustration with jars placed in recesses; this would seem to explain their function).

The minstrels play their instruments; the slaves scatter gold;
well-wishers drink wine, and ill-wishers grieve....

Below each palace people are gathered; it seems as if "their hands were pure gold, and their feet pure silver," as they compare the largesse they have received.

The like of this Afrīdūn did not own;
the like of this Iskandar did not build.

Why has the Amīr built all this? And why all this activity and effort? For the sake of his *ḥājib* (general) Ṭughril, in reward for whose praiseworthy service he has "bestowed upon him crown and belt" (the insignia of office) and has found him a noble bride.[32]

Here is nobility; here is lordship, generosity;
here is beneficence which has no limit or bounds,

says the poet, and proceeds to praise the Amīr, whose actions towards his servant testify to his own nobility and magnanimity.

Perhaps even more than the palace's architectural features, the decorations of its walls and ceilings inspire poetic description. We have already seen mention of inscriptions (*nibishta-hā*)—the Koranic verses inscribed in gold on the dome of Amīr Yūsuf's palace and on Maymandī's; the ornamental *ṭirāz* bands in the latter's "camphor room"—and of wall-paintings and figural friezes (presumably in stone, stucco, or wood).[33] Such features often come in for particular mention, as in ʿUnṣurī's description of Maymandī's palace. Maḥmūd's palace of Bāgh-i Naw boasts "ornamented porticoes" whose doors open onto the belvedere, "one [of which] is adorned with figures like Chinese brocades, the other filled with pictures like Mānī's *Artang*," among them "portraits of the Ruler of the East, now in battle, grasping a small spear; now feasting, a winecup in his hand" (Farrukhī 1932: 55). And while ʿUnṣurī does not describe the murals of the royal guard which adorned the audience hall at Lashgarī Bāzār, he does describe the guard itself, in terms virtually identical to those seen in the paintings (1944: 43),

> Their golden belts shining with jewels;
> their tunics of Chinese (silk) and scarlet brocade...
> Holding maces of gold and silver,
> each in a different color and of a different form.[34]

In these early Ghaznavid poems, the symbolic qualities of the palace-complex are balanced with concrete description: the palace is not only an emblem of the ruler's might (as well as of other qualities), but bespeaks an artistic creativity which excites the poetic imagination. Moreover, it is not merely an imposing edifice, but the scene of bustling activity.[35] But as we shall see, the nature of palace descriptions was about to change. After Masʿūd I's defeat by the Saljūqs in 431/1040, the Ghaznavid court withdrew eastwards, to Ghazna and to Lahore. The political instability of the next two decades appears to have been unfavorable to poetry; and when poetic activity revived in the late 5th/11th century, a new generation of poets was on the scene. In the regions conquered by the Saljūqs poetic activity seems also to have been disrupted; but towards the end of the 5th/11th century we find a remarkable poet who is both a continuator of the earlier Ghaznavid tradition and something of an innovator: Azraqī of Herat (dates uncertain), panegyrist to Malikshāh's governor of Khurasan Ṭughānshāh, who deserves special mention both because his poetry is not well known and because he appears to be the last great exponent of palace description in the style of the early Ghaznavid poets.

Azraqī devoted large portions of two *qaṣīda*s to Ṭughānshāh's palace in Herat. The first (1957: 11–13), which shows the influence both of

Farrukhī's description of Maḥmūd's Bāgh-i Naw palace (1932: 54–56)[36] and al-Buḥturī's Samarran poems, celebrates the ruler's installation in his new palace.[37] "With a new feast [Nawrūz?], into his new palace has come the wise lord and victorious ruler...Ṭughānshāh," says the poet, and describes the ruler's peregrinations in the palace's garden, whose "slave and servant are spring and Paradise." In the garden's court there is a deep lake (*birka*), "like the soul of the wise man, and the nature of the eloquent," in which "swim fishes of silvery countenance, like new moons in the brilliantly-lit heavens."[38] "A hair's breadth" from the garden is the palace-complex (*sarāy*), filled with *ṣuffa*s, palaces (*kākh*), *ayvān*s, and belvederes (*manẓar*). Though it may not be Paradise, the palace yet spoils the beauty of Paradise. It is so filled with silver-work (*nuqra-kārī*) that it resembles Solomon's palace; its foundations are as firm as Alexander's Wall. Its wall-paintings (*taṣāvīr*) "would amaze Mānī's talent;" its carved reliefs (*tamāthīl*) "would bring regret to Āzar's soul."

> The shadow, image and form of that *ayvān*
> are all depicted [*muṣavvar*] in that azure lake.
> You might ask: is this Kaykhusraw's Cup,
> in which are painted the images of the seven climes?

The parapets (*kangura*) atop the garden's walls "scrape, with their forms, the form of Gemini;" they look like "stags with full-grown horns, whose twistings are intertwined, one with another."

> Adorned in it are square colonnades [*ṣuffa*];
> painted in it are circular roundels [*shamsa*];
> In the *ṣuffa* are paintings of war-elephants;
> in the *shamsa*s the portrait of the victorious ruler...

This reference to *shamsa*s—ornamental "solar disks" which often contain inscriptions or arabesques, but which here contain portraits (*ṣuvar*) of the ruler—may shed new light on the Eastern tradition of wall-painting.[39]

The second *qaṣīda* (ibid.: 65–68) also begins with the garden. It is so bright one would think the moon and Jupiter had descended there from the heavens; it looks like Paradise on earth, filled by Riḍwān with brilliant forms like the moon and Jupiter. A long description of the garden leads, through a brief transitional passage on the lake, to the palace itself:

> That palace of mountainous form, with visage like the stars, in which
> is the breadth of the earth, and the loftiness of the heavens.

Because its top scrapes the sky, watchmen walk bent over on its parapets; when one looks at the crenellations from the garden's court, each image produces a manifest fancy:

> You'd say innumerable Sīmurgh chicks
> have put their sharp beaks out of the nest.

Here Azraqī introduces a new element: the "golden water-pipe" (*muzammil*) through which water is carried to a cistern (*ābdān*), water which is running (*ravān*) "clear as the soul" (or vital spirit, *ravān*).

> Turquoise, like drawn-out wire, it descends
> from the corner of the golden water-pipe to the reservoir.
> You'd say that skins of refined gold were being cast off
> by silver-bodied serpents with turquoise bones.
> A garden which looks like this, a building of this style:
> more pure and clean than Kawsar, more pleasant than Paradise.

Like the earlier Ghaznavid poets, Azraqī feels free to select whatever elements he chooses to describe. While some may be part of a standard repertoire (the palace's dome; its parapets), the poet may also introduce unexpected items (ʿUnṣurī's "camphor chamber", or the "picture-gallery", in Maymandī's palace; Farrukhī's "awnings"; Azraqī's "water-pipe"). This eclecticism, which relishes variety, vividness, and concrete detail, seems characteristic of the "Ghaznavid school" (if we may call it that). But with the panegyrists of the later Ghaznavids, as well as those of the Saljūqs and of other local rulers, not only are fewer palace descriptions to be found in the poets' *dīvān*s (with the exception of Anvarī, discussed below), but those that do occur are marked by a high degree of abstraction and a corresponding decrease in concrete description.

Let us look first at the later Ghaznavid panegyrists. Abū al-Faraj Rūnī (d. after 495/1102) composed several *qaṣīda*s which include references to palaces. The earliest of these, to Sultan Ibrāhīm (451–92/1059–99), contains only a cursory mention of the ruler's palace and *maydān* (1925: 44). Several poems addressed to Ibrāhīm's son and successor Mas'ūd III (492–508/1099–1115) include more extensive references, but the tendency towards hyperbole and away from concreteness is marked. (On Mas'ūd III's palace at Ghazna see Bombaci 1959; Scerrato 1959; Bombaci 1966.) One such poem praises the palace for its convivial setting, its paradisal qualities, and its safety from the ravages of weather and time (ibid.: 54–55). Another (ibid.: 24) states,

> The sphere saw his palace's *ayvān* and its *maydān*,
> and said, "It holds the entire world in its embrace."
> What *maydān*? A sea, whose waves are horses, elephants, men!
> What *ayvān*? A wall, (lofty and) magnificent!

Another poem (ibid.: 96–97) speaks of "this gilded *ṣuffa*," "this firm *gunbad*," "this indescribable *qubba*," "these unequalled paintings," and so on, but with no detail. Only in a *qaṣīda* addressed to Mas'ūd's favorite Bū Rushd Rashīd-i Khāṣṣ (ibid.: 121) do we find a bit more detail. Addressing the palace (in what may be perhaps the earliest example of such an apostrophe, which becomes frequent in later poetry), the poet comes (after the initial platitudes) to its wall-paintings. "Your walls' surfaces," he states, "boast so many images that they have taken on, from head to foot, the shape of the world."

> Therein are steeds full-flanked as onagers;
> therein are bold warriors wielding swords....
> Its prey has felt the harm dealt by the lion;
> its elephant's trunk remains (poised) in threat.
> Its harpist's hand (ever) strokes the harp;
> its flautist's lips (ever) breathe into the flute.
> Its wine-worshipper tastes a wine whose color
> is the envy of the rooster's crown and the osprey's eye.

These images of battle and of feasting have been rendered still and motionless, fixed in one place by the *mamdūḥ*'s magnificence.

'Uthmān Mukhtārī (d. after 513/1119?) opened two *qaṣīdas* to

Arslānshāh ibn Masʿūd (509–11/1116–17) with references to his palace. The first (1962: 51–53) begins,[40]

> The ancient sphere has founded the center of world rule,
> (and) from this Palace Jupiter exerts his heavenly influence.

The sun, observing its parapets from the heavens, "bowed its head to the ground, and set its eyes on that threshold;" the houris, gazing on the palace from Paradise, "took it as purest gold, and Paradise the mine." The poet continues in this vein, stressing the wonder of heaven and earth (and, not least, of other rulers) at the palace. The second example (ibid.: 371–73), which is similarly hyperbolic, begins with the conceit that, should God so command, Riḍwān, the guardian of Paradise, would rejoice were he to be ordered, "Go become the doorman of the sultan's royal abode." The poet then asks,

> Is this the sphere? It would seem so, if Saturn is its turret;
> Is it Paradise? It must be so, if Riḍwān is its doorkeeper.
> Its waters run in silvered streams, its earth is rained upon by gold;
> and when did Riḍwān's eyes e'er gaze upon such splendid chambers?...

Earth, having taken water from the skies, now "in turn, from these fountains, rains water on the sky," and "now with that silvery tongue, from that golden fountain's mouth," praises the ruler to the heavens for his support of "the Arab faith." Again, hyperbole triumphs over concreteness: the fountain (for example), which might have inspired an earlier poet to some detail (we may think of Azraqī's water-pipe), serves primarily to reflect the ruler's might and to emphasize his position.

A *qaṣīda* by Mukhtārī's younger contemporary, Ḥasan-i Ghaznavī (d. after 555/1160?), panegyrist to Bahrāmshāh (511–52?/1117–57?),[41] addressed to the vizier Ḥasan-i Aḥmad (1949: 178–9), also begins with an apostrophe to the building.

> O blessed building! What a pleasant place you are,
> whose head ever scrapes the heavens.
> To the eye you are a lofty building;

to nature you are an expansive plain.

Venus and Jupiter should enjoy the spectacle of "your garden-pavilion [*būstān-sarāy*]," says the poet; "you are like the world-seeing cup, for you show all that exists. Your belvedere rules the sun's zenith; you are no (mere) building, but the house [*burj*] of Gemini," he states, concluding this "description" with the prayer, "May you remain the abode of your lord till Resurrection." Ḥasan provides no details about the palace; it is simply more lofty, more impressive, more pleasing, more all-inclusive that anything that can be imagined. The reference to the "world-seeing cup" (for example) is not linked (as in ʿUnṣurī's *qaṣīda* to Maymandī) to a concrete element of the palace's decoration, but to its symbolic status as microcosm. In such a poem we cannot "see" the palace; we can only be impressed by its magnitude.

Another *qaṣīda* by Ḥasan (ibid.: 144–46, addressed to Bahrāmshāh, and, according to the rubric, celebrating the sultan's son's progress from the *imārat-khāna* to the *kūshk*, which appears to mean from a palace to a garden pavilion; the season is spring) is noteworthy only for its mention of the sun "begging light from the [*kūshk*'s] *shamsa* (which must here refer to the interior of its domed ceiling), and of the sky's (*āsmān*) amazement at the *kūshk*'s ceiling (*āsmāna*). Yet another poem (ibid.: 163–75; to the vizier Qavām al-Mulk Aḥmad ibn ʿUmar, said to have been composed *ex tempore*) states that "Paradise has received fresh currency, and a sphere has been added" by this palace. "Should I speak of the reflection of its gates and the image of its river," says the poet, "six things would become envious: the peacock's tail, the pheasant's wings, the falcon's eye; the elegant rose, fresh spring's season, and the multi-colored carpet.'

One wonders how contemporary audiences reacted (or how they were meant to react) to such resolute, and decidedly non-descriptive, hyperbole, which also characterizes poetry written in the Saljūq domains, such as that of Anvarī (d. after 560/1164–5?).[42] Anvarī composed at least nine *qaṣīda*s which include palace-descriptions, for two patrons: Nāṣir al-Dīn Ṭāhir, vizier to Sultan Sanjar (511–52/1118–57) from 528 until 548 (see the introduction to Anvarī 1994, 1: 52), and Abū al-Ḥasan ʿImrānī (described as *mudabbir-i umūr-i sulṭān Sanjar*, "manager of Sultan Sanjar's affairs), who was killed on the sultan's order in 545 (ibid., 1:

58–59). In a poem addressed to Nāṣir al-Dīn Ṭāhir (ibid., 1: 129; dated 542),[43] Anvarī, addressing the palace, hails it an "exemplar of the azure sphere" which, like the sphere, is "safe from hot and cold." But its lofty ceiling shames the sphere, and its court makes Paradise suffer pangs of jealousy: the sphere weeps bloody tears, "(red) like your vermillion paint," while Paradise's face "is yellow (with envy), like your orpiment [*zarnīkh*] hue."

> (But) you are still; otherwise, what difference
> is there between you and the world-turning dome,

he states, beginning what, in fact, seems like a description of the palace's wall-paintings: "You are a Paradise/garden [*jannat*] whose beasts and birds are free from (the need to) eat and sleep. Your nightingale cannot speak; your eagle and quail hasten without motion; your elephant and rhinoceros fight without enmity."

Most of Anvarī's palace descriptions, which serve as preface to the panegyric, take the form of an abbreviated catalogue of the palace's wondrous aspects. Another *qaṣīda* (ibid., 1: 103; probably addressed to the same patron), in the form of a *duʿā*, opens:

> May this august goal of world and religion flourish [*maʿmūr bād*];
> may it forever, (as long) as it flourishes, be far from calamities.[44]
> In its *ḥarīm* are he Kaʿba's qualities of safety;
> may its firm foundation be as stable as that of Mount Sinai!

"May the dust raised each dawn by its sweepers fill the sphere's roof with camphor," says the poet; "and each midnight, from its watchmen's cry, may the sweet music of a trumpet-call reach the sky." Should the sun pass over it without permission, may its bright day be dark as night from its eclipse; may the moon support its parapets each night, and may it ever hold the high throne of the vizier.

Occasionally we find a bit more detail in Anvarī's poems, as when, in another *qaṣīda* to the same vizier (ibid., 1: 182–87), he devotes a lengthy passage to the palace's wall-paintings. "The reflection of your wall," he states (again addressing the palace), "has made invalid the two colors day and night (once) owned;" "you are a temperate world" where "birds are continually both still and in flight," a "wondrous plain where wild beasts are forever all both fixed and moving."

> Your rhinoceros (bears) a slain elephant on its horn;
> your falcon (has) a wearied quail in its beak.
> Your lions and cattle are without struggle or rage;
> (they remain) forever fixed in idleness.

"Heaven has made the swords of the Turks of your battlefield safe from rust," he exclaims; from "the cup borne by the *sāqī* of your feast, the wine-drinkers (are) neither drunk nor sober." "The eyes of thousands have prostrated themselves before the magic of your paintings," he continues;

> The Daylamīs and Turks of your battlefield
> have no other occupation but warfare:
> The one's spear like a shooting star, burning like fire;
> the other's sword like the Milky Way, filled with pearls.
> To the beasts and birds of your hunting-ground
> the brush, untroubled, has given rest.

Everything here is calm, tranquil, at peace; and one wonders if this urge towards tranquillity reflects the troubled times in which the poet lived. For if, in reality, the "Daylamīs and Turks" of this world were ever fighting, in the paintings they are ever frozen; wild beasts and birds are no longer prey, but fixed in untroubled rest.

Considerations of space prohibit a detailed discussion of the poetry of this period; but we may note a few further examples in support of the argument that, in general, concreteness gives way to abstraction and hyperbole. In a *qaṣīda* to the vizier Abū al-Muẓaffar Naṣīr al-Dīn ʿAbd al-Ṣamad, the Saljūq panegyrist ʿAbd al-Vāsiʿ Jabalī (d. after 540/1145–6?) describes the vizier's palace (1960: 153–54). Now that the cold of autumn has come, the poet advises, it is time to "drink wine with beautiful heart-robbers and sweet-singing minstrels, (served) by the hand of a graceful, seductive *sāqī*,"

> Especially in this august building, which, when it comes to

> description,
> before its perfection (the poet's) thought falls short.
> A fortune-favored spot, a blessed building,
> marvelous in its beauty, a legend in its fairness;
> In brilliance a rarity, like your noble judgement;
> renowned for its freshness, like your subtle nature.

After more hyperbolic praise—the palace's ceiling leaves no place for the sphere; Paradise itself is without value when compared to its court—the poet concludes by saying that "four places have bestowed four gifts" upon the palace, each more fitting than the next:

> Iram its high degree, Shaddād's seven (palaces') worth;
> the Holy Shrine respect, Baghdad its royal *farr*.[45]

Nor is this phenomenon limited to panegyrists of the Saljūqs and their officials. Khāqānī Sharvānī (d. 595/1198–9) celebrated the buildings of his patrons, the Transcaucasian Sharvānshāhs (as well as those of other notables), in several *qaṣīda*s whose imagery is noteworthy chiefly for its unrelatedness to the building in question.[46] Of interest here is the third *maṭlaʿ* of a *qaṣīda* addressed to the Saljūq sultan Muḥammad ibn Maḥmūd ibn Muḥammad ibn Malikshāh (548–55/1153–60) (1959: 192–93; dateable to Muḥarram 550/mid-March 1155 on the basis of its astrological references), which begins:

> If you've not seen Iram's court, look at the ruler's garden;
> if you've not seen the Shrine's fort, pass by the ruler's palace.

Palace and garden possess the attributes of Paradise: the pool of Kawsar "has extended a canal [*kārīz*] into its fish-filled pools; (the tree of) Ṭūbā has grafted itself to the branches of its junipers." The phoenix nests in its basil; the sun sleeps in the shade of its pines. Like the trees of Vaqvāq, its birds speak, "reciting 'God be praised!' for the ruler's victories."

> His palace is like my thoughts, as I praise the sultan:
> the sphere is contained in it, the world depicted therein.
> That (ornamented) band [*juft*] from which the rainbow
> gained its hues;

that vault [*ṭāq*] which made the court of the heavens soar:[47]
Idrīs and Jam designed it; Moses and Khiżr built it;
the soul and the sphere adorned it; Noah and the angels were
its carpenters.
The stars are the images on its ceiling; and before every
image,
just as did Abraham, Āzar recites, "This is my Lord!"
Mercury wielded his brush, and with the sphere's azure
[*lājavard*],
wrote the sultan's name over the dado [*chift*] and lintel
[*maʿbar*].[48]

Here, despite Khāqānī's highly mannered imagery, we sense something of the lively atmosphere which animated earlier poems. Moreover, here the palace's attributes are identified not with the ruler but with the poet: the palace "is like my thoughts, as I praise the sultan: the sphere is contained in it, the world is depicted therein."

Despite the ravages brought by the Mongol invasions, princes continued to build palaces, and poets to sing their praises. I shall not dwell on post-Mongol poetry except to note the entry of new elements into the poetic repertoire.[49] In a *qaṣīda* to the Jalāyirid Shāh Uvays (757–76/1356–74) Salmān Sāvajī (d. 778/1376), addressing the palace (1958: 353–56), mentions its *tābkhāna*[50] ("You have a place where the sphere sets the sun, in place of a globe [*jām*])," its skylight (*rawzan*)[51] ("Like a mote, the sun, could it find the chance, would cast itself from the air through your *rawzan*"), and its kitchen (*maṭbakh*), "whose smoke makes the cloud ashamed." In another *qaṣīda* addressed to Shāh Shaykh Ḥasan (d. 757/1356; ibid.: 546–47) he observes, "So brilliant are the rays of the *shamsa*s on the wall[52] of your *ayvān* at night that the motes in the air cannot be counted one by one." Salmān's contemporary Khvājū Kirmānī (d. 753/1352), in a *qaṣīda* to the vizier Jamāl al-Dawla wa-al-Dīn Aḥmad (1957: 61–64), mentions the audience chamber (*ṣuffa-yi bār*), before which the sphere is a gilded chariot. The shavings left by its carpenter provide the columns which support the sky, its mortar the foundations of the holy Shrine; the sun's brilliance is the merest reflection of the *shamsa* (gilded tilework?) which adorns its ceiling; the "fixed nails" (which are said to hold the earth in place) are from the beams (*awtād*) of its doors; the moon's radiance is the glass bead (*munjūq*) of the lamp of its audience hall; at dawn the sun rises from the vizier's sleeping quarters (*shabistān*).[53]

The last poet I shall discuss is Ibn-i Yamīn (d. 769/1368), whose *dīvān* contains far more "building poems" than do those of his contemporaries,[54] and who appears as an emulator of the earliest "eastern" tradition, in that the balance between abstract and concrete is, to some extent, restored. Thus for example he begins a poem addressed to the vizier ʿAlāʾ al-Dīn Muḥammad (1966: 16):[55]

> What a marvelous palace, its foot firmly fixed in water,
> its head, in loftiness, stretched to the sun's zenith!...
> From the shame that must be (felt) from its beautiful images,
> Mānī's spirit will remain in torment till Resurrection.
> Bravo! to the hand of the master who painted its images!
> Could anyone in this way fix a picture upon water?

The conceit of "drawing upon water" (*naqsh bar āb bastan*; used proverbially for a futile action) links this first segment of the poem: unlike those whose designs (or plans) are of no avail, this palace stands firm. I take "fixed in water" to mean that the palace is beside, and reflected in, its garden's lake, which is mentioned a few lines later, and is likened to Kawsar, "if the water which springs forth from Kawsar were all rosewater."

> The baked bricks round its edges are the envy of jacinth and
> ruby;
> the pebbles within it are the envy of lustrous pearls,

states the poet, before turning to praise of the vizier.

Several of Ibn Yamīn's poems mention the *jāmāt* (sing. *jām*) that let in light through the ceiling (see e.g. ibid.: 23). In a *qaṣīda* to the Sarbadārid Tāj al-Dīn ʿAlī Chishumī (ibid.: 168–9; cf. the editor's introduction, *l–d*, and see *EI*^{2}, art. "Sarbadārids"), the poet states,

> Happy that palace in which, from the reflection of the globes
> in its *rawzans*,

you see the earth filled with stars, like the heavens.

Another *qaṣīda* to ʿAlāʾ al-Dīn Muḥammad (ibid.: 173–4) begins,

Dear heart, if you're inclined to see eternal Paradise,
or wish to see Iram's Garden manifest in the world,
Cast your eyes, in enjoyment, upon this lofty palace,
so, from the limit of delight, you may observe them both.
People build palaces in the world—indeed, that is the custom;
but has anyone ever built a palace in which you see the whole world?

Saturn is the watchman who patrols the palace roof; in the reflection of its courtyard's brickwork and the images on its ceiling one sees the sky, "filled with moon and sun," and the earth, "full of humans and *jinn*." This imagery is echoed in the praise of the vizier: since his justice is "the architect of the palace of creation," hereafter the world will, like the Holy Shrine itself, be safe from corruption.

May he ever, in this auspicious palace, rejoice, to the point
when you see, like Ibn Yamīn, the ancient sphere singing his praises.

What can we learn from these poetic texts? From a literary perspective, we see a progression from the relative concreteness of the early poetry to a greater degree of abstraction in the poetry of the later Ghaznavid and Saljūq periods,[56] with. perhaps, a slight return towards balance beginning in the late 7th/13th century.[57] Can this be attributed simply to a change in literary tastes? Not entirely; in my opinion it has much to do with the changing patterns of patronage which followed the collapse of the early Ghaznavids, and with the political instability which afflicted most of the Iranian world for some centuries thereafter.[58] As the base of patronage broadened, more and more poems were addressed to courtiers and officials, to military leaders, and to religious notables (*imāms*, *qāḍīs*), for whom the palace symbolized the power and status they had attained (often with difficulty, and often held precariously). For rulers, the palace becomes more a trophy than a locus of artistic creativity (cf. Bombaci

1966: 32, who suggests that Masʿūd III viewed his palace as just such a trophy of his Indian victories, "meant to raise the prestige of the dynasty"; one thinks also of such short-lived rulers as Arslānshāh, whose palace functions as an emblem of legitimacy). Palace descriptions therefore place greater emphasis on power (expressed hyperbolically) than on the palace's physical characteristics.

From a purely practical perspective, the evidence provided by poetic texts with respect to palace architecture and decoration cannot be ignored. While it is true that we may not be able to "see"—let alone reconstruct—a given palace from a given poetic description, the poetry enables us to discover not only what palaces meant, but how they appeared, to those who praised them. The information they provide (however impressionistic, and however sketchy) should not be disregarded by art-historians in the study of "Islamic" palace architecture. For in this context, as elsewhere, "the palace is set up as a mirror of the king"; and its "rhetorical function, as exemplified through its affect, is...as essential as its residential, administrative, productive, and ceremonial functions" (Winter 1993: 39). It is this "mirror effect," and this "rhetorical affect," that the poetry can help us to understand.

Bibliography

ʿUnṣurī. 1944. *Dīvān*. Edited by Yaḥyā Qarīb. Tehran.

ʿAwfī, Muḥammad. 1957. *Lubāb al-albāb*. Edited by Saʿīd Nafīsī. Tehran: Ibn Sīnī/ʿIlmī.

Allen, Terry. 1988. "Notes on Bust [I]." *Iran* 26:55–68.

———. 1989. "Notes on Bust [II]." *Iran* 27:57–66.

———. 1990. "Notes on Bust [III]." *Iran* 28:23–30.

Amin, M. M., and Laila A. Ibrahim. 1990. *Architectural Terms in Mamluk Documents (648–923H/1250–1517)*. Cairo: The American University in Cairo Press.

Anvarī, Awḥad al-Dīn. 1994. *Dīvān*. Edited by Taqī Mudarris Rażavī. 4th ed. 2 vols. Tehran: Shirkat-i Intishārāt-i ʿIlmī va-Farhangī.

Azraqī Haravī. 1957. *Dīvān*. Edited by Saʿīd Nafīsī. Tehran.

Ball, Warwick, and Jean-Claude Gardin. 1982. *Archaeological Gazetteer of Afghanistan*. 2 vols. Paris: Éditions Recherche sur les Civilisations.

Barnes, Ruth. 1987. "From India to Egypt: The Newberry Collection and the Indian Ocean Textile Trade." In *Islamische Textilkunst des Mittelalters: Aktuelle Probleme*, edited by Muḥammad ʿAbbās Salīm et al., 79–92. Riggisberg: Abegg-Stiftung.

Bayhaqī, Abū al-Fażl. 1995. *Tārīkh-i Bayhaqī*. Edited by ʿAlī Akbar Fayyāż. Tehran: ʿIlmī.

Blair, Sheila. 1993. "The Ilkhanid Palace." *Ars Orientalis* 23:239–48.

———. 1998. *Islamic Inscriptions*. Edinburgh: Edinburgh University Press.

Bloom, Jonathan. 1989. *Minaret, Symbol of Islam*. Oxford: Oxford University Press.

———. 1993. "The Qubbat al-Khaḍrāʾ and the Iconography of Height." *Ars Orientalis* 23:135–41.

Bombaci, Alessio. 1959. "Introduction to the Excavations at Ghazni (Summary Report on the Italian Archaeological Mission in Afghanistan)." *East and West* n.s. 10:3–22.

———. 1964. "La 'Sposa del Cielo'." In *A Francesco Gabrieli: Studi Orientalistici Offerti nel Sessantesimo Compleanno da suoi Colleghi o Discepoli*, 21–34. Rome: Università di Roma.

———. 1966. *The Kūfic Inscription in Persian Verses in the Court of the Royal Palace of Masʿūd III at Ghazni*. Rome: Instituto Italiano per il Medio ed Estreme Oriente, Centro Studi e Scavi Archeologici in Asia.

Digby, Simon. 1967, "The Literary Evidence for Painting in the Delhi Sultanate." *Bulletin of the American Academy of Benares* 1:47–58.

Dihkhudā, ʿAlī Akbar. 1993–94. *Lughatnāma*. Edited by M. Muʿīn and J. Shahīdī. "New Edition." 15 vols. Tehran: Dānishgāh-i Tihrān/Rawzana.

Farrukhī Sīstānī. *Dīvān*. Edited by ʿAlī ʿAbd al-Rasūlī. Tehran: Maṭbaʿa-yi Majlis, 1932.

Grabar, Oleg. 1978. "Palaces, Citadels and Fortifications." In *Architecture of the Islamic World: Its History and Social Meaning*, edited by George Michell, 65–79. London: Thames and Hudson.

———. 1990. *The Great Mosque of Isfahan*. London: I.B. Tauris.

———. 1993. "Umayyad Palaces Reconsidered." *Ars Orientalis* 23:93–108.

Gronke, Monika. 1992. "The Persian Court Between Palace and Tent: From Timur to ʿAbbas I." In *Timurid Art and Culture: Iran and Central Asia in the Fifteenth Century*, edited by Lisa Golombek and Maria Subtelny, 18–22. Leiden: E.J. Brill.

Ḥasan-i Ghaznavī, Sayyid Ashraf. 1949. *Dīvān*. Edited by M. T. Mudarris Rażavī. Tehran: Dānishgāh-i Tihrān.

Hillenbrand, Robert. 1994. *Islamic Architecture: Form, Function and Meaning*. Edinburgh: Edinburgh University Press.

———. 2000. "The Architecture of the Ghaznavids and Ghurids." In *Studies in Honour of Clifford Edmund Bosworth, Vol. II. The Sultan's Turrent: Studies in Persian and Turkish Culture*, edited by Carole Hillenbrand, 124–206. Leiden: Brill.

Humphreys, R. Steven. 1972. "The Expressive Intent of the Mamluk Architecture of Cairo: A Preliminary Essay." *Studia Islamica* 35: 69–119.

Ibn-i Yamīn Faryūmadī. 1966. *Dīvān-i ashʿār*. Edited by Ḥusayn-ʿAlī Bāstānī Rād. Tehran: Sanāʾī.

Jabalī, ʿAbd al-Vāsiʿ. 1960. *Dīvān*. Edited by Zabīḥ Allāh Ṣafā. Tehran: Dānishgāh-i Tihrān.

Jamāl al-Dīn Iṣfahānī. 1941. *Dīvān-i kāmil*. Edited by Vaḥīd Dastgirdī. Tehran: Armaghān.

Jāmī, ʿAbd al-Raḥmān. 1966. *Dīvān-i kāmil*. Edited by Hāshim Riżā. Tehran: Pīrūz.

Khāqānī Sharvānī. 1959. *Dīvān*. Edited by Źiyāʾ al-Dīn Sajjādī. Tehran: Zavvār.

Khan, Ghulam Mustafa. 1949. "A History of Bahram Shah." *Islamic Culture* 23:62–91, 199–235.

Khvājū Kirmānī. 1957. *Dīvān-i ashʿār*. Edited by Aḥmad Suhaylī Khvānsārī.

Tehran: Bārānī.

Manūchihrī Dāmghānī. 1996. *Dīvān*. Edited by Muḥammad Dabīr Siyāqī. 2d ed. Tehran: Zavvār.

Meisami, Julie Scott. 1999. *Persian Historiography to the End of the Twelfth Century*. Edinburgh: Edinburgh University Press.

———. 2001. "The Palace-Complex as Emblem: Some Samarran Qasidas." In *Proceedings, International Workshop on Interdisciplinary Approaches to Samarra*, edited by C. F. Robinson. Oxford: Oxford University Press (in press).

Melikian-Chirvani, A. S. 1974. "L'évocation littéraire du bouddhisme dans l'Iran musulman." In *Le monde iranien et l'Islam: sociétés et cultures*, 2: 1–74. Centre de recherches d'histoire et de philosophie de la IVe section de l'École pratique des Hautes Études. Hautes études islamiques et orientales d'histoire comparée. Geneva and Paris: Librairie Droz.

Mukhtārī Ghaznavī. 1962. *Dīvān*. Edited by Jalāl al-Dīn Humāʾī. Tehran: Bungāh-i Tarjuma va-Nashr-i Kitāb.

Necipoğlu, Gülru. 1993. "An Outline of Shifting Paradigms in the Palatial Architecture of the Pre-Modern Islamic World." *Ars Orientalis* 23:3–24.

O'Kane, Bernard. 1993. "From Tents to Pavilions: Royal Mobility and Persian Palace Design." *Ars Orientalis* 23:249–68.

Ruggles, D. F. 1993. "Arabic Poetry and Architectural Memory in Al-Andalus." *Ars Orientalis* 23:171–78.

Rūnī, Abū al-Faraj. 1925. *Dīvān*. Edited by K. I. Chaykin. Tehran.

Salmān Sāvajī. 1958. *Dīvān*. Edited by Manṣūr Mushfiq. Tehran: Ṣafīʿalīshāh.

Scerrato, Umberto. 1959. "The First Two Excavation Campaigns at Ghazni, 1957–1958 (Summary Report on the Italian Archaeological Mission in Afghanistan)." *East and West* n.s. 10:23–55.

Schlumberger, Daniel, et al. 1978. *Lashkari Bazar: Une résidence royale Ghaznévide et Ghouride*. Mémoires de la Mission Archéologie Française en Afghanistan, vol. 18. Paris: Diffusion de Boccaid.

Sperl, Stefan. 1989. *Mannerism in Arabic Poetry: A Structural Analysis of Selected Texts*. Cambridge: Cambridge University Press.

Wilkinson, Charles K. 1986. *Nishapur: Some Early Islamic Buildings and Their Decoration*. New York: The Metropolitan Museum of Art.

Winter, Irene J. 1993. ""Seat of Kingship"/"A Wonder to Behold": The Palace as Construct in the Ancient Near East." *Ars Orientalis* 23:27–55.

Ẓahīr Faryābī. 1959. *Dīvān*. Edited by Taqī Bīnash. Tehran.

Notes

1. Grabar (1978: 65) distinguishes between "the architecture of a culture, and the architecture of individuals within a culture;" it seems to me that the palace-descriptions to be discussed speak chiefly to this second category. As Grabar also notes (ibid.: 79), it is (perhaps ironically, in view of its evanescence) secular architecture which "penetrated into imaginative literature to a far greater extent than did religious architecture." One may speculate that this is connected with (the not unrelated) issues of power and prestige and of literary patronage.
2. See, for example, Necipoğlu 1993: 9, who appears to misread a passage from al-Masʿūdī's *Murūj al-dhahab* as referring to paintings in an audience hall, rather than figures on a carpet (the passage however requires further investigation).
3. This issue has of late received somewhat more attention. For example, in his study of the Great Mosque of Isfahan Grabar notes that, a year after the vizier Niẓām al-Mulk had built the south dome, his "main competitor and sworn enemy," Tāj al-Mulk Abū al-Ghanāʾim, built the north dome (which is "heavily inscribed" with Koranic verses which appear to be in part at least a response to those on the south dome, and with Tāj al-Mulk's Persian, rather that his Arabic, names and titles). Grabar observes that "something is going on here which does not deal simply with building a religious building we generally know as a mosque" (1990: 39–40), but does not pursue the issue. See also Bloom 1989, who however seems perhaps too prone to take a building—in this case the mosque, with or without minaret—only as a political statement; and see Humphreys 1972, who argues against a "purely functional interpretation" of buildings (73) in favor of examining "*why* a building is put together as it is, and what response it was intended to elicit from the beholder" (70; author's emphasis).
4. There are of course exceptions, notably with respect to the palace architecture of al-Andalus; see for example Ruggles 1993; Hillenbrand 1994: 440–41. In his recent study on Ghaznavid and Ghūrid architecture, however, Hillenbrand (2000) makes no use of poetic texts.
5. Little Persian poetry survives from earlier periods (the reigns of the Ṭāhirids, Ṣaffārids, and Sāmānids). As I am concerned here with Persian, i have not searched for Arabic palace-poems for these periods; but my general impression is that (with the exception of the Samarran and Andalusian poems) palace-poems are less common in earlier Arabic (at least) than in Persian poetry (although I am told that a substantial amount of poetry on buildings exists for later periods; Dr. Ruba Kanan, personal communication). I have also restricted myself to editions of the poets' *dīvān*s, although

other sources—e.g. anthologies, historical works—also require study.

6. The historian Abū Naṣr ʿUtbī (d. after 427/1036?) comments on the competition amongst the Ghaznavid nobility in building sumptuous residences on the hills outside Ghaznīn (Ghazna) itself (see Bombaci 1959, 20, 22 n. 50). That this activity was not limited to Ghazna is clear from the poetry (see also Allen 1990: 26, 30, on Ghaznavid residences at Bust; Wilkinson 1986, on Nishapur).

7. I have found no poems on Masʿūd I's (421–32/1030–41) building activities, although the Ghaznavid historian Bayhaqī tells us that he "was a master of building" and designed his palace of Shādyākh himself, as well as making additions to Maḥmūd's constructions at Lashgarī Bāzār (1995: 181; on Lashgarī Bāzār see n. 8 below). Had Bayhaqī included panegyrics to Masʿūd in his history we might have had some examples; but he did not, and such poems (if they existed) are lost. (On this problem see Meisami 1999: 291–92.) There is a fragment in Manūchihrī's *dīvān* (1996: 16)—clearly made up of lines (not necessarily consecutive) from a longer poem—which speaks of "that auspicious palace [*qaṣr*] which he [unidentified] built this year," its wood of sandal and aloes, its stone(s) of pearl and rubies, which is "lofty as your [unidentified] merit and open as your face; upright as your pact, and firm as your forbearance"; might this refer to Masʿūd?

8. Lashgarī Bāzār is cited copiously in the art-historical literature. See, in the first instance, Schlumberger *et al.* 1978; Bombaci 1959; *EI2*, art. "Las̲h̲kar-i Bāzār" (C.E. Bosworth; note that this is an inaccurate rendering of the local name for the site); Allen 1988 (especially 65–66, on the chronology of the site), 1989, 1990; Hillenbrand 2000: 147–52; and see also the relevant entries in Ball 1982. On Persian palace architecture see also *EI2*, art. "Sarāy" (S. Blair).

9. Farrukhī does not give the palace's location; but we may recall that the palaces of Ghazna were noted for their abundant use of marble, and that there was a marble quarry a short distance from Ghazna (cf. Bombaci 1959: 8). *Yashm-i Turkī* (a variant has *yashm-i ṣāfī*) is used specifically of jade. Cf. Dihkhudā 1993, s.v., who cites, among other *shavāhid*, Farrukhī's line, the anonymous 4th/10th century geographical work the *Ḥudūd al-ʿālam*, which states that jade (*sang-i yashm*) comes "from the rivers of Khotan," and references by Bayhaqī to jade objects, including a ring which once belonged to Sultan Masʿūd and decorations on ceremonially adorned horses. The earliest surviving jade objects date from the Tīmūrid period, and include a large block used as Tīmūr's cenotaph (see Blair 1998: 193). The use of precious stones in palace decoration is attested for the Īlkhānid period (see Blair 1993: 241–42), and was undoubtedly the practice in earlier periods as well.

10. Farkhār, the Soghdian term for a Buddhist sanctuary, occurs also as a place-

name (see Melikian-Chirvani 1974: 30); Kashmar is the site where a sacred cypress was planted by Zoroaster (cf. ʿUnṣurī 1944: 45).

11. Bloom argues that from around the 3rd/9th century onwards space replaced height (manifested by an externally visible dome) as reflecting the ruler's magnificence, although the dome remained both as a formal feature and as a metaphor (see 1993: 137–39). While this may be true of Abbasid architecture (Bloom bases his argument largely on the example of Samarra), progress through space (as in the caliphal palaces) does not seem to have been a feature of Persian palace architecture (cf. Blair 1993: 241), even though the physical space occupied by a palace-complex such as that of Lashgarī Bāzār was considerable. Domes figure prominently throughout Persian palace-descriptions.

12. On the various meanings of *īwān* (Persian: *ayvān*)—for which, in its sense of "a chamber or...a hall which is open to the outside at one end, either directly or through a portico," the term *ṣuffa* is often used in the texts—see *EI2*, s.v. (O. Grabar), and *EIr*, art. "Ayvān" (idem.). Cf. also Blair 1993: 241; Dihkhudā 1993, s.v. *ṣuffa*; Amin and Ibrahim 1990: 17–18.

13. Or perhaps this refers to the practice of strewing the palace floor with fragrant perfumes on feasts and other occasions.

14. Bayhaqī notes that on a visit to Maymand in 428/1039, Masʿūd I stayed in "the kingly buildings" built by (the now deceased) Maymandī (1995: 681).

15. Melikian-Chirvani translates this line as an address to the garden (1974: 69); but as the next line refers to "*its* nature," etc., this reading seems unlikely. The poet plays on *bahār*, meaning both "spring" and "temple" (specifically, a Buddhist temple, from the Sanskrit *vihara*; see ibid., especially 46–61), and on *mishkūy* ("pavilion"; also a term for a Buddhist temple [ibid.: 66]) and *mishk-būy* ("musk-scented"). Melikian-Chirvani translates the second *miṣrāʿ* as "the sanctuary of Mishkūy" (ibid.: 69), assuming that *mishkūy* is employed in the poetry as a place-name. My own feeling is that the joy is in the punning, and that we should not try to nail everything down to some exclusive meaning.

16. In other words, a *kūshk*, on the sense of which see Dihkhudā 1993, s.v. Dihkhudā makes no reference in his entry on *mishkū/mishkūy* (vowelled *mushk-*) to its meaning of "pavilion," although that meaning seems implicit here (ʿUnṣurī's line does not figure among his few *shavāhid*).

17. For *amthāl-hā-yi mīnā-rang* read *timthāl-hā*? (*Amthāl* is itself the plural of *mathal*, which is not used of images, whereas *timthāl* is used for carved figures, statues, and the like; see Dihkhudā 1993, s.v.) According to Dihkhudā, *mīnā-rang* is "green" (*sabz*), which is, traditionally, the color of the sky. For "Iram" perhaps read "Aram"; Melikian-Chirvani posits a confusion between

the Koranic Iram (in Arabia) and the Sanskrit Ārāma, "pleasure-garden" (see 1974: 70–72), and argues that in the early poetry the word should be read *aram* (though perhaps, again, the fun is in the pun). The *Artang* or (*Arzhang*) was a work attributed to Mānī which was said to have been illustrated with paintings, including astrological images and depictions of the final Judgement. It is the literary type of beautiful painting.

18. The *mizmār* is an oboe-like instrument, like a shawm.
19. In this description the garden's components are assimilated to adjuncts of palace life: for example, the sour orange tree (*nāranj*) looks as if someone had scattered vermillion over rust from a painter's brush, or like an enamelled censer from the grating (*mushabbak*) of which musky vapors emerge from flames of fire (*nār*; wordplay on the Arabic and Persian meanings of *nār*, "fire" and "pomegranate [blossom]"); the newly-opened narcissi are like golden cups filled with amber, silver cups filled with golden coins; not eyes, but like the eye, with onyx pupils and golden lashes; not a (royal) parasol, but like a parasol, and so on.
20. On the *shuruf* (sing. *shurfa*), the crenellations which adorn the tops of towers and ramparts, see Amin and Ibrahim 1990: 70. It is clear from the poetry that these early Ghaznavid buildings, like later Mamlūk ones, boasted *shuruf* in fantastic shapes, which gave rise to the use of highly fanciful descriptive imagery.
21. I have no idea what this might be: a room whose plaster is mixed with camphor? Cf. Anvarī 1994, I: 67, who speaks of "a dome [*qubba*] the brilliance of whose walls fills the sky with waves of light, (but) whose form does not put an end to desire, since its plaster [*gaj*] is mixed with camphor."
22. On *ṭirāz* as an architectural term see *EI2*, art. "Ṭirāz. 3" (Nasser Rabbat). Rabbat states that the term "came to architecture from textiles at an unknown date, but no earlier than the Fāṭimid period (10th–12th centuries)," and that its architectural application is not recorded in the Arabic dictionaries (it is, however, noted by Amin and Ibrahim, 1990: 76). Sheila Blair states that "in later times" (presumably Mamlūk? She cites as an example the inscription on the front of Sultan Qalāʾūn's tomb complex) the term was "used in the Arabic-speaking lands for the long bands inscribed with the ruler's name and titles decorating the façades of important buildings" (1998:165). This *ṭirāz* is clearly *inside* the palace; and since it is unlikely that the Ghaznavids "borrowed" the term from the Fāṭimids, ʿUnṣurī's poem provides an early instance of its use, outside the "Arabic-speaking lands," in connection with architectural decoration.
23. Kaykhusraw was said to possess a magical cup (which was later attributed to Jamshīd) in which he could see the entire world; the image recurs fre-

quently in connection with palatial domes.

24. *Vashy* (an unusual word in the poetry) designates an embroidered or painted fabric. Painted fabrics from India are attested for later periods (cf. Digby 1967: 55–56); however, if painted cotton fabrics were imported into Egypt as early as c. 1010 C.E. (Barnes 1997: 87–89), it is reasonable to assume that, in view of the Ghaznavids' far closer connections with the sub-continent, they might have used such fabrics.

25. Reading *bazmgāh*, "feasting place," for *razmgāh*, "battlefield," as seems called for by the standard *bazm u razm* ("feasting and fighting") doublet of Persian poetry, and preferring the variant *baqā-yi niʿmat* to the text's *baqā u niʿmat*.

26. *Farvār* refers to an upper room provided with doors and windows; cf. Dihkhudā 1993, s.v.

27. In later poetry (for example, that of Anvarī) the *ṭāram*, the domed (audience) chamber, seems to designate any domed structure, and the term *qubba* often replaces *gunbad*. Bayhaqī speaks of the *ṭāram* of Masʿūd I's palace(s) in terms which suggest that the administrative offices of the vizier and the chancery were housed there (see e.g. 1995: 175, 189, 210).

28. ʿUnṣurī (1944: 107) states that the *ruvāq* of Maḥmūd's palace at Bust (Lashgarī Bāzār) looks towards the water; this corresponds with the archaeological evidence for the audience chamber of the Southern Palace as opening onto the river (see Schlumberger 1978: 38). ʿUnṣurī's poem would seem to be a rare example, for this period, of a description of a palace whose ruins, at least, have survived.

29. One might interpret these "palaces" as temporary pavilions, or tents, set up for the feast which is about to take place (and which is further suggested by the reference to "awnings"; cf. O'Kane 1993: 250); but the general term for such temporary structures at this period seems to be *killa* (cf. Farrukhī 1932: 84), and I have found no attestation for the use of *kākh* in this sense.

30. *Panjara*, according to Dihkhudā (1993, s.v.), indicates a (window with) a latticed (*mushabbak*) grating.

31. This is the sole reference I have come across so far to "sunshades", presumably awnings made of fabric and attached to a wooden frame.

32. Amīr Yūsuf became smitten by Ṭughril (who was, at the time, one of Maḥmūd's favorite pages), was given him by Maḥmūd, brought him up, and, when he matured, found him a noble wife. Ṭughril repaid this generosity when, after Masʿūd's accession (and having been suborned by him), he betrayed his master, and brought about his arrest and death (see Bayhaqī 1995: 322–29).

33. Bombaci also notes "marble bas-reliefs representing human figures" found at Ghazna (1959: 9–14); see also Scerrato 1959: 41–42.

34. ʿUnṣurī's *qaṣīda* opens with a lengthy description of the sultan's *maydān*, a descriptive topic which merits further study. On the figural frescoes of Lashgarī Bāzār see Schlumberger 1978: 61–65; Hillenbrand 1994: 413; idem 2000: 201–02 (where he notes the central Asian parallels for the paintings); *EI2*, art. "Lashkar-i Bāzār". Compare Bayhaqī's description, in very similar terms, of Masʿūd I's Turkish guard in the account of that ruler's coronation in 429/1040 (1995: 713–15). On wall-paintings of approximately the same period in Nishapur see Wilkinson 1986: 159–87, 202–18, 242–58, 264–309. Wall-paintings were evidently so common that Ibn-i Yamīn saw fit to comment on their absence in the house of one of his patrons (1966: 23), a certain (unidentified) "Ḥakīm al-Dīn," who was perhaps a *qāḍī*.

35. I hope to deal elsewhere with the relation between palace descriptions and the activities which go on within the palace. These are (as S. Blair has pointed out with respect to the Īlkhānid period) less "elaborate ceremonial" (as was typical of the Abbasid caliphs) and more connected with "feasts and enthronements" (1993: 241), with the former definitely predominating.

36. It is in the same metre and rhyme, and its opening *miṣrāʿ* alludes explicitly to that of Farrukhī's poem (Farrukhī: *ba-farkhunda fāl u ba-farkhunda akhtar*; Azraqī: *ba-fāl-i humāyūn u farkhunda akhtar*).

37. This palace appears to have been built for Ṭughānshāh by his vizier, of whom the poet says, "A vizier who in a month has built [*pardākht*] a palace better than Kisrā's palace and Qayṣar's *ayvān*."

38. Compare al-Buḥturī's description of the lake in al-Mutawakkil's palace of al-Jaʿfarī; see Sperl 1989: 38–42; Meisami 2000.

39. On *shamsa*s in Mamlūk architectural decoration see Amin and Ibrahim 1990: 71; for the use of *shamsa*s in Fāṭimid architectural decoration see *EI2*, s.v. (H. Halm). See also Melikian- Chirvani 1974: 42–43 on the expression *shamsa-yi Chīn*, "rosace de Turkistan", and its connection with nimbused images of the Buddha. Hillenbrand refers to "Aufi's detailed description" of Ṭughānshāh's palace (1994: 414); in fact, the description is *not* ʿAwfī's, who only mentions the palace briefly before going on to quote in full the two *qaṣīda*s discussed here (ʿAwfī 1957: 311–17).

40. The poem appears to celebrate Arslānshāh's accession; cf. the poet's statement, "The garden of kingship became like a blooming bower, when he set up for the first time the royal throne in the garden."

41. Bahrāmshāh ibn Masʿūd was Arslānshāh's rival, and ultimate victor, in the struggle for Masʿūd III's succession. His reign saw a significant revival of poetry in Ghazna. See Khan 1949.

42. Anvarī is already late, and his palace descriptions (such as they are) were written in the East. The *dīvān* of Malikshāh's (465–85/1072–92) chief Persian panegyrist Muʿizzī (d. between 519–21/1125–27) appears to contain no palace descriptions in *qaṣīda*s dedicated either to the sultan or to Muʿizzī's other *mamdūḥ*s (amongst them, conspicuously, the vizier Niẓām al-Mulk; my thanks to Ms. G. Tetley, who is currently completing a D.Phil. thesis on the poetry of Farrukhī and Muʿizzī, for this information).
43. Nāṣir ibn Ṭāhir's palace-garden complex was called Manṣūriyya, "the [place of] Victory;" cf. Anvarī 1994: 1, 443–445, where the poet mentions, among other things, its lake (*birka*).
44. A variant—"May its expanse [*sāḥat*], like the *bayt-i maʿmūr*, be far from calamities"—is perhaps to be preferred in view of the ensuing comparison of the palace to the Kaʿba.
45. For other descriptions of palaces see e.g. Jabalī 1960: 222–23. Compare Ẓahīr Faryābī (d. 598/1201–2?), in a *qaṣīda* to the Atābak Nuṣrat al-Dīn Abū Bakr (1959: 156–57), in which the poet observes, "Riḍwān has painted [*takḥīl karda*] your inscription with ink from houris' locks; and each morning, from the *shamsa*s of your portico [*ruvāq*], the sun borrows light," and goes on to describe briefly the wall-paintings' scenes of hunting and feasting (on the sense of *takḥīl* see Dihkhudā 1993, s.v.); Jamāl Iṣfāhānī (d. after 588/1192?) who, in a *qaṣīda* to the Qāḍī al-Quḍāt Rukn al-Dīn Masʿūd (1941: 200–01), notes, in particular, the interior of the palace's "decorated dome" (*qubba-yi muzakhraf*), whose images have "rendered helpless this *muqarnas*-ed rosegarden" (i.e., the sky), whose *shamsa*s fill the air with sunlight, and whose ceiling is adorned with tilework (*mīnā*).
46. See e.g. Khāqānī 1959: 387–8 (to the Sharvānshāh Akhsitān [whose dates are uncertain]); 756 (to an unnamed patron, probably also Akhsitān; both poems stress the "newness" of palace and ruler, whom the latter poem describes as "seated in the *muqarnas* of his new palace [*ayvān*]); 774–75 (to the Sharvānshāh Manūchihr [again, dates uncertain, as is the actual dedicatee; the final line contains Manūchihr's title of Khāqān-i Aʿẓam, but the poet states that the palace is in Nīmrūz [Sistan]); 186–90 (to Sayf al-Dīn Arslān Muẓaffar, the ruler of Darband; the poet, longing to return to Mecca, where he had gone on pilgrimage shortly before, endows the ruler's palace, as well as his city, with the attributes of the holy sites).
47. The poet puns on *juft* and *ṭāq*, which also mean "pair" and "impair", i.e. even and odd (numbers). *Juft* occurs infrequently in Persian palace descriptions; I take it to mean a decorative band or dado around a window or other opening, as is attested for the Mamlūk period (see Amin and Ibrahim 1990: 29).

48. I must confess that the terminology defeats me here. *Chift* may refer to a hasp, *chuft* to a beam, a trellis, or shoring. For *maʿbar* cf. Amin and Ibrahim, s.v. *maʿbara*: the area over the lintel of a door (1990: 110).

49. These elements may not in fact be new; but I have not thoroughly studied later poetry, and merely note instances where I have come across something not seen before.

50. The *tābkhāna* was a heated chamber utilized in winter; the *jām* mentioned must refer to the glassed insets in a ceiling or skylight (*rawzan*) that let in light (cf. Amin and Ibrahim 1990: 27).

51. The *rawzan* or *rawzana* is a skylight (cf. Dihkhudā 1993, s.v.), or perhaps a light well such as those at Lashgarī Bāzār (cf. Allen 1988: 61).

52. Reading *dīvār* for *dīvān*, which seems meaningless.

53. In the poems of both Salmān and Khvājū one wonders whether it is palaces or tent-pavilions which are referred to; cf. n. 57 below.

54. Some of these describe other types of buildings, including the Friday mosque at Sabzavār built by the Sarbadārid Tāj al-Dīn (Ibn Yamīn 1966: 3–31); a dam constructed by the Kart ruler Muʿizz al-Dīn Ḥusayn (ibid.: 102); a *dār al-ḥadīth* (ibid.: 118–19); and a bathhouse (ibid.: 130). Also of interest is a *qaṣīda* in which the celestial spheres are compared metaphorically to (parts of) a building (ibid.: 87–89). I hope to deal with poetic descriptions of other sorts of buildings, and with buildings as metaphors, at a future date.

55. ʿAlāʾ al-Dīn (here, ʿAlāʾ al-Mulk) Muḥammad served the Īlkhānid pretender Tughātīmūr as governor of Khurasan until his fall from favor in 727/1327; see *EI2*, art. "Ibn-i Yamīn" (J. Rypka), art. "Sarbadārids" (C. P. Melville).

56. Although this move towards abstraction is a feature of the development of Persian poetry in general (and is especially notable in the *ghazal*, where the poetic vocabulary becomes a kind of allusive "shorthand"), it appears somewhat peculiar in passages whose primary purpose would seem to be ekphrastic.

57. The only Tīmūrid poet I have looked at is Jāmī (d. 848/1492). Of the 60 *qaṣīdas* in his *dīvān*, no less than eighteen contain references to and/or descriptions of palaces, typical features of which include *shamsas*, wall-paintings, arches (*ṭāq*), domes, crenellations, and so on. In one (1966:16), the palace itself "speaks," in much the same way as in a panegyric composed as a boast by the *mamdūḥ*: "I am (the one for whom) the crown on the sphere's head is dust beneath my feet" (etc.). Two points may be noted here: first, that these may not be palaces (despite their being generally termed *qaṣr*) but tents, which were a marked feature of Tīmūrid court life (see e.g.

Gronke 1992; O'Kane 1993, and especially 251, where he notes that tents were described in the same royal imagery as were palaces); and second, that many of these *qaṣīda*s conclude with an admonition to the *mamdūḥ* to build, not for this world, but for the next (see e. g. ibid.: 10: "Your difficulties will not be resolved by building this palace [*īn sarāy*], if in this world [*īn sarā*] you do not prepare for *that* palace [*ān sarāy*]." The relationship between architecture and literature in the Ṣafavid and Mughal periods is the subject of current research by Professor Paul E. Losensky of Indiana University.

58. In this connection it seems remarkable that the relatively stable reign of Malikshāh appears to have produced no poetry celebrating either that ruler's building projects or those of his vizier Niẓām al-Mulk; nor do those of Sultan Sanjar (511–52/1118–57) appear to receive mention. Similarly, the *dīvān*s of the panegyrists of the Khwārazmshāhs and the Qarakhānids seem to lack references to buildings in general and to palaces in particular. This issue, however, requires further research.

II

NARRATING ILLUSTRATIONS: TWO CASE STUDIES IN TEXT-IMAGE RELATIONSHIPS

Ferdowsi and the Illustration of the *Shahnameh*

JEROME W. CLINTON

This is an essay toward understanding the relation of text and image in Persian illustrated manuscripts. I wish to address here the thorny questions that are raised by any attempt to read the text and paintings in an illustrated manuscript as a single, composite whole. The focus of my remarks will be the *Shahnameh* of Abolqasem Ferdowsi. The choice of text is an obvious one. The *Shahnameh* was the first work of Persian literature to be enriched with paintings, and it has remained a principal choice for illustration down virtually to the present day.[1] It provides unusually rich and varied possibilities for the examination of the interrelation of poet and painter.

I approach the examination of the illustrated manuscript from the perspective of a literary critic, that is, as a scholar who starts from the text, not from the paintings. This point of view has gone largely unrepresented in the study of Persian book painting. I am tempted to qualify this by adding "for obvious reasons," but perhaps it should not be taken as given that a literary critic will have nothing to contribute to the discussion of paintings that are intended as illustrations of a narrative, and which are also invariably framed by written text. Literary critics have an established place as commentators on the relation of text and image in western cultural studies. This essay is an attempt to introduce this perspective to the study of one central document in the world of Islamic book painting.

When I first began to read paintings against the text they illustrated, I assumed that whatever the differences in detail between text and painting might be, I would find that they were unified in large measure by a shared esthetic. I quickly discovered that, on the contrary, illustrated manuscripts of the *Shahnameh*, were, both individually and collectively, arenas in which two very different visual esthetics and narrative strategies competed with each other. When Ferdowsi chose to, he could be a remarkable descriptive poet, and I shall have more to say about his visual style in the next section. But he was first and foremost a story teller, and in order to serve the needs of narration he diminished the role of description in his poetry to a degree far beyond that of the narrative poets who followed him. Painters, who came to his work centuries after its completion, were, by contrast, concerned principally with the look of the story, and altered the narratives of the *Shahnameh* in the process of illustrating them, adding some details not in the text, subtracting others that were, and changing those they retained. Their sense of what scenes should be illustrated differed strikingly from that of the poet, and their paintings were as likely to distort Ferdowsi's sense of the dramatic shape of a narrative as to support it. I shall return to these points in a moment.

My initial response to these striking divergences between text and image was to lodge complaints. I privileged the esthetics of the poet's narrative over those of painter, and interpreted divergences between them as painterly distortions or betrayals of the poet and his text. As I have pursued the question, however, I have come to realize that my complaints were based on a narrow understanding of the terms "illustrator" and "illustration," one that assumed that the task of the visual artist was to put his work at the service of the poet. In doing this I ignored the fact that the contemporary attitudes toward authorship offered little support for this view. Poets borrowed tropes and narratives from their predecessors and justified themselves by asserting that their work improved on the originals, and scribes and copyists felt free to interpolate lines and silently alter the text of the *Shahnameh* with an abandon that is the bane of modern editors.[2] When painters injected their own perception of a story or scene into the *Shahnameh* they were only following accepted practice.

In short, it would be truer to the esthetic conventions of pre-modern Iran to think of the painters who illustrated manuscripts of the

Shahnameh as providing alternative performances or interpretations of the scenes they chose to paint. Their work parallels that of Ferdowsi, but is not subordinate to it. Like the scribes and poets just mentioned, their attitude toward his poetry was admiring but not reverent. They saw nothing amiss in adding something of their own to what he had created, something not present in the original. Inevitably, such additions created tension between the visual and the poetic, and in the remainder of this essay I will examine several of these points of visual and narrative conflict. I would like to take the visual or pictorial dimension of Ferdowsi's poetry as my starting point since it is not as well known or studied as is that of the paintings that illustrate his poem. That is, how does Ferdowsi himself illustrate his work, and what is the place of the visual in his poetic style.

Ferdowsi's Style and the Visual

Let me begin with a few general assertions. As he tells us quite emphatically, Ferdowsi wishes the narratives that make up the *Shahnameh* to be widely read or recited. To that end he employs all the varied skills of a master craftsman to make his poetry memorable as well as instructive. Although he does not say this explicitly, he clearly feels that the value of these tales lies in their historical and moral content. Of necessity he must depict, or give some visual sense of, both the world in which his narratives take place and the characters that populate them, but this is of secondary importance. These are not courtly lyrics, but instructive narratives. His dominant concern is to reveal to his audience the interior landscapes of his characters and the moral geography of their world. As a consequence, he uses pictorial description, and uses it skillfully, but he subordinates it to the needs of narration. At times images command the foreground of the poem, but always to some practical end. To paraphrase Shafi'i-Kadkani, Ferdowsi, contrary to the practice of other poets, does not create images for themselves alone, but as a means of revealing the events and circumstances of the narrative.[3]

As an example of this emphasis, consider his treatment of one of the most vividly pictorial and strikingly Iranian icons from the imaginative world of Persian literature—Simorgh, the legendary bird that nests atop

Mount Alborz. Although her origin is in pre-Islamic Iran, she survived and flourished in the Islamic period, most notably as the patron and protector of Zal and his family, but in many other contexts outside the *Shahnameh* as well. She is a favorite of Iranian artists, and one does not have to look far to find colorful and fantastic interpretations of the Simorgh in a variety of media. Ferdowsi, however, does not exploit the striking appearance of Simorgh at all. In fact, in her first appearance in the *Shahnameh*, she is reduced pictorially to a shadowy but threatening presence with wings and talons, and plays a supporting role to a howling infant. I am referring here to the scene in the "Story of Sam and Zal" that leads to her becoming the family's totem. At Sam's order, the suspiciously white-headed infant Zal has been left to die on the slopes of Mt. Alborz. Simorgh initially seems destined to assure that his end will be swift and horrible. That is, when she sets out from her nest at the mountain's peak that day she is searching for food to nourish her own young. The first thing she sees is Zal, and she swoops down to investigate.[4] The poet gives us a detailed picture of the wretched child whose cries have attracted her.

> She saw an infant far below whose cries
> Had set the land to boiling like the sea.
> Granite was his cradle, the earth his nurse.
> His body bare of clothes, his lips of milk,
> Around him dark and gloomy earth, while high
> Above the sun had reached its apogee.

Simorgh snatches the child from the ground, not to rescue him, but to provide a meal for her chicks.

> Simorgh descended from the clouds and with
> Her talons seized him from the fiery rock,
> Then bore him flying up toward her nest
> Atop the peak of Mount Alborz.
> She gave him to her young to feed upon, and not
> Be moved by his laments and cries.

The next line is the central one in the scene from the point of view of the larger narrative structure in that it shows how the intervention of God

(Yazdan) transforms the remorseless hunger of these wild creatures into love and compassion.

> But then Yazdan, who gives the good, but holds
> All things within His soul, preserved the child.
> Simorgh and all her hungry brood looked at
> The child whose eyes wept bloody tears, and in
> Amazement showered love upon poor Zal,
> Enchanted by the beauty of his face.
> She chose the softest morsels of her prey
> For him so he might chew them with his gums.

This sequence offers a number of other pictorial possibilities—Simorgh and her chicks in the nest, Simorgh swooping down from the clouds or carrying Zal in her talons back up to the nest, Simorgh and her chicks adoring the infant, and so on. Instead of these, Ferdowsi has given us an indelible image of a visually less promising moment, but one that more effectively dramatizes Yazdan's compassion by emphasizing Zal's pathetic vulnerability. The wretched and unhappy infant suits his end, the visually spectacular Simorgh does not. Objects whose presence is necessary to set the stage in a minimalist fashion—mountain, clouds, Simorgh, nest—he names but does not describe, leaving it to his audience to supply from their own experience and imagination the additional details necessary to fill out the scene. In describing Simorgh as "visually spectacular" I am, of course, referring to the later interpretations of the great bird by illustrators.[5] In the *Shahnameh*, Simorgh is only a large, awesome presence with wings and claws.[6]

This scene illustrates several other characteristic features of Ferdowsi's style. The first is his minimal use of adjectives and adverbs. The earth is dark and gloomy (*tireh va nezhand*), and the rock from which Zal is snatched is "fiery" (*garm*), but the remaining nouns—granite, earth, sun, clouds, etc.—are presented in their unmodified generic form. Under the general heading of nouns, one category is noteworthy for its absence, and that is color. On the occasions when he finds color useful, as in the scene where Sohrab looks out over the Iranian army from the heights of the White Fort and describes the heraldry of Iran's Shah and heroes for Hojir, Ferdowsi employs the colors necessary to accurately depict their tents and banners.[7] But these occasions are rare, and for the most part Ferdowsi's palette is limited to six colors: black, white, gold, silver, red, and blue, all of which have strong metaphoric content. Gold and silver appear as emblems of wealth and luxury. Black and its synonyms indicate night, moral depravity, psychological confusion, and whatever is ominous or threatening, as in the black earth on which Zal lies. White sometimes suggest the opposite of black. A white beard or white hair denotes wisdom, and pale skin is a mark of beauty, but white often has negative associations, as in the name, and hair, of the White Div. Sam also sees his infant son's white hair as a bad omen. Blue, which appears as both indigo (*nil*) and sky blue (*lâzhvard*), evokes the darkness of night as well as the more usual water and sky. The true antonym of black is light which Ferdowsi associates with the sun and the forces of good, and does not describe as a color. The most common color of all is blood red, which by signifying both death and mourning (in the form of bloody tears), is the recurrent adornment of the many violent encounters that pepper the text.

Verbs are similarly unmodified. Cruelty is implicit in Simorgh's instructions to her chicks, as is loving kindness in her selection of the tenderest morsels for Zal, but neither quality is expressed explicitly. So also we assume without being told that her flights down from her nest and up to it are swift and powerful. When Ferdowsi does employ more elaborate metaphors and similes he rarely extends them beyond a single line, nor does he link them to complementary images. The evocation of the earth as boiling like the sea is powerful and memorable, but it is contained within a single half line. Shafi'i-Kadkani remarks on this stylistic economy and cites it as a mark of Ferdowsi's superiority to other poets, who, he says, are inclined to heap up similes and metaphors in excess.[8] This is a matter of taste, however, and I am simply interested in drawing attention to the use of brief, vivid, and independent images as a characteristic feature of Ferdowsi's style. If this sequence is poor in pictorial detail, it is rich in feeling, energy, and movement. It provides the reader with a sure sense of where the characters are relative to each other, of their movement between the base of the mountain and its peak, and of their emotions, but not of what they look like or of the settings in which they find themselves.

Ferdowsi characteristically uses a very poetic and unpainterly sleight-of-hand to evoke the physical presence of his characters. Even in the most pictorial lines of the passage Ferdowsi conveys Zal's misery to the audience by indirect means. That is, he does this either by implying it or by showing us not the emotion itself, but its effect on Zal's surroundings. The two techniques overlap, but are subtly different in their effects. He says that Zal is weeping, but not that he is intensely miserable. Once we see his condition, however—he has no clothing or milk, his cradle is granite, and the sun is beating down on him—what other assumption could we make? Moreover, his lamentations are gigantic. Again, we know this not because Ferdowsi says so, but because he shows us their effect on the world around him ("whose cries/Had set the earth to boiling like the sea").[9] That is, his wretchedness is a furnace so hot that it dissolves stone.

This technique of making a thing known by its effects, pervades the poem. Over and over we see the world of the *Shahnameh* principally through its reflection. Just as we understand the intensity of Zal's unhappiness through its impact on the earth around him, so also we know the ferocity of heroes through the terror they inspire in demons, wild beasts, other heroes, and even in nature. To give only two examples from among many possible ones, when Tahmineh describes for Rostam how she has become infatuated with him through the tales she has heard of him, she first describes his strength directly, "No crocodile or lion is so fierce," and then gives a catalogue of the terrible impact of his presence:

> When you approach them with your mace in hand,
> The leopard rends his claws, the lion his heart.
> The eagle when he sees your naked blade,
> Dares not take wing and fly off to the hunt.
> The tiger's skin is branded by your rope.
> The clouds weep blood from fear of your sharp lance.[10]

Later, in the story of Esfandiyar, Rostam says of his grandfather, Sam, that "Male lions fled their lairs at his approach," and also that Sam had defeated an elephant "the very thought/Of whom would make a joyful heart despair."[11]

While the use of description in Ferdowsi's narrative style tends, as I have suggested, toward the minimalist and focuses on action and emotion, when it suits his purposes, he can create images that are both richly pictorial and essentially static. A scene of mourning follows immediately on the fatal wounding of Esfandiyar. When, at the conclusion of his death bed soliloquy, he breathes his last and his body must be transported to the court, Ferdowsi composes a mourning tableau to honor the prince. He describes the coffin and the funeral procession in vivid, luxurious detail, reminding us by the use of this image that here lies the scion of a royal family, and slowing down the action in order to prolong the moment of intense grief.

> A splendid iron coffin was made for him,
> And lined with Chinese silk. The sides were sealed
> With pitch on which they sprinkled sandalwood,
> Musk, and fragrant herbs. His winding sheet
> Was made of gold brocade. The famous lords
> Assembled by his bier, and wept. And after,
> They clothed his glorious body, and set a crown
> Of turquoise on his head, then firmly closed
> The lid upon his narrow coffin. So passed
> Away that fruitful, royal tree.

At this point the narrative might naturally take on a more dynamic character as horses and camels are brought forward and the procession makes ready to move out along the road, but again Ferdowsi uses descriptions of the funeral accoutrements to halt that movement. The army is marching by Esfandiyar's bier, but by calling attention to the signs of mourning on their faces, Ferdowsi makes them appear to us as a crowd of mourners, and not a funeral procession. He introduces Pashutan leading Esfandiyar's horse, then freezes that image by describing how the horse's mane and tail have been docked as a sign of mourning, and listing the possessions of its late master with which it is now burdened.

> Rostam chose forty camels from the best he had,
> And these he draped with fine brocade. Two carried
> The coffin of the shah, while left and right,
> And front and back, the army marched with them.

> Faces bloody, their hair torn out in hanks,
> They called his name, longing to see his face.
> At the army's head rode Pashutan, who led
> His pitch black horse, its mane and tail cut short,
> Its saddle front to back. Esfandiyar's mace
> Hung from the saddle tree together with
> His warrior's helmet and mailed shirt, his bow
> And quiver too.[12]

Note that Ferdowsi has not changed his style here so much as he has shifted its emphasis. There is no appreciable increase in the frequency of adjectives and adverbs. He piles up nouns—camels, brocade, coffin, faces—but does not describe them more richly. The verbs denote action, but action that is directed toward evoking a scene of mourning—the preparation of the coffin, the clothing of the corpse, and acts of grieving.[13]

Another scene in the "Story of Rostam and Esfandiyar" has this same essentially static and pictorial character. In accordance with the dying Esfandiyar's wishes, Rostam takes his son, Bahman, under his wing at his court in Zabol, and teaches him the arts of ruling. When Goshtasp calls him back to court, Rostam opens the doors of his treasury and sends him back with a caravan of precious goods. The effect of luxury is achieved here not by detailed descriptions of his gifts, but by the number and variety of items he includes.

> [Rostam] chose fine gifts from what he had within
> His treasury, mailed shirts and tempered blades
> From India, maces, bows and arrows,
> Armor; and camphor, musk, fresh ambergris,
> And aloes wood; gold, silver, precious gems,
> Fleet horses, bolts of uncut cloth; female slaves—
> Both children and full grown—golden stirrups
> And bridles, two ruby goblets inlaid with gold
> As well—all these he gave Bahman.[14]

Again, we have a listing of luxurious objects, but in their generic forms, naming them, but not describing them.

To illustrate the contrast between Ferdowsi's pictorial style and that of his contemporaries here are a few lines here from a lyric poem by Manuchehri of Damghan (d. 1059), a poet who was famous for his vivid renderings of nature. In this poem he describes an autumn orchard on the cusp of winter, depicting the various fruits at their ripest. Manuchehri creates a memorable and highly individual image of a single object, transforming an ordinary apple into something magical and luxurious.

> That apple like a smooth turned ball of sugar
> That has been dyed three hundred times with saffron.
> Upon its cheeks are spots of coral hue.
> An emerald saddle cloth lies by its stem.
> The tiniest of domes fill up its belly,
> In each of these there is a Zangi child,
> As black as pitch, who's sound asleep.[15]

Not every simile or metaphor in Manuchehri's poetry is as richly visual as this one, but such painterly images are characteristic of his metaphoric repertory, as they are also, with some variation, of the metaphoric repertories of other lyric poets of this time.[16] The qualities most central to Ferdowsi's poetry—narrative movement, intensity of affect, economy of expression—are marginal to Manuchehri's lyrics. What he offers instead are a static image for the eye to dwell upon, a varied palette of colors, and an abundance of visual details and textures.

There is another difference to be noted here. As readers we observe Manuchehri's world from over his shoulder, or through his eyes, much as we look at paintings, and with the same sense of distance and separation from the object observed.[17] The relative paucity of descriptive details in the *Shahnameh* reduces this sense of distance. As we ourselves supply the lack of specific details our imagination moves us into the text. In addition, Ferdowsi further bridges the divide between audience and text through his reliance on depicting an object or person through their impact on those within the story. By some subtle poetic alchemy we become the recipients of that impact—the joyful heart that despairs at the thought of the elephant that Sam will defeat.

Picturing Narrative

With these general characteristics of Ferdowsi's poetry in mind, I would like to comment briefly on some points where the poetic and pictorial esthetics of the illustrated *Shahnameh* sharply contrast with each other. Two obvious ways that the painter's representation differs from the poet's are the addition of color and the freezing of narrative movement. The ways that they impinge on the audience's perspective are quite different. The addition of color supplies something that is missing from the poetry of Ferdowsi without, in my view, altering the flow and rhythm of the narrative, or the evocation of character and affect. The role of color while not altogether neutral, in this regard, is not dramatically intrusive. The static quality of painting, by contrast, is. Poetry shifts easily between static and dynamic. Painting does not. It immobilizes characters and action even when the event depicted is embedded in a fluid, ongoing narrative.

This difference between the two media generates tension, and the degree of that tension varies greatly both with the amount of detail in the painting and the degree of movement in the narrative. The more detailed the painting the more it interrupts the narrative's movement. Conflict is not inevitable, however. Even when the tension between poetry and painting is at its greatest, these two representational strategies can complement each other, as when heroes meet not to fight but to parley, or when a newly crowned monarch delivers himself of the ascension speech that convention seems to require [Plate 1].*

There are also scenes in which movement through time and space are slowed down in order to focus on the interplay between characters. This interplay can be emotional, as in the erotic interlude between Rostam and Tahmineh, can be tensely confrontative such as the moment when Esfandiyar challenges his father, Shah Goshtasp, or can have a more formal ritualistic quality as in the courtly tableaux that mark the coronations of new rulers.[18] Tension is generated when, as is frequently and unsurprisingly the case, artists chooses to paint scenes of great dynamism rather than relative stasis. I mean here the many scenes of armed combat between armies or individual heroes, where arrows fall as thick as rain, the combatants wheeling and charging with lightning speed, are frozen into a tableau.

In addition to the innate differences between the two media, the way an artist chooses to illustrate a scene can radically alter the dramatic focus of a narrative. A notable example of this occurs in the Story of Rostam and Esfandiyar. A favorite subject of artists is the moment just after Rostam's arrow has penetrated Esfandiyar's eye.[19] In all the versions of this scene that I have come across (ranging from the 14th to the 17th centuries) the two horsemen face each other, both seated erect on their horses, Rostam with bow in hand and Esfandiyar with an arrow protruding from his eye. It is a chilling, poignant tableau, as though death had brought the angry energy that has been driving the two heroes up to this point to a sudden and complete halt.

In Ferdowsi there is no such moment of arrested time. The arrow strikes, and Esfandiyar, wounded and stunned but still alive, crumples slowly from his saddle and falls to the ground. His followers rush to him, and he like Sohrab before him, has a decent interval between receiving his fatal wound and the moment of his death in which to deliver his dying thoughts. He strips away the mask of loyalty and obedience that he has worn throughout his mission to Zabol, and expresses both his respect and affection for Rostam, and his bitterness toward his father, Shah Goshtasp. By focusing on the moment when Esfandiyar receives the mortal blow, paintings of the scene shift the dramatic focus of the narrative away from this final dramatic revelation.[20]

Similar alterations in the dramatic shape of a story can be brought about not by the choice of a scene, but by the way it is represented. Painters, especially, after the 15th century, regularly fill up their paintings with people and animals that are not mentioned in the text.[21] In some scenes their presence is of little or no consequence, in others the illustration is so busy that it is difficult to distinguish immediately who the principal characters in the drama are. In the text this is never an issue. And at times an audience is provided for a scene that is explicitly identified as taking place in private, as in the last of the three battles between Rostam and Sohrab[22] [Plate 2].* Here the two protagonists dismount and, engrossed in their struggle, drift far from the battlefield where their two armies are stationed. As a result, when Rostam, having thrown Sohrab to the ground and stabbed him in the chest, learns that Sohrab is his son, he does so in private. This leads to a moment of tragic irony. The day has waned, and Rostam's soldiers, anxious to know how their leader is faring, come looking for him. Seeing his horse, Rakhsh, standing riderless and caked with mud on the plain, and knowing that Sohrab has already overthrown their hero once, they fear that Sohrab has defeated Rostam again and killed him.

A messenger is sent to the Kay Kavus who is understandably distressed. The loss of Rostam would leave Iran vulnerable to invasion from Turan. The Shah sends Tus to the battlefield to learn the awful truth. As he is about to set out Rostam suddenly appears and the Iranian army, overwhelmed with relief, falls prostrate in grateful prayer to God for their deliverance. And so, at the very moment when Rostam, heavy with the terrible knowledge that he has slain his own son, crosses the plain toward his camp, he is confronted with the sight of his comrades in arms rejoicing and thanking God for his triumph. It is a moment of great poignancy, and one that depends for its effect upon the fact that no one in the army knows either that Rostam has defeated Sohrab, or that Sohrab has revealed to him that he is his son. The large audience that painters supply for this scene undercuts that ironic moment and makes the anxiety of the Iranians groundless.

Poet and painters also use very different means to identify the leading characters of the narratives. One of the few descriptive features that is iconic in the *Shahnameh* is size. Rostam's huge body allows others to distinguish him from his companions on a number of occasions, and, of course, it is Rakhsh's unusual size that suits him to be Rostam's mount. In book painting, however, the absence of perspective makes the representation of relative size problematic. Lacking this marker, painters rely on others. Since facial features are generic both in the text and in painting, Rostam's "tiger skin cuirass" (*babr-e bayan*) becomes the one sure means of identifying him visually. In the fifteenth century, illustrators added a distinctive leopard skull helmet as well, although it does not appear in the text. Rostam thus becomes not the physically dominant hero, but the one with a distinctive costume. (No similar identifying mark was introduced for Rakhsh.)

Sohrab presents a special problem since in the text much is made of his strong family resemblance to Rostam, including his great height.[23] The only notable difference between them is age. Some illustrators make him shorter than other heroes to suggest youth, and most rely on a widespread convention in both painting and poetry and depict him as beardless. In the *Shahnameh*, however, Ferdowsi rarely if ever mentions beards, and never uses them to mark the difference in age between Sohrab and his father. So, again, a notable hero looks very different in one medium than he does in the other [Plate 2].*

Illustrators often give their characters faces that are altogether devoid of affect at moments when the text indicates that they are overwhelmed with rage, grief, or passion. There are, of course, means other than facial features by which painters can depict emotion—torn clothes and disheveled hair for grief, eyes tilted down for submission, and so on. Ferdowsi regularly employs these devices as well, as, for example, when he tells us that Esfandiyar stands before his father, Shah Goshtasp, "like a willing slave,/Distressed and anxious, hands upon his chest."[24] But the faces of his characters also flush with joy (or wine), crease with rage or pain, and so on. He does not describe every facial expression, but he accustoms his reader to thinking that the characters in the *Shahnameh* show their feelings in their faces and bodies as well as in their words. As a result, the blank faces of the figures in illustrations seem strangely incongruous.[25]

Painter and Poet

The works of manuscript illustrators are usually described and evaluated exclusively in terms of their relation to each other and to the tradition of book painting. An understanding of Ferdowsi's own approach to illustrating his work suggests an alternative set of criteria for describing the work of the painters who added their representations of scenes from the *Shahnameh* to his, one that starts from a consideration of how well, or in what way, their vision meshed with that of Ferdowsi. He leaves the painter a very free hand since he provides few visual cues, iconic or otherwise. Painters, like the rest of the audience of the *Shahnameh*, are implicitly invited to supply all missing details from their own imaginations, and this they have done, often drawing on sources from outside the

Shahnameh for thematic content as well as artistic inspiration and guidance. In the earliest illustrated manuscripts, however, the illustration is clearly derived from a specific line in the poem, is placed in close approximation to it, and is clearly intended to depict the narrative content of that line.[26] Moreover, despite a good deal of variation in the abilities of the artists, they employ a style that is remarkably like that of Ferdowsi. Portraits are generic, details of dress and setting are kept to a minimum, and there are no backgrounds.[27] They are also small and obviously contained within the text. This moment of esthetic harmony did not endure long, however, and, to simplify a great deal, as the art of manuscript illustration developed, individual paintings diverged ever more widely from the text which framed them.

Graphically, too, paintings, which started as inserts within a page of manuscript, expanded to fill more and more of the page, and, eventually, to reverse the physical relation of painting and text, surrounding the poetry as the poetry once surrounded it. So also in later manuscripts the linkage between painting and text grew so tenuous that at times paintings become not just a version of the scene, but, as I have already suggested, alternative performances of it.

Increasingly the painted version of a scene comes to dominate the audience's perception of it. A notable case in point is that of how one is to represent the most frequently illustrated scene in the whole of the *Shahnameh*, Rostam's defeat of the White Div (*div sepid*).[28] Ferdowsi describes the White Div as not white, except for his hair. His face and body are black and he wears iron brassards and an iron helmet. Size is a significant element of his appearance. He is so large he "fills the world," and he moves toward Rostam "like a black mountain."[29] Painters, by contrast, consistently substituted horns for hair, ignored his iron armor and changed the div's skin color to milky white. They represent him as large, but his cave home contains him and Rostam comfortably. While the reason for this striking transformation of the White Div may be inspired by some external source, it may be that the whitening of the div was initially a response to the extraordinary difficulty of rendering him in paint as he is in the poetry. This large, dark demon would be almost invisible in the obscurity of his cave, and so the artist takes his cue from the demon's name and shows him as white against the cave's blackness. Later painters followed the earliest painters' lead, and the White Div became white in person as well as in name. Whatever the origins of this tradition of representation, the point to make here is that by now virtually all readers of the *Shahnameh* visualize the White Div as, indeed, white, and are astonished to learn that this not at all how Ferdowsi describes him [Plates 3 and 4].*

Having drawn attention to how greatly text and image diverge, I should also add that the two are not always in conflict, even when they seem at first to be so. Some paintings, or painters, seem to have developed deeper affinities with the text in lieu of the superficial ones just mentioned. The series of paintings of Simorgh, Zal, and Sam mentioned above are, with their richly detailed images and complex visual structure, stylistically, a world apart from the text as I have described it. Yet by dividing the paintings vertically into two dramatically different halves—a wild and craggy world on the left that is dominated by the figures of the gorgeous mythical bird and the saintly, pale Zal, and on the right a sedate and well-ordered plain that is defined by the shah and his courtly retainers—the artist powerfully enhances the text's message that by returning to his father's court Zal is entering a new and very different world than the one he inhabited as a child. It also provides a compelling visual witness to the recurring theme of Zal's connection to the magical realm of his foster parent.[30]

Reading Paintings, Visualizing Poetry

Examining individual examples of the tension between text and illustration will take us only so far. The next step is obviously to carry out studies of individual manuscripts, and to compare the ideological programs of painter and poet in an extended and systematic way. At present, virtually no such studies exist for the *Shahnameh*, and few for other illustrated Islamic manuscripts. In 1969, A. S. Melikian-Chirvani published a brief monograph on the illustrated manuscript of Ayyuqi's *Varqe va Golshah* that incorporated careful, parallel examinations of the poetic and the pictorial esthetics of the work. Despite this promising beginning, however, his work remains—30 years after its publication—

virtually unique.[31]

Historians of Persian and Islamic art have usually treated illustrated manuscripts more as albums of pictures than as works of literature. There are some honorable exceptions. M. S. Simpson includes both texts and translations of the relevant passages in her discussion of the miniatures from the Freer Gallery's *Haft Awrang* of Jami. Her study sets a new standard for incorporating the text as an essential adjunct to the study of the paintings.[32] Such exceptions are still very few. At best there is a careful identification of the appropriate textual passages and sometimes translations or paraphrases of them. This is true even in the case of studies that are otherwise exemplary. The study of the Great Mongol *Shahnameh* by Grabar and Blair already mentioned includes a provisional analysis of the ideological program of the whole manuscript. The discussion of Grabar and Blair is devoted almost exclusively to the paintings in the manuscript, however, and the text is represented only by allusions to one or two recurrent motifs.[33] Robert Hillenbrand's essay on the illustration of the Iskander Cycle in the Great Mongol *Shahnameh* has the advantage of a clear and specific focus, a series of paintings in a single remarkable manuscript. His discussion of the relation of the paintings to the contemporary social and political context and the other sources for the Alexander material is both exhaustive and illuminating, and clarifies the degree to which particular artists drew their inspiration from sources outside the text they were illustrating. In his view, the artist's presentation of Alexander's adventures improves on the Ferdowsi's rather pedestrian treatment of the legend, although in fairness to the poet one should add that Hillenbrand's analysis of the text fails to make clear where he thinks it is lacking.[34]

Both studies are the result of art historical scholarship of a very high order, and any disappointment I feel at their having slighted the text has to be balanced both against the realization that literary scholars have contributed even less to the study of the relation of text and image. Moreover, disappointing as this neglect of the text is to the literary scholar, it is not altogether surprising. One would have to be wearing blinders not to recognize that the paintings in an illustrated manuscript invariably provide a significant motive for its production, and, in the case of the masterpieces from royal workshops, the determining one. The paintings and all the other extra textual components of the manuscript are newly created especially for the manuscript. The text is not. On the contrary, in general only well known and highly admired works of literature were chosen for illustration. How else could the patron justify the expense of commissioning paintings for a manuscript and, in the case of works of royal provenance, the staggering cost of hiring all the other artists and craftsmen necessary to produce a volume of an excellence to match the paintings? Yet the full understanding of illustrated manuscripts requires a vision that includes both poet and painter. That is the dilemma.

In order for individual scholars to make explicit what is implicit in this esthetic dialogue they would have to be not just gifted amateurs like the elites of the Il-Khanid, Timurid, and Safavid courts who were the work's first audience, but real intellectual amphibians, equally comfortable in the two disciplines of art history and literary criticism. Few if any contemporary scholars can make that claim, and certainly, I do not make it for myself. What is needed is a dialogue between literary critics and art historians, or, rather, a dialogue in which they jointly interrogate text and illustration to illuminate the nature of the relations of text and image. What I have attempted to do here is to initiate that dialogue by asking the kinds of questions that occur to a literary critic when he reads an illustrated *Shahnameh* with more than a casual, admiring eye on the pictures.

*The plates included here may also be seen in color online at <princeton.edu/~jwc/shahnameh/illustration.html>.

Plate 1—Ferdowsi and the Illustration of the Shahnameh. "Luhrasp enthroned." Princeton University Library, Islamic Manuscripts, Third Series, no. 310 "Peck," folio 222b.

Plate 2—Ferdowsi and the Illustration of the Shahnameh. "Rostam stabs Sohrab." Princeton University Library, Islamic Manuscripts, Third Series, no. 310 "Peck," folio 22b.

Plate 3—Ferdowsi and the Illustration of the Shahnameh. "Rostam fights with the White Div." Princeton University Library, Islamic Manuscripts, Third Series, no. 310 "Peck," folio 62b.

Plate 4—Ferdowsi and the Illustration of the Shahnameh. "Rostam slays the White Div." Princeton University Library, Islamic Manuscripts, Garrett no. 57, folio 62a.

Plate 1—The Lover, His Lady, Her Lady, and a Thirteenth-Century Celestina. Riyāḍ Faints at the Mention of Bayāḍ's Name; f. 3v.; *Ḥadīth Bayāḍ wa Riyāḍ*, Vat. Ar. Ris. 368; photograph courtesy of the Vatican Library.

Plate 2—The Lover, His Lady, Her Lady, and a Thirteenth-Century Celestina. Riyāḍ Sings and Plays the Lute at the Sayyida's Maclis; f. 10r; *Ḥadīth Bayāḍ wa Riyāḍ*, Vat. Ar. Ris. 368; photograph courtesy of the Vatican Library.

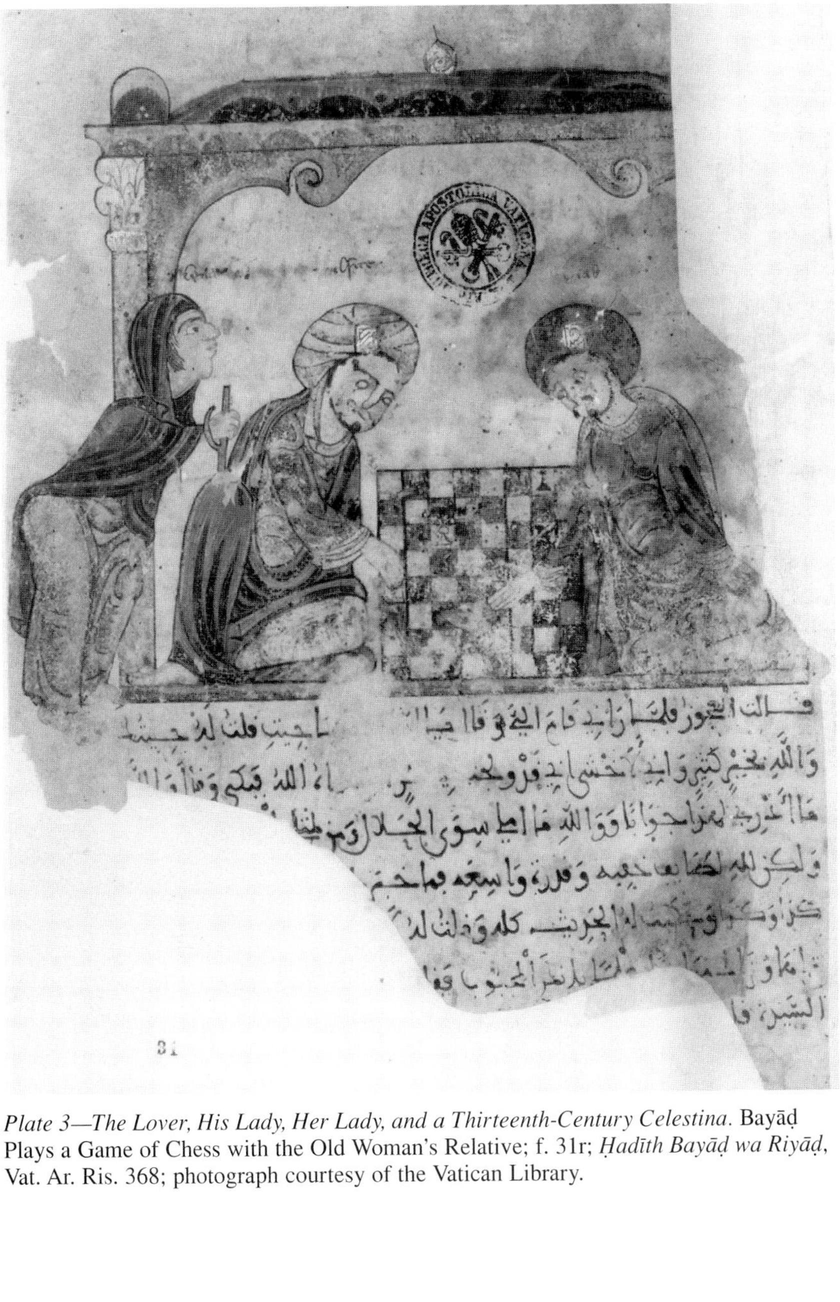

Plate 3—The Lover, His Lady, Her Lady, and a Thirteenth-Century Celestina. Bayāḍ Plays a Game of Chess with the Old Woman's Relative; f. 31r; *Ḥadīth Bayāḍ wa Riyāḍ*, Vat. Ar. Ris. 368; photograph courtesy of the Vatican Library.

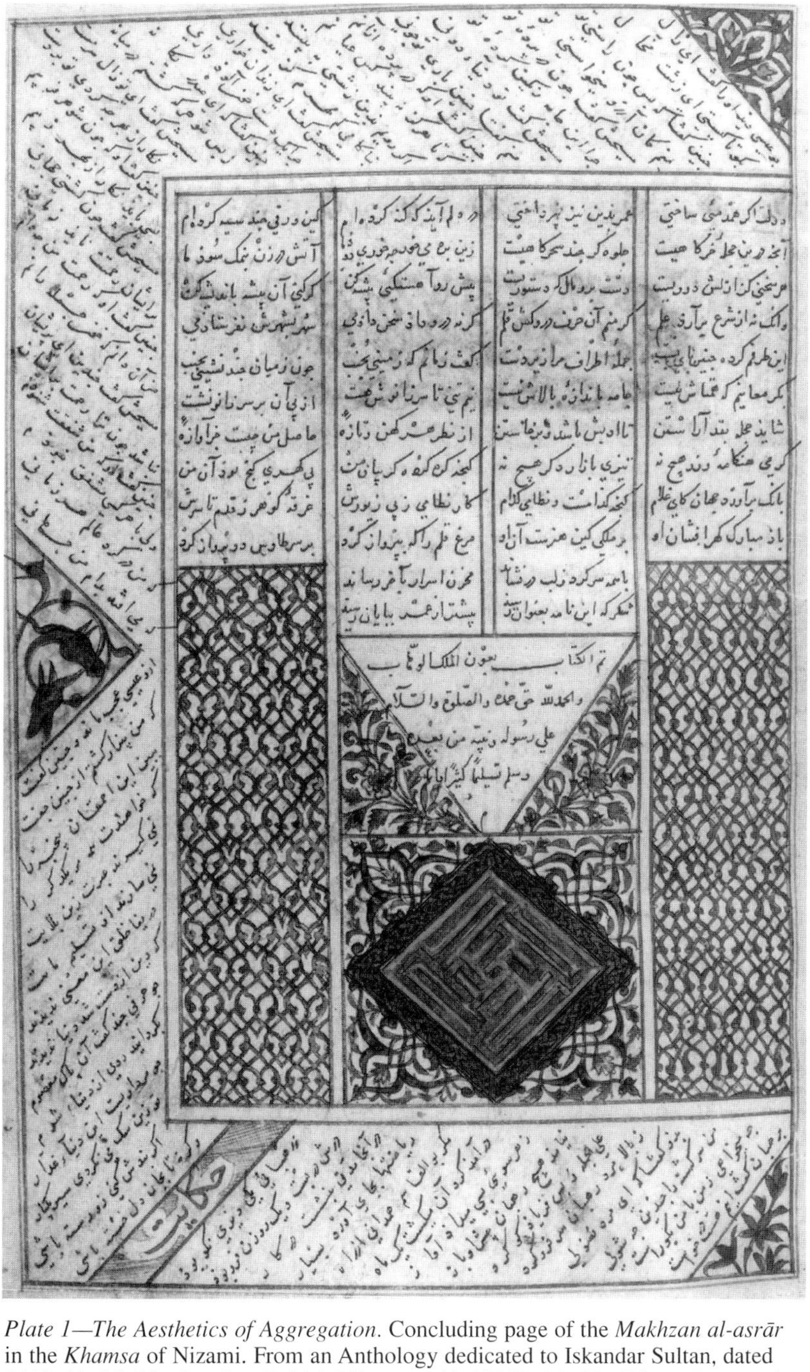

Plate 1—The Aesthetics of Aggregation. Concluding page of the *Makhzan al-asrār* in the *Khamsa* of Nizami. From an Anthology dedicated to Iskandar Sultan, dated 1410–11, fol. 28a. London, British Library, Add. 27261, fol. 28a (Photo: By permission of the British Library, London).

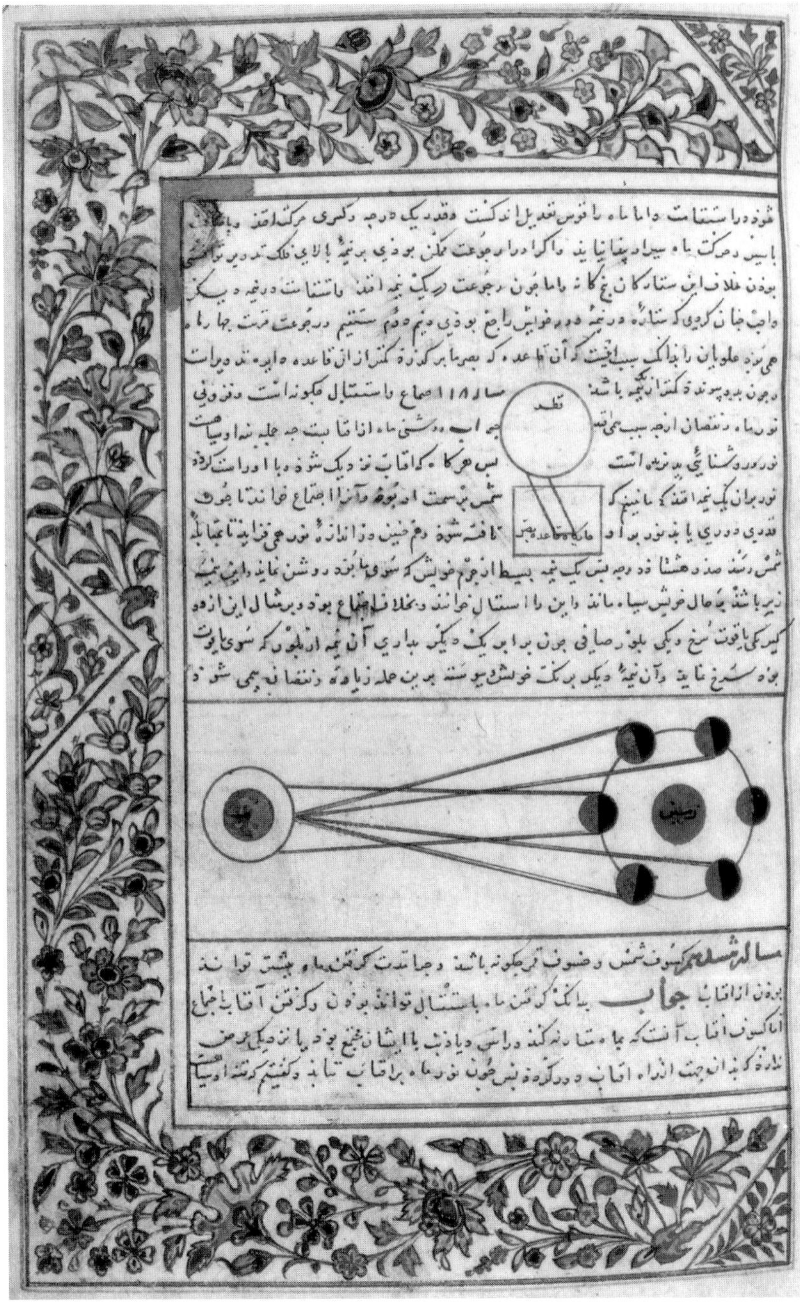

Plate 2—The Aesthetics of Aggregation. Pages from a "Treatise on Astrology." From an Anthology dedicated to Iskandar Sultan, dated 1410–11, fols. 409b–410a. London, British Library, Add. 27261, fols. 409b–410a (Photo: By permission of the British Library, London).

Plate 2A—The Aesthetics of Aggregation.

Plate 3—The Aesthetics of Aggregation. Page depicting designs for bookbinding components. From an Anthology dedicated to Iskandar Sultan, dated 1410–11, fol. 543a. London, British Library, Add. 27261, fol. 543a (Photo: By permission of the British Library, London).

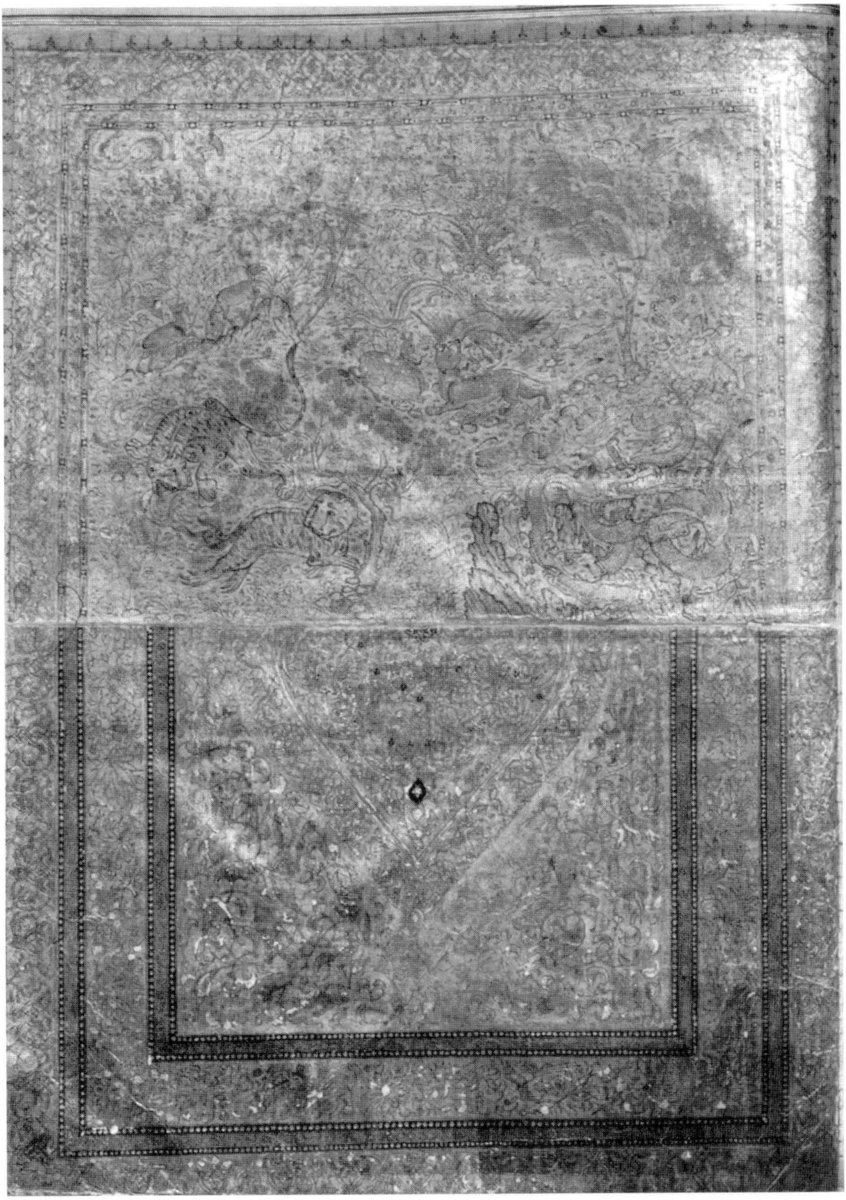

Plate 4—The Aesthetics of Aggregation. Painting in gold and ink showing alternative designs for a bookbinding. Page from an Anthology dedicated to Iskandar Sultan, dated 1413–14, bound into a Timurid-period album (B. 411), fols. 138a–166a, fol. 164a. Istanbul, Topkapı Palace Museum, B. 411 (Photo: Topkapı Palace Museum).

Plate 1—The Sound of the Image/The Image of the Sound. "The Old Man and the Youth," Riżā ʿAbbāsī, Fletcher Fund, 1925.68.5, Metropolitan Museum of Art.

Plate 2—The Sound of the Image/The Image of the Sound. "Young Portuguese," 1634, Riżā ʿAbbāsī, Gift of Robert H. Tannahill in memory of Dr. Wilhelm R. Valentiner. Photograph The Detroit Institute of Arts.

Notes

1. Oleg Grabar expresses this idea in greater detail in the introduction to Jill Norgren and Edward Davis, *Preliminary Index of Shah Nameh Illustrations* (Ann Arbor: Center for Near Eastern and North African Studies, University of Michigan, 1969).
2. I have discussed the question of how pre-modern poets viewed translation and imitation most recently in, "A Sketch of Translation and the Formation of New Persian Literature." *Iran and Iranian Studies: Studies in Honor of Iraj Afshar*, edited by Kambiz Eslami (Princeton: Zagros Press, 1998), pp. 288–305, and earlier in "Xaqani's Mada'en Qaside (I)," *Edebiyat* vol. i, no. 2 (1976):153–70.
3. M. R. Shafi'i-Kadkani, *Sovar-e khial dar she'r-e parsi* (Tehran: Nil, 1969), p. 350.
4. Abolqasem Ferdowsi, *Shah Name*, ed. Ye. E. Bertels, et al., 9 volumes (Moscow: AN, 1961–1972), vol. i, p. 140, l. 78 (hereafter Bertels). Translation from J. W. Clinton, "The Story of Sâm, Son of Narimân and the Birth of Zâl," *Textes et Mémoires*, vol. xvi, *Iranica Varia: Papers in Honor of Professor Ehsan Yarshater* (E.J. Brill: Leiden. 1990), p. 42.
5. Simorgh appears as not only large but brightly colored in even the earliest manuscripts. In later paintings she becomes ever more splendid. To choose one example from among many possible, the *Shahnameh* of Shah Tahmasb includes three paintings of the Simorgh in sequence to illustrate this story, a rare clustering of images, and in each of these the Simorgh is large and brilliantly colored, with tail feathers that trail behind her like an iridescent banner. She can be described without exaggeration as "visually spectacular". The first and third images are reproduced in Stuart Carey Welch, *Wonders of the Age: Masterpieces of Early Safavid Painting 1501–1576* (Cambridge: Fogg Art Museum, Harvard University, 1979), pp. 66–69, the second in *Persian Painting*, by the same author (New York: George Braziller, 1976), pp. 48–49. Note also that in his brief paraphrase of this incident, Welch elides God's role in bringing about Zal's miraculous transformation from an object of prey to the focus of intense affection, "*...[Simorgh] grasped him in her talons and carried him off to her nest, where she reared him with her own young.*" (Italics original). See also the paintings of the Simorgh from Hazine 2153 and Hazine 1479 on the Topkapı Palace Museum website <www.ee.bilkent.edu.tr/~history/topkapi.html> in the section "Miniatures from the Topkapı Museum" under "Mongols and Painting under the Jala'ir" and "Secular Illustrations and Persian Painting," respectively.
6. In the story following this when Simorgh appears to assist the birth of

Rostam, Ferdowsi describes her as like a dark cloud that rains coral (Bertels, vol. 1, p. 237, ll. 1477–78). When Zal calls on her again in the story of "Rostam and Esfandiyar," her appearance is only hinted at—"then suddenly it seemed/The clouds turned iron black." (Bertels, v. 6, p. 293, l. 1241). For a translation, see J. W. Clinton, *In the Dragon's Claws: The Story of Rostam and Esfandiyar* (Washington, D. C.: Mage Publishers, 1999), pp. 109–10. (Henceforth *Dragon's Claw.*) Earlier, her mate appears as one of Esfandiyar's seven labors, where he is portrayed as so large ("like a flying mountain") as to be able to carry off an elephant, crocodile, or tiger with ease. He is so terrifying in flight that the earth faints and the sun's light is dimmed (Bertels, v. 6, pp. 180–2, ll. 243–48 and 261). Since both Simorgh and her mate are consistently presented as resembling huge, dark clouds, the source of the rainbow colors in which they are depicted in paintings must lie outside the *Shahnameh*. Robert Hillenbrand suggests China (personal communication).

7. Bertels, vol. ii, p. 212–14. For a translation see Abolqasem Ferdowsi, *The Tragedy of Sohrab and Rostam*, Persian text with a verse translation, introduction, and notes by Jerome W. Clinton, 2nd ed., revised (Seattle: University of Washington Press, 1996), pp. 93–101. (Henceforth *Tragedy.*)
8. Shafi'i-Kadkani, *Sovar-e khial*, p. 349.
9. My translation makes the link between weeping and boiling more causative than it is in the text, which reads literally, "He saw a nursing infant crying (*yeki shir khâreh khorushandeh did)*/He saw the earth boiling like the sea *(zaminrâ cho daryâ-ye jushandeh did*)."
10. Bertels, vol. ii, p. 175, ll. 78–80. Translation (*Tragedy*), p. 15–16.
11. Bertels, vol. vi, p. 257, line 654; *Dragon's Claws*, p. 72.
12. Bertels, vol. vi, p. 313, lines 1528–38; *Dragon's Claws*, pp. 128–29. The translation adds one phrase ("and fragrant herbs") not in the text.
13. There is a rare and wonderful depiction of this scene in the *Great Mongol Shahnameh* (New York, Metropolitan Museum of Art 33.70. Purchase, Joseph Pulitzer Bequest, 1933). A black and white photograph of the scene is included in Oleg Grabar and Sheila Blair, *Epic Images and Contemporary History: the Illustrations of the Great Mongol Shahnameh* (Chicago: University of Chicago Press, 1990), pp. 100–101.
14. Bertels, vol. vi, p. 320, lines 1657–61; *Dragon 's Claws*, p. 136–37.
15. Manuchehri Damghani, *Divan*, edited by M. Dabir-Siyaqi (Tehran: Zavvâr, 1347/1969), p. 149, "Mussamat #1", lines 1914–16.
16. See note 3.
17. Andras Hamori remarks on the distancing effect of detailed description in

On the Art of Medieval Arabic Literature (Princeton: Princeton University Press, 1974), p. 28.

18. According the to the *Preliminary Index*, Tahmineh's visit to Rostam has been illustrated in 18 manuscripts, but Esfandiyar's challenge to his father has been depicted only twice. Farhad Mehran has assembled the data from the *Preliminary Index* into a useful table in "Frequency Distribution of Illustrated Scenes in Persian Manuscripts," *Student* (Neuchâtel, Switzerland) vol. 2, no. 4 (1998): pp. 351–79.

19. The *Preliminary Index* lists 66 separate illustration of this scene as opposed to 1 of Rostam and Zal with the dying Esfandiyar and 6 of his mourning procession.

20. The *Great Mongol Shahnameh* already mentioned is unusual in containing images of both scenes (see note 13). There is a colored reproduction of Rostam slaying Esfandiyar following p. 18 in *Epic Images*, and a black and white photograph on p. 99. In this illustration Esfandiyar has begun to slump in his saddle, but has not yet fallen.

21. Simpson indicates that this is common even in the earliest illustrated manuscripts (*The Illustration of an Epic: The Earliest Shahnama Manuscripts* [New York: Garland Publishing, 1979], p. 252).

22. This scene appears in Bertels, Vol. II, p. 239–40; *Tragedy*, p. 158–59.

23. Before their final battle Sohrab says of his yet unknown opponent, "His shoulders, chest and neck are so like mine/It seems some craftsman marked them with a rule." (Bertels, vol. 2, p. 232; *Tragedy*, p. 137). Earlier, Gazhdaham has remarked on his great height, saying "His stature far exceeds a cypress tree's." (Bertels, vol. 2, p. 191; *Tragedy*, p. 49).

24. Bertels, vol. 6, p. 221; *Dragon's Claws* p. 34. I should except the *Great Mongol Shahnameh* from this general stricture. As in so many other ways, it is exceptional in this regard. In many of its paintings, such as the funeral procession for Alexander already mentioned, the figures show their feelings in their faces as well as their bodies.

25. Here, as elsewhere, Iranian painters may be imitating the style of painting on Chinese porcelain. Whatever the source of their inspiration, however, the point to make here, as with the possible Chinese origin of the visually spectacular Simorgh, is how this stylistic feature contrasts with that of the poet.

26. Simpson, Marianna S., "The Pattern of Early *Shahnama* Illustration," in *Studia Artium Orientalis et Occcidentalis* vol. 1, *Problems in the Relation of Text and Illustrations*, (Japan: SAOO, 1982); Farhad Mehran, "The Breakline Verse in *Shahnama* Illustrations" (submitted to *Ars Orientalis*). I am grateful to Dr. Mehran for allowing me to make early use of this remark-

able paper.

27. Simpson, *Illustration of an Epic*, p. 251. See also the illustrations from Hazine 1479 on the Topkapı Palace Museum website (See note 5 for address).
28. Farhad Mehran, "Frequency Distribution," pp. 351–79.
29. Bertels, vol. II, p. 107 (*be rang-e shabah ruy o chon shir muy/jahân por ze pahnâ-y o bâlây-e uy. /Su-ye rostam âmad cho kuhi seyâh/az âhansh sâ'ed ze âhan kolah*).
30. I should like to thank Ileana Drinovan for suggesting this interpretation to me.
31. A. S. Melikian-Chirvani, "Le Roman de Varqe et Golsah: essai sur les rapports de l'esthétique litteraire et de l'esthétique plastique dans l'Iran prémongol, suivi de la traduction du poéme," *Ars asiatiques* 22 (1970).
32. Marianna Shreve Simpson, *A Princely Manuscript from Sixteenth-Century Iran*. (New Haven; London: Yale University Press, 1997).
33. Grabar and Blair, "The Ideological Program of the Manuscript," in *Epic Images*, pp. 13–28.
34. Robert Hillenbrand, "The Iskander Cycle in the Great Mongol Shahnameh," in *The Problematics of Power: Eastern and Western Representations of Alexander the Great*, ed. by M. Bridges and J. Ch. Bürgel (Bern; New York: Peter Lang, 1996), pp. 203–30. I should like to thank Professor Bürgel for drawing this work to my attention.

The Lover, His Lady, Her Lady, and a Thirteenth-Century Celestina: A Recipe for Love Sickness from al-Andalus

CYNTHIA ROBINSON

The most direct and intimate relationships between textual and visual idioms, of course, are those which exist between the covers of an illustrated book. The manners in which these relationships are experienced by the public(s) to whom the book is available at a particular time or in a particular place are ideally approached through comparison with the processes of visual and aural or textual reception of other books belonging to the same cultural and chronological context. In the case of (Arabic-speaking) al-Andalus, however, such an approach is impossible for, despite the proliferation of medieval Andalusī literary texts which would seem to contain the possibility for programs of illustration and/or illumination, only one example is known to have survived from more than eight centuries of Muslim and Arabic-speaking presence in present-day Spain. The manuscript in question, moreover, is doubly problematic, in that it also contains the only known surviving version, both in terms of text and of image, of the love story of *Bayāḍ wa Riyāḍ* (Vat. Ar. Ris. 368; hereafter, *BR*).[1] Reconstructing a culture of illustrated books on secular themes in Arabic on the basis of one surviving example is a delicate business, but nevertheless, I feel, a worthwhile one: *BR* is certainly not the only illustrated Arabic manuscript to have been produced in al-Andalus. It is, indeed, impossible to imagine the absence of this facet from an otherwise thriving book culture; thus, it is doubly incumbent upon scholars to, as it were, get their money's worth out of this one surviving example. It is in many ways surprising that the wealth of visual, literary and larger cultural information contained in *BR*'s tattered and moisture-damaged pages has, for the most part, been ignored, and one of the broader objects of this essay is to bring *BR* back into the field of actively considered texts and images (or, at any rate, to make it visible) in the world of those who study medieval Mediterranean culture. This essay will, primarily, address the interior mechanisms through which *BR*'s text and images interact, thus laying the groundwork for a future and broader consideration of *BR*'s function(s) and audience(s). I will suggest a dual instructive and performative function for *BR*; the full implications of the performative function for the manuscript's resonances in contemporary Latinate and Romance spheres of culture, both in recently-conquered Seville and further afield, will be left for a lengthier study to be undertaken in the near future.[2] Certain characteristics of *BR*'s text-image-audience relationships might even eventually be proved to be particularly Andalusī (i.e., products of a culture whose hybridity is often hidden or smoothed over by categories based on presumed divisions along linguistic lines—Hebrew, Latin, Romance, Arabic—which are applied to the visual and literary realms), and to differentiate them from others which might have been received and/or appropriated from cultural contexts further east.

Its status as an *unicum* certainly explains, to a great extent, the paucity of scholarly attention that *BR* has received since its first two publications by Nykl and Monneret de Villard shortly after 1940.[3] When this consideration is added to the tendency of both scholars of medieval Arabic literature and historians of Islamic art to consider anything Andalusian as *a fortiori* derivative of cultural artifacts produced closer to the center of the Islamic world, the fact that *BR*'s images have been considered (with a general neglect of content) almost exclusively in terms of the stylistic similarities and differences they evidence when compared to the 13th-century illustrations of the *Maqāmāt* is not particularly surprising.[4] The fact that such comparisons have been made with only tangential (at best) considerations of *BR*'s textual component, however, is more difficult to explain, although the rather pedestrian quality of both narrative prose and lyric insertions probably constitutes one reason. It will be one of the objects of this study to suggest a field of both visual and literary comparanda for *BR* which will situate it more exactly within the Andalusī cultural milieu in which it was produced.

The manuscript is housed in the Vatican library in Rome (Vat. Ar. Ris. 368), and is composed of thirty paper folios, fourteen of which contain illustrations. The first, last, and an undetermined number of the middle folios are missing—if date and/or place of production or dedicatee were originally indicated, this information has been irretrievably lost.[5] The typically sepia ink and characteristic script (in the case of *BR*, vocalized almost completely throughout) are clearly localizable in the Western half of the Dār al-Islām, almost certainly Andalusī,[6] and most probably datable to the thirteenth century.[7] All illustrations are of roughly the same size, each occupying a large part of its respective page (see Plates 1–3). The images are completely without framing elements, marginalia or extraneous illumination of any sort: an especially direct relationship between text and image thus seems to be implied, along with the necessity for a viewing and/or reading public to react accordingly. Khemir, in support of a 13th-century date for *BR*, also points out strong connections between the illustrations which contain architectural material and what we know of architecture and ornament produced under Almohad patronage.[8]

First, a word about the plot. Nykl, in his 1941 edition and Spanish translation, refers to *BR* as a "love epic." Although the term "epic" is not the one which springs most readily to mind, given the complete absence in *BR* of themes of travel and battle, the first word in Nykl's phrase could not have been more aptly chosen: *BR*'s plot is entirely centered around love, and more particularly around the proper and improper (or, "courtly" and "uncourtly") ways in which one might approach love's practice. The story concerns a pair of young lovers, Bayāḍ (a merchant's son from Damascus) and Riyāḍ (a slave-girl who belongs to a powerful *ḥājib*, or minister, in an unidentified but almost certainly Andalusian city).[9] Bayāḍ has fallen hopelessly in love with Riyāḍ after having seen her only once, and has enlisted the help of an Old Woman (the *ʿajūz*, in whose voice the story is also narrated)[10] in securing a *rendez-vous* with her. Following a visit by the Old Woman to the palace in which Riyāḍ is housed, the lovers meet in a *majlis* organized by Riyāḍ's Lady (hereafter, the *Sayyida*), who is the daughter of the *ḥājib* to whom Riyāḍ ultimately "belongs."

Following an extended session of singing and wine-drinking, Riyāḍ, along with the rest of the assembled company, listens enraptured to Bayāḍ's description (*waṣf*) of her, first in prose and then (given somewhat reluctantly, probably due to his knowledge of the portentous nature of the *tashbīb* (to rhapsodize about a beloved [woman]; to speak of her charms in verse) he is about to "commit") in verse. After Bayāḍ's performance, Riyāḍ loses control of herself and, amid tears and sighs, imprudently (i.e., sincerely, and in a decidedly *uncourtly* fashion—according to the text's standards of courtliness, at any rate) declares *her* love for *him* in verse.[11] The fact that she commits *her* indiscretion (understood in the text and, presumably, by the audience as more much indiscreet, somehow, than Bayāḍ's) in such public and elegant/"courtly" company serves, as comments to that effect by the *Sayyida* and the Old Woman underline, to exacerbate the gravity of her misdeed. Although what has gone on and been said would in no way fit beneath the rubric of *mujūn*, "courtly" norms *have*, we are given to understand in no uncertain terms, been transgressed. The *Sayyida* is gravely offended, and she makes her anger publicly known by shouting and rending her (very costly) gown. The *majlis* breaks up immediately, with the Old Woman resorting to disguising her *protegé* as a slave girl in order to get him home without further mishap. The rest of the story consists of exchanges of impassioned letters in verse between Bayāḍ and Riyāḍ through mysterious third parties, and of manipulations of situations, and particularly of language, by the Old Woman in service of the two distraught, and lovesick, lovers. A modern audience is, because of the manuscript's incomplete state, in the end left wondering as to the ultimate results of these machinations, but the content of the final surviving folios bodes well for a second try at a *majlis* for Bayāḍ and Riyāḍ, at which it is hoped they will conduct themselves properly.

The manuscript was certainly not cheap to manufacture. Despite the fact that we lack any knowledge of its binding or of the other texts, perhaps also illustrated, with which it might originally have been combined, we may say that *BR* was clearly intended to function, on at least one level, as an expensive luxury object: fourteen illustrations in a book containing only thirty folios translate as a very labor-intensive project. Moreover, the amount of careful detailing in the images—apparent in the rendering of noses, folds of cloth, specifics of setting and architectural ornament—bespeaks high-quality work; touches of gold (on bottles, *tirāz* bands, columns, capitals) suggest luxury,[12] both for the manuscript's owner and for the setting into which the story is placed. The consistent size and format of the *BR* images would also seem to be the product of a thoroughly organized enterprise of book production and illustration,[13] as would the easy division of the *BR* images into several types, upon which variations are produced according to the specific needs of the narrative moment in question. Interiors (*Riyāḍ's Fainting Spell*, f. 3v [Plate 1]; *Bayāḍ Receiving Riyāḍ's Letter*, f. 22; *Bayāḍ Asleep*, f. 29r; *Bayāḍ Playing Chess with the Old Woman's Relative*, f. 31 [Plate 3])[14] are presented frontally in almost identical size and proportions, with similar treatment of turrets or other exterior architectural features.[15] Garden scenes (the three *majlis* scenes, ff.4v, 9 and10 [Plate 2], with *Riyāḍ's Reunion with the Sayidda*, f. 27r, constituting a potential variant on this theme) are similar and at times identical in their use of architectural features to frame a group of figures, as well as in their presentation of water, grass or other details of setting. Likewise, the two scenes which depict Bayāḍ receiving counsel or advice from the Old Woman (ff. 2v and 9) conform to a type (in this case, moreover, the specifics for each narrative situation are provided solely by the text).

The first surviving image, f. 1, also probably conforms to a type of frontispiece which finds heavy resonances in the author portraits of some roughly contemporary examples of *Maqāmāt* mss.[16] The image is badly damaged, but it is framed by a clearly legible architectural setting hung with an elaborate curtain (the only of the *BR* images to be so presented). Four personages are positioned frontally: one is certainly a slave girl playing the lute (Riyāḍ?), one is the Old Woman, while a third, lounging on a low throne as does the *Sayyida* in his absence, is probably intended to represent the *ḥājib*.[17] A clearly male figure, sporting a strikingly large turban, stands behind the slave girl and the Old Woman toward the center of the area framed by the curtain; his face is all but erased due to the damaged state of the image, and I have thus far not been able to firmly identify him. The image might well illustrate the *majlis* at which we find the Old Woman when we as readers enter the narrative on f. 1r, *in medias res*, to find the *ḥājib* calling out to his slave girls one by one, or in pairs, and parading them in front of the Old Woman for her visual delectation: one would almost say he is asking for trouble during his upcoming voyage, about which we are informed only obliquely, and only once we get to f. 16-17, where Shamūl inadvertently advises Bayāḍ of the *ḥājib*'s absence in the context of news concerning his beloved. Riyāḍ's entrance onto the scene, flanked by two *qiyān* (singing slaves) on either side, constitutes the climactic moment of this *défilé*. Probably significantly, though, the image which would otherwise appear to pertain specifically to this narrative moment is not accompanied by the usual discursive subtitle, a fact which suggests that it might have been intended more as a frontispiece or a presentation of *dramatis personae* (in this case, the standing male figure might be identified as Bayāḍ, whose presence would be logical in a presentation of major characters, and would not make much sense in the context of the *ḥājib*'s *majlis*) than as an illustration *per se*.

In addition to image type and structure, the details which bring grass, hands, and particularities of clothing to life in the *BR* illustrations are handled in a consistent and self- assured manner which should put to rest any supposition concerning this manuscript's having been a rarity in its original cultural context. Rather, it is certainly the product of an established Andalusī tradition of secular book production and illustration. Given that we lack similar material from the "Islamic" sectors of Andalusī society, I would like to suggest here that a productive source of comparanda for *BR* (in addition to the more-familiar *Maqāmāt*, a body of texts and images most likely produced in the related but hardly contiguous context of 13th-century Syria and ʿIrāq) is the contemporary Alfonsine manuscript enterprise. The body of densely illustrated texts, which includes the four famous copies of the *Cantigas de Santa María* and the *unicum* example of the *Libros del Ajedrez*, have important ramifications for a conceptualized interpretation of *BR*, in the realms of practice and production, as well as in the larger project of the construction of cultural meaning. It would even seem possible that an infrastructure for the making, illustrating and illuminating of luxury-category books might have existed in Seville before the Alfonsine apparatus was put into operation; given the numerous and striking similarities between the *BR* illustrations and, particularly, those of the *Libros del Ajedrez*, such an assertion would seem to merit (and will, elsewhere, receive) detailed consideration.

The Alfonsine book-production machine was a large and well-organized one,[18] and it is probably not amiss to consider *BR*'s circumstances of production and reception as in some way intersecting with the conditions under and owing to which this machine functioned. Certain of the most salient similarities and differences—doubtless culturally significant ones—between *BR* and the Alfonsine manuscripts might be briefly sketched here before turning to a more detailed consideration of *BR*. First, it is worth observing that, at least as far as we know, the products of the Alfonsine *talleres* were tailored exclusively to the tastes, needs, political and aesthetic concerns, and pocketbooks of a royal patron and his immediate entourage. *BR*, on the other hand, because of its mutilated state, is impossible to associate definitively with any particular or identifiable social *milieu*; several factors, however, would indicate that the economic *milieu* to which *BR* most immediately responds was not able to match the Learned King's outlay of funds in exchange for the best materials. *BR* is also considerably smaller than the better-known Alfonsine products, and (I believe conspicuously) lacks the color blue, an expensive one[19] to produce, and one used lavishly and ostentatiously in the Alfonsine codices. The difference in size and the absence of expensive blues in the *BR* images are almost certainly related to the circumstances of recent Christian conquest in many parts of the Iberian peninsula, and to the strictures placed (at least officially) on possession and public use by Muslims of numerous substances and materials viewed by 13th-century society as rare or prestigious.[20] The fact that *BR* was produced on paper would seem to confirm this restriction, given that the Alfonsine de luxe manuscripts were all produced on parchment.[21] Nevertheless, the striking similarities one may observe between the actual images in one case and the other are worth remarking: these consist especially in architectural framing motifs which at times are almost identical and, in the case of the *Libros del Ajedrez*, a gamut of figural types and details (clothing included) which would seem to suggest interaction on several different levels; in the case of the *Cantigas*, it is precisely in the use of figural types that the Alfonsine products differ most pointedly with *BR*, a matter which I believe to be of significance, and which I have addressed elsewhere.[22] Detailed and extended comparisons between *BR* and the illustrated codices produced under the patronage (and, perhaps to a certain extent, the supervision) of Alfonso X are not the specific point of focus here, but the idea of an Alfonsine cultural panorama for the production and reception of *BR* is intended to underlie many of the principle points I shall make.

In light of the question of *BR*'s intended public, the quality of the *BR* images is, in truth, far superior to that of the text they accompany. As Nykl observes in his introduction, *BR* contains several grammatical errors (although some are arguably due to carelessness in copying rather than to a faulty command of the language).[23] Moreover, the prose and verse in which the story is told are of a caliber probably best described as pedestrian: even when a particular passage (generally recited or improvised by Bayāḍ) is lauded, by the *Sayyida*, as "original," or as "real *adab*" (f. 10r), the verses are in fact repetitive in terms of content and vocabulary, and are both sparse and clumsy when it comes to the use of devices such as metaphor. Nor, it should be added, are they noticeably different in quality from the verses sung by the *qiyān*.[24] The instance of Bayāḍ's description (*waṣf*) of Riyāḍ, requested by both the *Sayyida* and Riyāḍ's fellow slave girls, is a perfect example of this mediocrity passed off, or possibly perceived, as high-end literature (f. 11r). Probably as a result of his choice of the *least* transgressive of the two possible ways in which a poet might speak literarily of the object of his (or her) desires, Bayāḍ sidesteps the *Sayyida*'s request for a description of Riyāḍ by, first, modestly demurring—his powers of description could not possibly be up to such a task, etc.—and then naming those of his beloved's qualities of physique and of character which he *would* praise *were* he to undertake the task.[25] Bayāḍ's oral and improvised performance in the ordering of these attributes, however (despite the fact that the *Sayyida* later proclaims herself bowled over by the brilliance of his *nathr*, or prose), is a far cry from the complexities of properly composed *sajʿ* (rhymed prose): he merely lists single words[26] which appear to be randomly chosen, rather than arranged in accordance with the strictures of meter or rhyme. This discrepancy in quality between image (as well as the proportionately large number of these) and text leaves the door open for the asking of questions concerning public(s) and access to the "arts of the book" (particular among the so-called "luxury arts" in that its products, especially when illustrated, are most often assumed to be restricted to a patron class of royalty, nobles and only the wealthiest of merchants). The discrepancy also hints at interesting possibilities for comparative assessments of access in Arabic- and Romance-speaking circles to illustrated books: following his first performance at the *Sayyida*'s *majlis*, when Bayāḍ is asked by his hostess concerning his *akhbār* (f. 7v), he makes a point of the fact that he is the son of a (Syrian) merchant (*tājir*). It would thus seem at least possible that the original owner of this manuscript was not a noble, a sharp contrast with what is currently agreed to be the case in terms of Alfonsine illustrated-manuscript production.

In terms of a discussion of *BR*'s probable function, it is important, first, to insist on the illustrative quality and narrative content of the images.[27] They occur either in the middle of or following the section of text or the narrative moment which they sum up. One might even imagine the images, along with their titles, serving a narrator as a basis for oral performance or improvisation, providing that she or he were well-acquainted with text and plot and thus able to, as it were, fill in the blanks. The images alone do not tell *BR*'s story completely, but they consistently and accurately reflect events or descriptions related in the text, and often contain details, at times piquant or amusing, which elaborate or comment on features of the narrative; these details, in turn, depend on an audience's familiarity with the story in order to achieve their greatest effect. For instance, in the illustration of Riyāḍ's fainting spell upon the Old Woman's mention of Bayāḍ and his interest in her (see Plate 1), the room in which the action takes place is presented frontally, as is customary in the *BR* illustrations (as well as in those of the *Maqāmāt*, to which they are usually compared), and in those of the Alfonsine *Cantigas* and the *Libros del Ajedrez* (to which they are not). In addition to its belonging to a certain type or genre of image (i.e., the interior), this particular *version* of the type was manipulated (through the pointed addition of a closed door) both to suit and to gloss the narrative occasion to which it corresponds: to wit, in addition to representing Riyāḍ's attack and the reaction of slave girls and Old Woman, the image's details comment ironically on the necessity for secrecy (in the words of the Old Woman, *kitmān*; *sitr*) at such moments as the delicate one it depicts. The closed door (which is employed in the context of *BR* only in images of interiors in which secrecy might, on the basis of the text to which they correspond, be said to be an issue) constitutes a visual implication that all gazes but the Old Woman's—and ours—are blocked. Up in the turret of the tower, though, is a small but very widely opened window (the only one thus depicted in the *BR* illustrations) which seems to hint at the shameful disclosures to come, a theme with which the text is imminently preoccupied; if an audience were already familiar with the story, such a detail might foreshadow or even amuse. Another instance of this visual glossing is found in the three consecutive *majlis* images. The *Sayyida*'s *majlis* constitutes the context in which all of the love songs-proper in *BR* are sung, and through the singing of which, it seems, the miseries of lovesickness are visited upon the protagonists. All three *majlis* images, like the interiors and the counseling scenes, conform in their most general characteristics to a *type*. Upon closer inspection, though, an attentive observer might note that in the first of the *majlis* images, no props for wine-drinking (cups or bottles) appear. In the second, however, which corresponds to Riyāḍ's first performance (see Plate 2), Bayāḍ's hand holds a cup from which he is clearly sipping as he, likewise, drinks in his beloved's every (sung) word. In the third image, in which Bayāḍ takes up the lute, Riyāḍ now also holds a cup (the two would-be lovers, visually mimicking the mirroring which goes on throughout the text, have in essence simply swapped places). Riyāḍ's drinking-and-listening gestures are also ambiguously echoed by the unidentified slave girl at her side, and slightly later in the narrative, it becomes clear that such a juxtaposition might have moral implications: Riyāḍ has not known how to keep her head about her, or perhaps the "wine" has gone to it, whereas the other slave girls were aware that the songs and their singing were not to be taken seriously, and thus were able, so to speak, to handle their liquor. Moreover, in the third *majlis* image the Old Woman (her profile is clearly legible toward the back left corner of the group of figures) rather ostentatiously wields a wine flask, which viewers might remember as sitting innocently to one side on a table in the first *majlis* scene, at which the *ḥājib* was present. She—in addition to, or perhaps despite, protestations concerning her noble intentions in bringing the two lovers together—has been distributing the ruby-red elixir consumed by Bayāḍ, Riyāḍ, and the unidentified slave girl, and perhaps fomenting a bit of metaphorical trouble to boot. These visual points would have been driven home for their audience by the (probably performed; see below) text which, interspersed with the images, contains lyrics filled with pointed references to the contrast between drunkenness brought on by wine (remediable) and that resulting from love's onslaught (irremediable). The song performed just preceding Bayāḍ's arrival (after a break in the singing activities so that everyone could drink some [more] wine) by a slave girl named ʿUqār ("Remedy," or "Cure," an irony which is unlikely to have escaped any of those present at a reading of *BR*) on ff. 5v–6r, likewise, refers to the bitter cup which Love has given her to drink, and (as if that were not enough), the slave girl called upon by the *Sayyida* to perform immediately following ʿUqār's song (f. 6r) is named *Mudām*, one of whose possible translations is "wine," and whose multiple associations surely would not have been lost on an audience. Each of the two *majlis* images which follow display, ostentatiously, the accoutrements of wine-drinking, in the hands of the principle characters—Bayāḍ, Riyāḍ, and the Old Woman. In short, the images, in their function *as* illustrations—i.e., through their construction as specific units of summed-up narrative and their clear and forceful communication of this purpose to an audience, as well as their lack of marginalia or other devices potentially visually distracting—would thus lead a viewer to examine them closely, and to interpret the additional details—such as windows and cups—as comments on the narrative and/or larger didactic messages born by the images. This process of the construction of meaning then leads the viewer, ultimately, back to the now-visually-glossed text with new levels of interpretation, both ironic and didactic, to apply.

In addition to its existence as a luxurious object, *BR* would also seem to have functioned (possibly with a certain degree of implied irony) as an instructive handbook intended to guide its affluent (but perhaps not noble or extremely highly educated) readers and larger audience in the proper ("courtly") manner in which to conduct a love affair (and to set up and host/attend the parties where one might do this). The elegant and literate class of *ẓurafāʾ* (sing., *ẓarīf*) to which many of *BR*'s principle characters are presented as belonging is vaguely defined as including kings (f. 3r: "...for kings love to take their pleasures in gardens..."), the largely absent *ḥājib*,[28] elegant ladies like the *Sayyida* and her singing, poetry-reciting slave girls (of whom Riyāḍ [ff. 1r–1v] we are given to understand, is the most beautiful and accomplished), and the Old Woman's relative, who consoles Bayāḍ in his lovesick misery, first listening to his woes and then distracting him (as is proper in such cases) with conversation, outings, and games of chess. The characters, although they do evidence individualities in their personal sentiments,[29] conform in large measure to literary and/or social types which would have been clearly identifiable to members of a 13th-century audience, and the plot centers around the potentially didactic dilemma of how to maintain socially accepted "courtly" norms when confronted with lovesickness (which perhaps translates in actual social terms as the temptation to transgress these norms). Each character might be read as constituting a lesson (or, in Riyāḍ's case, an anti-lesson...) in loving elegantly and nobly. The *Sayyida*'s (despite her loss of control and her decidedly *un*courtly hurling of an ivory inkwell at her favorite), the Old Woman's relative's, and the slave girls' (from among which Shamūl is singled out) belonging to this class of noble lovers is never questioned. With the exception of Riyāḍ (whose case is special, punished, and thus also exemplary), each responds to the demands placed upon her or him by specific narrative situations in ways which are presented to readers (whether or not there may be, as I suspect but will doubtless have difficulty in proving, some irony intended) as laudable and, implicitly, worthy of emulation. Bayāḍ's acceptance into the class of noble lovers, though, hangs somewhat in the balance during the opening pages (might his status as the son of a trader be at the root of this ambiguity?): the Old Woman appears to reserve judgment on this issue until she shall have observed his behaviour at the *Sayyida*'s *majlis*. She does express her surprised approval, though, when she notes, as they walk along the river toward the appointed place for the *majlis*, that her young *protegé* is carrying a "nice" lute. This fact seems to bode well for Bayāḍ's potential as a courtier, and—at the end of the trials and tribulations to which his lovesickness subjects him—he does eventually prove himself to be a worthy member of the society of the *ahl al-ʿishq* (or of their descendants, given that most of the names of famous lovers reeled off by the Old Woman [f. 2r] belong to figures from the earliest days of Islam). Riyāḍ, on the other hand, is presented as the antithesis of proper, or "courtly," behaviour in matters of love. She falls from grace despite her privileged beginnings (she, as the Old Woman and the *Sayyida* both note, was raised in the *ḥājib*'s palace and given every advantage, so perhaps it could be argued that she should have known better),[30] and is reinstated in her Lady's good graces (and into the fold of the noble descendants of *ahl al-ʿishq*) only after much suffering and due to the *Sayyida*'s clemency.

BR's dictums and advice concerning proper (i.e., "courtly") behaviour (usually pronounced in the Old Woman's voice) are somewhat reminiscent in tone of passages in Ibn Ḥazm's early 11th-century *Tawq al-Hamāma*, and they find even more specific resonances in al-Washshāʿ's 9th-century *Kitāb al-Muwashshāʿ*.[31] *BR*'s striking novelty with respect to these two texts, however, is constituted by its didactic passages' having been seamlessly interwoven with the threads of narrative which both occasion and justify them, and illustrated; on this note, I would also suggest that *BR*'s images are highly implicated in the manuscript's didactic concerns. Despite the already-noted high percentage of images to text in *BR*, it is also certain that not *every* narrative moment which would seem to suggest illustration gets memorialized (and, thus, singled out) in an image.[32] The *Sayyida*'s rending of her gown in anger, for instance, following Riyāḍ's *faux pas*, might easily have inspired a painter to pick up his or her brush, and Bayāḍ cross-dressed as a slave girl (which happens twice in the narrative as it is preserved) would also potentially constitute interesting visual fodder; nevertheless, neither moment is illustrated. Nor are we shown an image of Riyāḍ in her languishing state (whereas, on the other hand, we are *told*, and in great detail, in the voice of Shamūl (f. 12v), of the specific physical changes wrought in her companion by lovesickness, and we are also given a very exact description of the place in which Riyāḍ has been enclosed, within the palace, to either recuperate or die). Instead, we are shown (certainly deliberately) the scene in which her ostracism *begins* (a scene in which her bloody face places particular emphasis on the fact that she has been wounded by the inkwell that her very own Lady has thrown at her), following which Riyāḍ is not pictured again until her reconciliation with the *Sayyida*. Moreover—and in another example of visual glossing of the text—she is represented as already *physically* distanced from both the *Sayyida* and the Old Woman, who has appeared in order to set matters aright with her glib tongue, by a pond of which no mention is made in the text (mention is made, rather, of the separate room into which the Old Woman coaxes the *Sayyida* following her outburst, which is also represented in the image—the pond thus constitutions an addition).

To state the case another way, *BR*'s program of images appears to consciously avoid—except for the one (certainly very intentional) exception of the moment immediately preceding Riyāḍ's exile as a result of her *transgression* of "courtly" norms—depicting *un*courtly behaviour. They concentrate, instead, on images of behaviour considered worthy of emulation according to "courtly" standards. It might even be argued that the scene in which Riyāḍ's ostracism is made apparent was also chosen in order to avoid depiction of the specific moment of the *Sayyida*'s (who is presented, by and large, as a positive example) *un*courtly injuring of her favorite. In short, the choice of *what* (and what *not*) to illustrate reinforces a particular aspect of the text's contents, and amplifies this message into a visual didactics similar to that recently proposed by Sandra Hindman for French manuscripts containing stories by Chrétien. These narratives are also, incidentally, concerned with "courtly" and uncourtly behaviour, and Hindman suggests that they have been illustrated with a clear agenda of the glossing, emphasizing or elision of certain (didactic or socially relevant) aspects of the text's content.[33]

Viewed as part of an instructive program concerned with courtliness, the *BR* images might be summed up as follows. Seven of the surviving images are dedicated to events surrounding the *Sayyida*'s *majlis*, at which Bayāḍ and Riyāḍ are united for the first time, with the disastrous results of Riyāḍ's loss of control depicted in the seventh. These are: the frontispiece or presentation of *dramatis personae*, which also corresponds to the *ḥājib*'s *majlis* (where, incidentally, all behave properly); the first scene of Bayāḍ's receiving advice from the Old Woman; Riyāḍ's fainting scene (which is still within the realm of proper "courtly" behaviour [Plate 1]: Riyāḍ, upon being brought to consciousness by the rose water sprinkled on her cheeks, declares to the worried group that this "isn't what they think," and then enjoins her fellow slave girls to keep what they have seen a secret); the three consecutive images of performance at the *Sayyida*'s *majlis*, discussed above (exhibiting, when considered together, the progressive intrusion of wine flasks and cups, along with their implied dangers of a loss of control; see Plate 2); and, finally, the image of Riyāḍ's ostracism. The second group of images—which also number seven—are devoted to the resolution (through, it is implied, exemplary "courtly" behaviour) of the disaster wrought by Riyāḍ, and contain the most obviously programmatic "laundry list" of proper, "courtly" postures and activities for the lovesick lover. These images include: the second instance of Bayāḍ's receiving advice from the Old Woman; Bayāḍ's receiving of a letter from his beloved at the hands of *her* faithful intermediary and fellow slave girl, Shamūl; Bayāḍ's fainting spell beside the river (observed by the Old Woman's relative, who begins to improvise verses of *rithā'* (elegy) because he assumes that the young foreigner is dead); Bayāḍ playing a game of chess with the Old Woman's relative (the two are observed by the Old Woman herself, positioned—probably tellingly—at the very margins of the interior space in which the two young men are depicted; see Plate 3); Bayāḍ's reception of yet another letter from Riyāḍ through the *waṣā'if* (slave girls) of the *Sayyida*'s palace; Riyāḍ's reconciliation with her Lady; and the Old Woman's observation of her *protegé* as he slumbers, having doubtless dozed off, as writing implements and a book-stand (not mentioned in the text; probably references to Bayāḍ's qualities as an *adīb* (literatus); these references might be ironic, for the Old Woman notes that he was drooling as he dozed) prominently displayed in the background of the much-damaged image seem to suggest, while composing a "courtly" love letter to his beloved.[34] The latter half of the manuscript in its surviving state is the most damaged; thus, even more images of these topical and approved postures for the lovesick but always "courtly" lover might originally have been included.

Each half of the manuscript and its particular group of images contains, early on in its narrative sequence, an image of Bayāḍ being counseled by the Old Woman in the (loving) customs and mores of the *ẓurafā'*: each group of images (and the text they accompany) is probably colored, governed or categorized as didactic by these scenes of the imparting and absorbing of information. The first group of images is especially preoccupied with two themes. First is the *majlis* itself (how to set it up, and how to behave at it): note again that four of the seven images contain *majlis* scenes which correspond to passages in which the Old Woman either admonishes Bayāḍ concerning how he should behave at the *Sayyida*'s *majlis*, or describes approvingly the appointments—which are appropriate to "women such as they" (f. 4r)—of that *majlis* once she arrives with her charge. As the Old Woman notes when she arrives at the palace to set up the fateful *rendez-vous* (f. 3r), Riyāḍ is an expert at setting up for such festivities, and her narration also pays particular attention to the manner in which, upon their arrival the following day, Bayāḍ is received, greeted, fed and given to drink (f. 7r), and to the fact that he, in turn, receives these attentions in a manner befitting a *ẓarīf*.[35] Second—and of ultimately greater import—as a theme of concern or emphasis in this first group is the nature of the engagement with love which behooves the *ẓarīf*. In the passages of text most immediately surrounding the first counseling scene, the Old Woman and Bayāḍ engage in something of a debate on this issue (ff. 2r–3r). Bayāḍ champions love as the adornment of the elegant, while the Old Woman's tone is reserved and cautionary—she counsels secrecy as the only way, pointing to the ultimate irony that it is precisely of those who could not keep their mouths shut that we *know*, whereas those whose behaviour was exemplary (i.e., who kept their secrets closely guarded) have fallen into oblivion. She thus problematizes speech—and particularly *poetic* speech—as a dangerous vehicle of revelation (in this case, of lovers' secrets, but perhaps also with wider implications); her position is somewhat ironic, though, considering the amount of secret-revealing verse about to be visited upon the reader/hearer, and also in light of the fact that it is she herself who will relate the large part of the story...to us, and in her own (i.e., first-person) voice; ironically, too, almost all of these images are concerned with the most dangerous form of speech in this context, the love poem or song. *Textual* admonitions concerning secrecy and choosing the path of moderation (*qaṣd*; f. 6r) are repeatedly offered, even (and almost certainly ironically) in the context of the very *majlis* at which the transgressive revelation is to be made: even as she promotes (and demands!) the performance of (an *im*moderate quantity of?) lyrics whose powers of emotion-evoking *ṭarab*[36] were clearly more than the two protagonists could withstand,[37] the *Sayyida* invokes divine protection against a love which won't even permit itself to be enjoyed because of its very bitterness. Likewise, Riyāḍ, just moments before her decisive performance, lauds (in prose) the virtue of sincerity, and declares blameworthy those who (note that the "courtliness" of this next dictum is somewhat questionable), when the possibility presents itself, do not take the opportunities to unite themselves with their beloveds; Bayāḍ responds (somewhat cryptically?) that those worthy of trust are few (f. 10r). Given the situation (a *majlis*) in which both characters *and* audience find themselves (again assuming that *BR* was at least partially intended to function as a performable/performative text) while this didactic material was presented and absorbed, it seems at least possible that these discussions between *BR*'s characters concerning love's merits and disadvantages, and the most elegant ways to go about loving, might have constituted (as we know they did, for instance, at the court of French nobles such as Marie de Champagne, probable patroness of Andreas Capellanus' treatise[38]) occasions for the assembled company ("courtly," at least in their own eyes) to engage in similar debates based on the characters' decisions and actions.

The second group of images, as discussed earlier, constitutes a visual list (seconded by the text) of postures and actions for the lovesick lover who wants to remain this side of "courtly," and it is in this second half of the manuscript, following Riyāḍ's emotional blunder, that Bayāḍ shows himself to be a truly "courtly" lover even in lovesickness. Once the second half of the story has begun, the text, the images, and the Old Woman are in agreement: Bayāḍ is truly deserving of the title of "*adīb*," and he is to be accorded a place among the honorable descendants of the *ahl al-ʿishq*. Nevertheless, the question appears *throughout* the manuscript to be (deliberately?) open to debate among the public. Once inside the castle on her mission to secure the first *rendez-vous*, for example, the Old Woman manages to speak alone with Riyāḍ, and to communicate to her the desires of a certain *refined and educated* young man for a meeting with her (f. 3r: "*al-ghulām al-adīb al-shāʿir...*"). Nevertheless, in her own words, the Old Woman also informs us (by way of prompting Riyāḍ's memory, upon her claims to have forgotten her first encounter with the Syrian dandy—the girl has asked guilelessly, "Who is Bayāḍ?") that Bayāḍ has *already* recited verses to her (f. 3r): she says, to be exact, that, he is the one Riyāḍ has seen from atop a tree.[39] Bayāḍ apparently thought it strange (the "it"—*istagharaba*—is probably the fact that Riyāḍ was atop a tree), and recited verses to her. Given the problematic nature of such possible *tashbīb*,[40] and the dangers of betraying the secrets of one's desire (which have been expounded by the Old Woman herself as she counseled Bayāḍ for the first time), the "courtliness" of Bayāḍ's first bold recitation (to which we have not been privy, either because it was not recorded, or because those pages of the manuscript have been lost) might well be called into question by an audience aware that they were permitted, or perhaps *expected*, to debate the courtliness of the characters' actions.[41] Also potentially of questionable (and debatable) propriety is the fact that there seems, according to the Old Woman at any rate, to already have been a meeting planned between the two lovers before their encounter at the *Sayyida*'s *majlis*: "...and you two had a *rendez-vous* (*waʿd*) for Friday!...," she states triumphantly in a final jarring of Riyāḍ's memory, at which point the latter drops onto the ground in a dead faint. Another utterance of Bayāḍ's which might appear to an audience to be of potentially debatable "courtliness" is his *waṣf/tashbīb* of his beloved, rendered at the *Sayyida*'s *majlis* in a *nathr* (rhymed prose) of decidedly lackluster quality which, nonetheless, was lauded by the *Sayyida* as "real *adab*." The *waṣf*, it will be remembered, comes in the form of a telegraphic listing of Riyāḍ's laudable qualities. While Bayāḍ starts off with attributes of the maidenly variety—things like silence, shyness, and the pallor of her skin, the roses of her cheeks—his *waṣf* then begins at a certain point to travel down and around the lovely body beneath the rose-bud mouth and delicate chin, and to linger over such features as thighs and haunches (f. 11v), as well as her coquettish behaviour. Although neither the *Sayyida* nor anyone else appears to be in the least offended by Bayāḍ's fetishizing of his beloved's body, one does wonder a bit about how an audience might have reacted to it—and, for that matter, to the *Sayyida*'s *failure* to react.

A case for *BR*'s belonging to a 13th-century Andalusī/Christian conquest cultural context in which the "courtly" (and anti-"courtly") literary and social models are familiar (even to the point of having become *cliché*), fully absorbed and widely known certainly needs no special pleading. Indeed, it would seem that the text and its unknown author(s) play upon the certainty of an audience's recognition of these *topoi*, alternating between a serious/didactic mode (to which the images purport to correspond) and a potentially parodic or ironic one: here we might recall the Old Woman's characterization of Riyāḍ's manner—*bayna al-hazl wa-l-jidd* ("half-joking and half-serious;" f. 3r)—as she, overseeing the *majlis* preparations, laughingly swats the male slaves under her direction with a switch. In this context it seems worthwhile to mention the consistent use of character names which comment, probably ironically (at least in some instances), on the purportedly didactic nature of text and images. The allegorical and—according to the particular narrative situation in which they might be placed—potentially ironic connotations of the names of the two principle characters—Bayāḍ and Riyāḍ—are obvious, and a glance at the names of the *Sayyida*'s slave girls would seem to further emphasize the text's potential for (ironic or parodic) allegory. Each of the *qiyān* called upon by the *Sayyida* to perform (performances which, in the end, invoke upon characters the very woes and devastations they bemoan within the fictive world of the lyric) bears a name which directly relates her to the excessive emotional ammunition agreed upon by 13th-century audiences to be contained by the love lyric—*Kāʿab* ("She of the Full Breasts"; because it derives from the same root as "*kaʿba,*" it also carries connotations of "object of veneration or devotion"), *Surūr* ("happiness"), *ʿAqqār* ("cure"), *Shamūl* ("fine, chilled wine"), *Ṭurūb* ("perturbed state of woeful joy"), *Mudām* (one of its possible translations is "wine"), *Ghayḍāʾ* (succulent or tender), etc.[42] Finally, in a truly memorable touch, *BR*'s anonymous author has chosen the name "*tharthār*"[43] for the river beside which Bayāḍ first sees Riyāḍ, which also forms the backdrop for the fateful *majlis* for Bayāḍ's lovesick wanderings, and for his meeting with Shamūl.

* * *

Evidence of *BR*'s performative or oral aspect may be found both in characteristics internal to the manuscript itself, and in associations between the *BR* images and contemporary or slightly earlier material culture. As already mentioned, the manuscript is small (particularly when compared to the products of Alfonsine workshops). It is therefore probable that it was intended for relatively private use. It is not so small, however, as to exclude the possibility of "reading-over-the-shoulder," or of being placed on a book stand (such, perhaps, as the one discussed earlier which appears in the image of Bayāḍ sleeping), and several persons, rather than only one, being able to follow along. Owing to its manageable size, it might also have been held easily (this of course assuming, probably logically, that the original thickness of the manuscript, before *BR* was separated from other texts with which it might have been bound, would not prohibit this) in the hands of someone who read or recited from it, or perhaps improvised on the basis of some combination of memorized knowledge of the prose, poetry and songs, and prompting from the lengthy subtitles which appear beneath each image. I would also mention again, in this context, the relatively large percentage of page space occupied by each image and the absence of any marginalia or ornamental framing devices which might distract the attention of a viewer from narrative content: it seems at least possible that the images could have been shown, as part of *BR*'s performance, to a small group of listeners such as might have been gathered—in an irony which would certainly not have escaped that public—for a *majlis* of singing, recitation, wine, and merriment similar to the one organized by the *Sayyida* for the benefit (and, ultimately to the detriment...) of Bayāḍ, Riyāḍ, and her other guests.[44]

Certainly the strongest argument in favor of a performative function for *BR* is found the overwhelmingly large proportion of fully-cited songs and lyrics to narrative prose text.[45] The most dense concentration of song appears in the first half of the manuscript, devoted to the events which lead up to and include Riyāḍ's inspired, improvised, and sung declaration of genuine love for the young stranger who has come into the midst of the Lady's carefully organized *majlis* and disrupted its symmetry (many of the interpolations in the more "serious" second half are to be understood as recited or written, rather than sung). Interspersed with the three *majlis* images (in view of the manuscript's didactic function, it is interesting to note that the precise moment of Riyāḍ's sung declaration is *not* illustrated; rather, the illustration of her playing to the lute corresponds to her performance prior to Bayāḍ's *tashbīb/waṣf* of her) are more than half-a-dozen songs placed back to back, with only a few necessary fragments of prose narration to carry the characters (and the readers or audience) from song to song. These songs are introduced through formulaic phrases such as "...and she (or, in Bayāḍ's case, he) took up the lute, tuned it, and began to sing[46] some verses that "go like this" (*haytha ta/yaqūl*). This phrase generally occupies an entire line of text, and is always rendered in thick, black letters (roughly proportional in size to those used for the subtitles beneath the illustrations; both *haytha ta/yaqūl* and subtitles are generally thicker and larger than the phrases uses to separate narrative moments between images, these come in the form of "*qālit al-ʿajouz*" [the old woman said][47]). This both adds significance to these phrases (and to the subtitles) and (I would argue, equally importantly) makes them more immediately visible. A reader, member of an audience, or especially a performer would thus be aware that either a song or narration was "coming up" and, with the prompting of subtitles, would possibly be able to sum up the narrative prose largely from memory, and perhaps render (either alone or accompanied by members of the "public") the verses and/or songs contained beneath the rubric-like phrases, *haytha ta/yaqūl*. Songs are clearly indented from the surrounding prose narrative, and are marked by small double-slashes at the beginning and end of each line, devices which seem to pointedly separate them from the rest of the text, and to render them visible as a unit, thus easy both to see and to extrapolate from. Once a song is finished, this closure is underlined by a thick red, or occasionally black, "and the Old Woman said," as if to say, "now the song is over, let's get back to the story."[48] The ironic implications of audience members' having themselves listened to, or perhaps even sung, the very songs which lead *BR*'s principle characters to their downfall would, I think, have constituted one of the most enjoyable aspects of the text's performance.

In terms of connections to the world of performance suggested by contemporary material culture, a number of textiles of Andalusī manufacture, surviving today in various collections, are adorned with paired or grouped figures of notable similarity to those in the *BR* images. They are engaged in the activities of drinking, and playing or listening to music. One of the best-preserved examples is the pillow, or *almohada*, which belonged to the Queen Berengaria (mother of Alfonso X's father, "San" Fernando, to whom the Christian conquest of Seville is owed); it was found in her tomb at the royal Cistercian convent of Las Huelgas, near Burgos, founded by her parents.[49] In a roundel located in the center of the piece, two female figures with facial features strikingly similar to those which characterize the visages of Bayāḍ, Riyāḍ, and the *Sayyida* dance round a central stem or tree. One plays a tambour. The pillow was probably made about 50 years before *BR* was produced, and is roughly contemporary to fragments of wall paintings—whose subjects also dance and play musical instruments—uncovered by Julio Navarro in a 12th-century dwelling in *Siyāsa*, near Murcia; Navarro presumes the context to be "Islamic."[50]

Equally intriguingly, the manner in which gardens are depicted in the *BR* images—sunken beneath the level of the salons which flank them, and navigated through a system of small, stepped bridges and peripheral passageways—corresponds almost exactly to what archeologists have recently determined to be the original configuration of the Almohad-period patio known today as that of the old Casa de Contratación, nestled within the complex of the Alcázares Reales in Seville.[51] Almagro suggests that these sunken gardens were typical only of the most luxurious and high-end of Andalusian residences. Although the alterations in the patio during the presumed period of Alfonsine use of the Alcázares are still being studied, it seems clear that the newly (at least partially) Christian elite of post-conquest Seville would have had at least some contact with that patio; it is doubtful that the contemporary Christians would have been ignorant of its intrinsic worth as a cultural signifier. Presumably those who produced the *BR* illustrations would also have been aware of the *de luxe* implications of this particular sort of patio: the clear and consistent presence of a bi-level garden in the *Sayyida*'s palace was surely intended to further emphasize the luxuriousness and nobility of the place, and of those who frequented it. Finally, a particular element of what survives of the patio's ornamental program suggests strong connections to the *BR* images: around the perimeter of the lower level of the garden, false doors were painted into the interiors of slightly raised blind arcades fashioned of brick, and these doors are all but identical to those employed so pointedly in the *BR* images to refer to the need for (or lack of...) secrecy in certain narrative situations. One wonders as to the purpose of the false doors around the periphery of the Almohad patio: might they not also reflect some connection to the "illusions" particular to the world of song and performance to which *BR* itself belongs? In other words, the *BR* images interact with a group of objects and architectural adornments which, when considered as a whole, show a marked (Andalusī?) preference for subject matter related to the world of the *majlis* and performance; this body of cultural artifacts, in ways yet to be fully articulated, clearly crossed presumed linguistic and cultural "boundaries" and was manipulated by an as yet nebulously defined variety of patrons.

Further investigation is also merited, in the field of Arabic literature, into *BR*'s connections, in both written-text and potentially performative spheres, to Ibn Saʿīd's collection of love songs and stories, the *Murqiṣāt*, to the *Maqāmāt* themselves, to the near-contemporary farces by Egyptian "playwright" Ibn Dāniyāl, and to the *1001 Nights*.[52] Considered in its performative context, *BR* also opens many doors for possible comparative study across linguistic boundaries: in light of the intensely hybrid nature of the social forum provided by Spanish/Andalusī cities during the 13th century, if performed, the manuscript's possibilities for reaching an audience wider than that uniquely (Arabic-speaking) Islamic one most often tacitly assumed for books written in Arabic, whether illustrated or no, become exponentially greater. It is probably not entirely coincidental that the short narratives in Provençal referred to as *vidas* and *razos*, along with the surviving corpus of troubadour song (sometimes in the troubadour songbooks the prose texts are recorded alongside the compositions of the pertinent troubadour, and sometimes they are preserved in a separate section of the ms.) was written down at approximately the same historical moment as *BR* and the *Murqiṣāt*; like *BR* and the *Murqiṣāt*, the troubadour songbooks yield a combination of narrative prose and lyric, both of which many now believe to have served, among other things, as material for performance. Interest in combining narrative prose and situations with lyric, often composed significantly earlier than the prose, may also be seen in the developing traditions of song-and-story in Romance-language literatures; such texts as Jean Renart's *Guillaume de Dole*, when considered comparatively, demonstrate striking resonances with *BR*, as well as with Ibn Saʿīd's *Murqiṣāt*.[53] Lovesickness, moreover, within the general context of a concern with courtliness and courtly etiquette such as that exemplified in *BR*, is a preoccupation at this time in all linguistic camps toward the western part of the Mediterranean world, in ways which do not appear to be as much the case in contemporary Arabic literature from places further east; comparative study of lesser-known Andalusī texts from the 13th century with the near-contemporary body, for example, of lyric poetry in Gallego-Portugués, as well as the production of the Sicilian courts under the patronage of Frederick II and those associated with him, will probably yield interesting results. Finally, an air of nostalgia—it permeates both 13th- and 14th-century reception of earlier troubadour literature, particularly in Spanish (Christian) and Northern Italian court contexts, and the Andalusī fascination with the *ahl al-ʿishq* from long ago—is a characteristic which marks the two traditions both as similar (perhaps inadvertently) and as (pointedly) different. Both Arabic and Latinate-Romance traditions, in the cities, ports, and fortresses in which they are most often obligated to rub shoulders, seek to create a cultural present through the invocation of lovers past. It is premature, though, to paint the backdrop for the minutiae of interchanges, desired or no, produced by varied and sustained contact between distinct or overlapping social groups in the complex circumstances of the 13th and 14th centuries. First, it is to be hoped that comparative research will more clearly articulate the specifics of these resonances, starting—perhaps—with why the dancers on Queen Berengaria's pillow look so much like Riyāḍ.

Notes

1. None of the usual sources—Ibn al-Nadīm, Muḥammad ibn Isḥāq (fl. 987), *al-Fihrist* (Beirut: Dār al-Kutub al-ʿIlmīyah, 1996); Carl Brockelmann, *Geschichte der arabischen litteratur*, 2 vol. (Weimar: Felber, 1898–1902); Fuat Sezgin, *Geschichte des arabischen Schrifttums* (Leiden: Brill, 1967–) —which one normally consults for comparanda in such cases have yielded results.

2. Even if it were ultimately shown that the ms. was produced in Granada, Murcia, or Valencia instead of in Seville, these resonances would remain valid. I do at present, however, feel that the *BR* images are most strongly related to Alfonsine manuscript production, which we know to have been centered in Seville, probably in the Reales Alcázares themselves. For recent considerations on the Alfonsine *talleres*, see Joaquín Yarza Luaces, "Reflexiones sobre la iluminación de las Cantigas," in *Metropolis Totius Hispaniae: 750 Aniversario Incorporación de Sevilla a la Corona Castellana, Real Alcázar de Sevilla, 23 de noviembre 1998 a 3 enero 1999* (Seville, 1999), pp. 163–182. Ugo Monneret de Villard ("Un codice arabo-spagnolo con miniature," *La Bibliofilia*, XLIII [Ottobre-Dicembre 1941], pp. 210–211), in one of the few publications *BR* has elicited, mentions in passing connections between *BR* and both the *Cantigas* and the *Libros del Ajedrez*, but in the end does not pursue the matter, and appears to suggest that *BR* has little in common with the products of the Alfonsine workshops. Likewise, Raquel Arié ("Le Costume des Musulmans de Castille au XIIIe siècle d'après les miniatures du *Libro del Ajedrez*," in *Mélanges de la Casa de Velazquez*, 2 [1966], pp. 59–66) notes that the *Libros* and the *Cantigas* were, at the moment the article was written, beginning to be seriously considered as sources of information on the material culture of Seville and other Spanish/Andalusian cities during the second half of the 13th century. She does not, however, specifically pursue the idea of connections between *BR* and the *Libros* or the *Cantigas*. A preliminary overview of this comparison in visual terms is undertaken in Cynthia Robinson, "Preliminary Considerations on the Illustrations of *Qiṣṣat Bayāḍ wa Riyāḍ* [Vat. Ar. Ris. 368]: Checkmate with Alfonso X?," forthcoming in a festschrift volume for Christian Ewert; I will explore other terms and manners in which the texts interact in a forthcoming collection of essays, *Under the Influence*, ed. Cynthia Robinson and Leyla Rouhi (in preparation).

3. Monneret de Villard, *Bibliofilia*, pp. 209–223, in which the program of illustrations is the primary subject of consideration. Initial comparisons between the *BR* images and those of the 13th-century illustrated *Maqāmāt* are proposed, and other potential, roughly contemporary comparanda are dis-

cussed. A.R. Nykl, *Historia de los amores de Bayad y Riyad, una chantefable oriental en estilo persa (Vat. Ar. 368)* (New York: The Hispanic Society of America, printed by order of the Trustees, 1941), introduction. Nykl's publication (an edition and un-annotated Spanish translation) is concerned uniquely with the text. Although ten of *BR*'s fourteen illustrations are reproduced in black and white, they do not appear alongside their proper captions. Rather, they have often been extracted from their proper text-image sequence; thus, from the very beginning, text and image are each accorded to a member of their respective "fields" for study, and visual and textual/verbal elements of what was meant as one cultural product are implicitly presumed by scholarship to be separate. In a very brief introduction, Nykl sketches two primary comparative directions for *BR*: Fernando de Rojas' *Celestina* (written and/or adapted around the turn of the 16th century) and the Old French *Aucassin et Nicolette* (probably composed sometime during the first half of the 13th century). Citations and discussions of editions of *Celestina*, as well as valuable summaries and pertinent bibliography of past, present, and future directions in Celestina scholarship may be found in the recent collection of studies edited by Ivy A. Corfis and Joseph T. Snow, *Fernando de Rojas and Celestina: approaching the fifth centenary: proceedings of an international conference in commemoration of the 450th anniversary of the death of Fernando de Rojas, Purdue University, West Lafayette, Indiana, 21–24 November 1991* (Madison: Hispanic Seminary of Medieval Studies, 1993); on *Aucassin et Nicolette*, there is the edition and modern French translation by Gustave Michaut, with preface by Bédier, *Aucassin et Nicolette, chante-fable du XIIème siècle* (Paris: Fontemoing, 1901); it was later re-edited and re-dated to the 13th century by Mario Roques in *Aucassin et Nicolette, chantefable du XIIIe siècle* (Paris: E. Champion, 1929; reprinted, 1973). A modern French prose translation by Gustave Cohen can be found in *Aucassin et Nicolette: chantefable du XIIIe siècle* (Paris: H. Champion, 1974); for suggestions on further reading, see Barbara Nelson Sargent-Baur and Robert Francis Cook, *Aucassin et Nicolette: a critical bibliography* (London: Grant & Cutler, 1981). Both directions (neither has been pursued since the initial publication of *BR* in the early 1940's) merit further investigation, and will be considered in a larger study of *BR* in the near future.

4. For the illustrations, see Oleg Grabar, *The Illustrations of the Maqamat* (Chicago: University of Chicago Press, 1984), and for more accessible reproductions of some images (Grabar's come in the form of microfilm), see Shirley Guthrie, *Arab Social Life in the Middle Ages: an illustrated study* (London: Saqi Books, 1995). For the *Maqāmāt* themselves, see Ḥarīrī (1054–1122), *Kitāb al-maqāmāt al-adabīyah* (Egypt: al-Maṭbaʿah al-Ḥusaynīyah, 1326 [1908 or 9]); for an English translation, Ḥarīrī, *The*

Assemblies of al-Harīrī; Student's edition of the Arabic text; with English notes, grammatical, critical, and historical introduction. By F. Steingass (London: Sampson Low, Marston & Co., 1897). The differences between the *BR* and *Maqāmāt* illustrations are implicitly characterized by Monneret de Villard (*Bibliofilia*, esp. pp. 212–213) as qualitative ones. The dependence of Andalusī cultural products on Eastern models is also implicitly assumed by Nykl, despite his expertise in matters Andalusī, in his characterization of the text, in the title of his publication, as "*una chantefable oriental en estilo persa*."

5. Nykl (*Chantefable*, introduction) believes that *BR* might have been temporarily removed to Paris' Bibliothèque Nationale during the early 19th century; one of the folios bears a stamp from that institution. Monneret de Villard (*Bibliofilia*, p. 211) for his part, suggests that it may have entered the Vatican's collection during the first half of the 16th century along with "other Arabic mss.;" these mss. are not specified, and I have not yet identified them.
6. Monneret de Villard, *Bibliofilia*, pp. 211–213, cites and concurs with Levi della Vida, stating that the script is unquestionably Andalusī. He also, however, concurs with Levi concerning a probable 14th-century date for the ms., a conclusion with which I am in disagreement. I concur with Khemir (see below, note 8) on the probability of a 13th-century date.
7. Monneret de Villard, *Bibliofilia*, pp. 210–11. North Africa might also be considered as a provenance for *BR*. No illustrated manuscripts are known to have survived from a Maghrebī Almohad, Ḥafsūnid, or Merinid context, but one imagines that they certainly must have been produced.
8. Sabīha Khemir, in *Al-Andalus: the art of Islamic Spain*, ed. Jerrilynn D. Dodds (New York: Metropolitan Museum of Art: Distributed by H.N. Abrams, 1992), pp. 312–313, also observes, somewhat in passing, relationships between certain features of the *BR* images and near-contemporary textiles which were probably produced in Seville (or, possibly, Almería; the textiles will be briefly considered in the conclusion to this essay) to signal a Sevillan workshop as the manuscript's most likely point of origin. The images do—as Khemir also observes, particularly in terms of certain architectural details which have an unmistakably "Almohad" look about them—tend to shore up the argument for a 13th-century date, which might be pushed back to the very late 12th century at the earliest. In particular, there are striking similarities between the architectural representations in the *BR* images and the "Almohad" patio which has been uncovered in the old Casa de Contratación within the complex of the Reales Alcázares in Seville; I will further consider the wider implications of these similarities in a forthcoming essay in *Medieval Encounters*; on the patio see *El Jardín Musulmán de*

la Antigua Casa de Contratación de Sevilla, v. 1 and 2 (Seville, 1992) and, now, Antonio Almagro, "El Patio del Crucero de los Reales Alcázares de Sevilla," *Al-Qantara*, XX, fasc. 2 (1999), pp. 331–376. The images also resemble to some extent reconstructions of late Almoravid- or Almohad-period dwellings excavated by Julio Navarro Palazón in the region of Murcia (Cieza/*Siyāsa*); see Julio Navarro Palazón, "La Dār As-Sughrā' de Murcia. Un palacio andalusí del siglo XII," in *Colloque international d'archéologie islamique*, ed. Roland-Pierre Gayraud, *Textes Arabes et Études Islamiques*, 36 (Damascus, 1998), pp. 97–140. The paleographical aspect of this project is perhaps the one which still needs the most attention, but at present, my admittedly somewhat unsystematic comparison of *BR*'s script with that of other Andalusī manuscripts also leads me to incline toward a 13th-century date.

9. No geographical indications besides Bayāḍ's Syrian origins are actually given in the text. During his interview with the *Sayyida*, following his performance which was such a hit, he simply says that he has come to rest "in your country"—*fī baladikum* (f. 8r). The only other possible reference comes in the form of the designation of the Old Woman as "from Babylon" (16 v): this latter, however, is probably more an indication of an exotic or somehow marginal or *other* quality which the narrator and her/his public attach to her, a view clearly communicated throughout the text. It might also be an indication that the story (or the character) had, indeed, migrated into al-Andalus from elsewhere and had, even for Andalusī speakers of Arabic, an aura of the exotic about it. It is an avenue worth further investigation.

10. Two valuable comparative studies on the theme of the "go-between" (or, "Celestina") character in Medieval literature have appeared recently; neither, however, includes *BR*'s Old Woman seriously in its considerations; see Robinson and Rouhi, *Under the Influence* (in preparation). See Francisco Márquez Villanueva, *Orígenes y sociología del tema celestinesco* (Barcelona: Anthropos, 1993) and Leyla Rouhi, *Mediation and love: a study of the medieval go-between in key Romance and Near-Eastern texts* (Leiden; Boston: Brill, 1999).

11. Riyāḍ's transgression of "courtly" norms through the sincere use of verse to speak of her beloved mirrors, of course, the transgression of that most famous of all famous lovers, *Majnūn*. Despite the fact that the drama surrounding *Majnūn*'s lovesickness unfolds, first in Bedouin camps and, later, in the wilderness, while Bayāḍ's and Riyāḍ's saga is essentially an urban one, the parallels would have probably been obvious to a 13th-century public. Moreover, the surviving Andalusī text which appears most closely connected to *BR*, 13th-century poet and anthologist Ibn Saʿīd al-Andalusī'(1213-1286)'s *Murqiṣāt fi-l-Muṭribāt* (Bayrūt: Dār Ḥamad wa-Miḥiū, 1973), con-

tains a lengthy version of Qays' woes, pp. 240 ff., complete with *isnād*, verses and directions for performing them, similar to those found in the *Kitāb al-Aghānī*; for an example of these performance instructions (which are quite common in the *Aghānī*), see Abū al-Faraj al-Isbahānī (897 or 8–967), *Kitāb al-Aghānī*, 27 vols. (Bayrūt: Dār al-Kutub al-ʿIlmīyah, 1992), vol. 1, p. 58. A possible link in the chain between the *Aghānī* and Andalusian literature is also the 10th-century Tunisian Ibn al-Raqīq's *Quṭb al-surūr fī awṣāf al-khumūr*, ed., Aḥmad al-Jundī (Dimashq: al-Muqaddimah, 1969, a compilation of, among other *majlis*- and wine-related matters, drinking songs with *isnād* for both verses and music and performance instructions). Given its presence in Ibn Saʿīd's anthology, we may suppose that *Majnūn*'s story was experiencing particular popularity in literary circles at the moment in which *BR* was produced. I plan to address the relationships between these texts in the near future.

12. The *Sayyida*'s palace is clearly intended to be perceived as a particularly luxurious place; this is achieved through careful detailing of architectural and ornamental features, down to stained or colored glass for the windows (see, esp., the image of Riyāḍ's fainting spell); Julio Navarro Palazón has demonstrated that colored glass was a present, although not terribly common, feature of upper-class urban dwellings in 13th-century Murcia; see Julio Navarro Palazón, *Una Casa Islámica en Murcia: Estudio de su ajuar (s. XIII)* (Murcia: Centro de Estudios Arabes y Arqueologicos "Ibn Arabi", 1991), esp. pp. 76–78. Likewise, Antonio Almagro ("El Patio del Crucero") proposes that the particular sort of two-leveled patio-and-garden he identifies in the original configuration of the "Almohad" patio in the Casa de Contratación in Seville was relatively uncommon in Andalusī patio-garden typology during the period in question; given its location in the Reales Alcázares, this is probably to be interpreted as an "elite" feature. The *Sayyida*'s garden as represented in the *BR* images was, I think, specifically intended to be perceived as of this type; see below.

13. In light of this suggestion and of the comparisons which I wish to establish between *BR* and Alfonsine books, it is interesting to remark the existence of a treatise, in Old Portuguese but written in Hebrew characters, on the subject of the mixing and preservation of various colors used in the illumination of books; D.S. Blondheim, "An Old Portuguese Work on Manuscript Illumination," *The Jewish Quarterly Review* XIX, no. 2 (October, 1928), pp. 97–136. The treatise, according to Blondheim, was produced by Abraham b. Judah ibn Hayyim (it is signed by him, at Loulé, Portugal; although the document in question probably represents a later copy) sometime around 1262 A.D., a moment of intense activity on the part of Alfonsine workshops, and most likely contemporary to the production of *BR* as well. While Blondheim

implies that the treatise pertains particularly to the illumination of *Hebrew* manuscripts, it certainly has a wider cultural "semantic field." The existence of such a treatise suggests that the illustrating and illuminating of manuscripts in the middle of the 13th century was a large enough business to warrant the production of such documents for the instruction of painters. Moreover, the colors which are given pride of place (first gold, then blues, reds) correspond to the colors most used in the illuminated/illustrated Alfonsine codices. It is also interesting to note that the treatise contains information concerning the gilding of sword handles and varnishing, which its author appears to consider as within the professional ballpark of those who illuminated/illustrated books.

14. This folio is bound out of order.

15. There are also striking similarities between the *BR* images and paintings produced under Fatimid patronage or "spheres of influence," as well as the paintings from the ceiling of the Cappella Palatina in Palermo. These similarities are much stronger, particularly in terms of the rendering of specific figural and architectural details, than are the more general ones they exhibit to the *Maqāmāt* illustrations; they perhaps argue for more intense interchange based on the practicalities of geographics, but have probably not been noted before due to the simple fact that the Fatimid products are less well-known to scholarship than are the *Maqāmāt* illustrations.

16. See Eva R. Hoffman, "A Fatimid Book cover: Framing and Re-framing. Cultural Identity in the Medieval Mediterranean World," in *L'Egypte Fatimide: son art et son histoire*, ed. Marianne Barrucand (Paris: Presses de l'Université de Paris-Sorbonne, 1999), pp. 403–420.

17. This suggestion is lent greater credence by the fact that the almost completely mutilated part of the ms. page closest to this image contains a word which is almost certainly "*ḥājib*." The words immediately surrounding this one are too damaged to reconstruct, and Nykl does not include the sentence in his edition of this folio.

18. Basic bibliography on the *Cantigas*, in addition to Alfonso X, King of Castile and León. *Las Cantigas de Santa María: edición facsímile del Códice T.I.1 de la Biblioteca de San Lorenzo el Real de El Escorial, siglo XIII* (Madrid: Edilán, 1979), John E. Keller and Annette Grant Cash, *Daily life depicted in the Cantigas de Santa María* (Lexington, Kentucky: University Press of Kentucky, 1998), and broader cultural studies such as Robert I. Burns, ed., *Emperor of Culture: Alfonso X the Learned of Castile and his thirteenth-century Renaissance* (Philadelphia: University of Pennsylvania Press, 1990), and Joseph F. O'Callaghan, *Alfonso X and the Cantigas de Santa María: A poetic biography* (Leiden and Boston: Brill, 1998), and ibidem, *The Learned King: The Reign of Alfonso X of Castile*

(Philadelphia: University of Pennsylvania Press, 1993), include: *Cantigas de Santa María*, ed., Jesús Montoya (Madrid: Cátedra, 1988); *Cantigas de Santa María*, ed., Walter Mettmann (Vigo: Edicións Xerais de Galicia, 1981); *Cuarenta y cinco cantigas del Códice Rico de Alfonso el Sabio: textos pictóricos y verbales*, trad., intro. and commentary, Luís Beltrán (Palma de Mallorca: J.J. de Olañeta, 1997); *Rimario e lessico in rima delle Cantigas de santa Maria di Alfonso X di Castiglia*, ed. Maria Pia Betti (Pisa: Pacini, 1997); Amparo García Cuadrado, *Las cantigas, el códice de Florencia* (Murcia: Universidad de Murcia, 1993); Jesús Montoya Martínez, *O cancioneiro marial de Alfonso X, o Sabio* (Santiago de Compostela: Universidade de Santiago de Compostela, 1991).

19. See note 13; Abraham b. Judah ibn Hayyim's treatise informs its readers on how to manufacture a color *like* that made across the Mediterranean (which, it is to be presumed, was either too expensive or too rare to be found in the author's immediate surroundings). Likewise, Michael Baxandall's work on 15th-century Florence emphasizes the great esteem in which this color was held by painters and patrons alike, presumably because of its rarity and costliness. See Michael Baxandall, *Painting and experience in fifteenth century Italy: a primer in the social history of pictorial style* (Oxford [Oxfordshire]; New York: Oxford University Press, 1988, c. 1972).

20. Many of these strictures are preserved in the form of sumptuary laws, discussed briefly in Arié, "Le Costume des Musulmans." In Robinson, "Preliminary Considerations," I have suggested that these restrictions may have carried implications for the production of both *BR* and Alfonso's *Libros del Ajedrez*.

21. Indeed, the primary grounds for comparison between *BR* and the Alfonsine products—besides our knowledge that they were produced roughly at the same time and in the same place—are found in the images themselves—at a first glance, in terms of content, the two texts would appear to have little or nothing to do with one another; Robinson, "Preliminary Considerations." Moreover, it should be noted that Abraham b. Judah ibn Hayyim's treatise on the fabrication of colors for ms. illumination *assumes* the use of parchment, a fact which suggests that the makers of *BR* would probably have used parchment if it had been readily available to them. See Blondheim, "An Old Portuguese Work on Manuscript Illumination."

22. Robinson, "Preliminary Considerations."

23. Nykl, *Chantefable*, introduction.

24. Bayāḍ's relatively brief poetic description (*waṣf*) of the garden in which he is currently seated with the *Sayyida*, the *waṣāʿif* and Riyāḍ (f. 10r), for instance, would have struck contemporary critics as mediocre at best, if in

fact they would have dignified it with their consideration. To name only one of its faults, six of the seven lines begin with "*ka'anna*," and what follows is a list of simple comparisons based on the colors of the flowers of the *Sayyida*'s garden.

25. Bayāḍ's reticence to employ verse in the description of his beloved is, of course, in direct contrast to Riyāḍ's soon-to-come rash belting out of not one but several consecutive love songs in which her true feelings are (all too clearly) revealed. More on the ms.'s didactic function will be said shortly.

26. The copyist, or perhaps the author, however, clearly perceives these words as *sajʿ* and intends for the audience to perceive them in this way as well: the words are separated by small circles with dots at their center, identical to the graphic devices used elsewhere in the ms. to signify pause or punctuation. Likewise, such separations appear between the discrete segments of *sajʿ* in mss. of works filled with dexterously wrought rhymed prose, such as al-Fath ibn Khāqān's *Qalā'id al-ʿIqyān*, or the more closely contemporary Ibn Saʿīd al-Andalusī's *Murqiṣāt fi-l-Muṭribāt* which, while not rendered entirely in *sajʿ*, contains competent examples of it.

27. Here, I would like to modify statements made in Robinson, "Preliminary Considerations," concerning the ambiguity of the narrative function of the *BR* images. That essay was written at a much earlier stage of this project's research, and I now believe that the images are *primarily* narrative, and that therein lies their power to comment or to gloss the primary meaning of the text.

28. The *ḥājib* is present in the scene with which the ms. opens, when the Old Woman casts an eye on *Riyāḍ* for the first time, and is referred to several times as the plot thickens as an authority figure whose wrath is to be feared but, for the most part, events take place in his absence, and his court connections remain unspecified.

29. The Old Woman is the most developed in this respect, a fact which suggests yet another intriguing parallel with *Celestina*. Note particularly her explanation of her own emotional reactions and intentions in the instances when Bayāḍ's spirits are at their lowest; ff. 2v–3r, 15r–15v. On the character development of *Celestina*, see Joseph V. Ricapito, "People, Characters and Roles: A View of Characterization in *Celestina*," in Corfis and Snow, eds., *Fernando de Rojas*, pp. 181–192.

30. The Old Woman, though, true to her character-type, is able to manipulate to her *protegée*'s advantage even Riyāḍ's privileged existence as the favorite of both the *Sayyida* and the *ḥājib* (from whose lecherous advances we are given to understand that the *Sayyida* has thus far been able to guard her...i.e., she has not had to "pay" at all for her privileges). She convinces the *Sayyida*

that Riyāḍ's protected upbringing (i.e., maybe she *didn't* know any better) in some way relieves her of responsibility for her actions. Immediately following this statement on the Old Woman's part, the *Sayyida* begins to blame herself for the unfortunate turn taken by the *majlis* (it is, perhaps, *she* who should have known better), and then breaks into inspired verse for the first time, bemoaning her own irresponsibility with respect to her favorite.

31. ʿAlī ibn Aḥmad Ibn Ḥazm (994–1064), *Ṭawq al-ḥamāmah fī al-ulfah wa-al-ulāf*, ed. Ḥasan Kāmil al- Sīrfī (Cairo: al-Maktabah al-Tijārīyah al-Kubrā, 1964); English translation, *The Ring of the Dove* (New York: AMS Press, 1981). Muḥammad ibn Isḥāq ibn Yaḥyāʾ al-Washshāʿ (d. 936) *Kitāb al-Muwashshāʿ*, ed. ʿAbd al-Amīr ʿAlī Muhannā (Bayrūt: Dār al-Fikr al-Lubnānī, 1990); Spanish translation by Teresa Garulo, *El libro del brocado* (Madrid: Alfaguara, 1990). *BR*'s importance as a partial solution for the lack of firm evidence of knowledge among later medieval authors, in both Arabic and Romance contexts, of Ibn Ḥazm's text, is capital; Márquez comments several times on this *lacuna* in the available evidence in *Orígenes y sociología*, but only mentions *BR* (not in the context of that particular discussion) in a footnote.

32. Although, as already stated, an undetermined number of folios are missing from *BR*, the narrative moments signaled here as (perhaps surprisingly) *not* illustrated are not located near problematic *lacunae*.

33. See Sandra Hindman, *Sealed in Parchment: rereadings of knighthood in the illuminated manuscripts of Chrétien de Troyes* (Chicago: University of Chicago Press, 1994).

34. The order of these last two images, I believe, is meant to be reversed: several of the final pages of the manuscript in its current state of preservation are bound out of order. Nykl's 1941 edition presents the pages (and, thus, the images) in the order in which they have been bound, without comment.

35. Yet again, one wonders about the possibility of ironic or humorous intent—the Old Woman's comment is that Bayāḍ received the *Sayyida*'s attentions in an exemplary manner like a *ẓarīf* (f. 7r; "*fa-akala aklan ẓarīfan nabīlan mathīlan...*"). The passage could really be interpreted either way, but given the ambiguities in play here concerning the characters' observation of proper etiquette, the fact that his manners were considered at all probably indicates that the possibility of parody or irony should not be ruled out.

36. Joy, pleasure; delight or rapture; also amusement or entertainment involving the performance of music.

37. The emotive powers conceded by 12th- and 13th-century literati to the well-wrought love lyric are excellently summed up in Ibn Saʿīd al-Andalusī's introductory passages to *Murqiṣāt*.

38. André le Chapelain, *De amore et amoris remedio*; English translation, *The Art of Courtly Love*, by John Jay Parry (New York: Columbia University, 1941 and 1990). Recently on the "Art," see Paolo Cherchi, *Andreas and the Ambiguity of Courtly Love* (Toronto; Buffalo: University of Toronto Press, 1994). Spanish & Latin, *De amore = Tratado sobre el amor*, ed. and trans., Inés Creixell Vidal-Quadras (Barcelona: Sirmio, 1990); in terms of parallels with potentially debatable narrative situations in *BR*, I am thinking specifically of the "iudicia" of Chapter VII (Creixall, pp. 324 ff.), particularly XVIII, "Quidam milites intima turpiter et secreta vulgavit amoris..."—"a certain soldier-gentleman shamefully disclosed the intimate secrets of his love..." The result, after judgment by a group of courtly ladies, is ostracism from the court of love (Creixall, pp. 342–345). The offending party, of course, in the case examined by the Chaplain is male instead of female, but the parallel is nonetheless suggestive.
39. The motif of seeing or observing from atop a tree seems a bit out of place here, or perhaps not to have much purpose. Yet, it is insisted upon twice: it recurs when Bayāḍ arrives at the *Sayyida*'s *majlis* and Riyāḍ becomes so agitated that she attempts to climb a tree, and a slave girl has to coax her down. It is tempting to compare it to King Mark's spying down on Tristan and Isolde from atop a tree, a motif known to have had, as it were, something of a life of its own. See the essay by Michael Curschmann in Adrian Stevens and Roy Wisby, eds., *Gottfried von Strassburg and the Medieval Tristan Legend: Papers from an Anglo-North America Symposium* (Suffolk: D. S. Brewer; London: Institute of Germanic Studies, 1990); see also Michael Camille, in *The Medieval Art of Love: objects and subjects of desire* (New York: Abrams, 1998), p. 15, fig. 7, for the "Forrer" casket, made in Cologne (today in the British Museum) c. 1180–1200, a bone casket which gives particular visual emphasis to the *topos*. The fact that the *topos* is also intertwined with that of Riyāḍ's failure to remember (recognize?) Bayāḍ, a motif which finds several echoes later in the narrative, might also suggest this as a productive direction for comparative consideration: following Riyāḍ's lapse of memory concerning their previous meeting and supposed tryst, Bayāḍ fails then to recognize Riyāḍ when he sees her at the *majlis* until prompted by the *Sayyida*. He later fails to recognize Shamūl when she approaches him by the river; he also fails to recognize the garden as the one in which he was united with Riyāḍ, and appears to have forgotten the lines of his own composition, which Shamūl recites to him in order to prove to him that she has indeed made his acquaintance. Like the motif of Riyāḍ continually climbing up trees, the lack-of-recognition motif does not really make a great deal of sense in the narrative contexts in which it occurs in *BR* (especially in the cases of Bayāḍ and Riyāḍ failing to recognize one another), a fact which might argue for its being foreign to the story's (unfortu-

nately lost) tradition.

40. To rhapsodize about a beloved [woman]; to speak of her charms in verse.
41. The idea of *BR* having been put together with an eye toward possible debates concerning properly "courtly" behaviour on the part of the audience might also provide an explanation for certain ambiguities in the text, given that the text fails to do so (i.e., perhaps they, because of their incongruity within the codified system of elegant or "courtly" behaviour certainly very familiar to *BR*'s audience, were intended to call an audience's attention to themselves and thus to elicit debate).
42. For the clearest statement by a 13th-century poet and anthologist of these perceptions concerning the emotive power of the love lyric, see Ibn Saʿīd's *al-Murqiṣāt al-muṭribāt*. The treatise is organized according to the principle of "most moving=most original."
43. One of the possible translations of *tharthār* is "chatterbox" or "prattler."
44. I have actually tried this myself, and given the bold, clearly distinguished areas of color defined by dark, relatively thick (and easily visible) outlines, I think it is quite plausible to assert that the images might have been read, and were probably intended to be read, from a short distance as well as up close.
45. As indicated by Nykl's earlier suggestion of *Aucassin et Nicolette* as comparanda for *BR*, narratives with lyric insertions were also becoming popular in Romance literature during the first half of the 13th century. The issue has recently been investigated by Maureen Barry McCann Boulton, *The Song in the Story: Lyric insertions in French narrative fiction, 1200–1400* (Philadelphia: University of Pennsylvania Press, 1993); thanks to John van Engen for bringing this study to my attention. Boulton proposes distinct functions for these lyrics according to the narrative contexts in which they appear, and many of the cases she sketches find more than superficial parallels with the lyrics in *BR*. Particular parallels are notable between BR and Jean Renart's also roughly contemporary (12th/13th cent.) *Guillaume de Dole*, available in two recent editions and translations: Jean Renart, *The Romance of the Rose or of Guillaume de Dole = Roman de la Rose ou de Guillaume de Dole*, ed. and trans., Regina Psaki (New York: Garland Pub., 1995), and *The Romance of the Rose, or, Guillaume de Dole*, trans. and intro., Patricia Terry and Nancy Vine Durling (Philadelphia: University of Pennsylvania Press, 1993). Jean Renart's romance is similar to *BR* particularly in terms of its interest in lavish courtly festivities, and the introduction of outsiders or interlopers into these latter.
46. The arabic word "*indafaʿa[t]*" is used almost exclusively in the first half of the ms., that which corresponds to the fateful *majlis*, to name the action of

"beginning to sing." Whether the desired interpretation tends toward rashness or spontaneity is not entirely clear; both implications of the term could certainly be taken into account.

47. There is one instance of "*qālit al-sayyida*" [f. 6r] which occupies the place and performs the separating function following a song of "*qālit al-ʿajūz*," possibly a scribal error or a case of convenience, for the *Sayyida* does begin to speak at this point.

48. Ibn Saʿīd, *al-Murqiṣāt al-muṭribāt,* p. 7, notes that the best lyrics are easy to memorize, presumably because this would aid in performance.

49. For the pillow, see *Al-Andalus*, no. 89, p. 321. The use of these themes in (secular) luxury objects for a Christian (female) patron should probably be given more case-specific consideration than it has received in the past. Berengaria, daughter of Alfonso VIII of Castile and Eleanor of England, was the *infanta* of that kingdom, was a "key player" in some very complex political situations during the late 12th and early 13th centuries (including a marriage to Alfonso IX of León which was later effectively annulled with the excuse of consanguinity by Pope Innocent III—he placed the kingdom on León under interdiction and excommunication). Thus, the creation and propagation of a royal identity would have been part of the agenda of any object commissioned by and/or for her. The issue of the queen's association of herself, through the pillow, with what are probably *qiyān* clearly merits further investigation. See also the also 13th-century "Drinking Ladies" silk textile, cat. no. 106 in Vivian B. Mann, Thomas F. Glick, Jerrilyn D. Dodds, eds., *Convivencia: Jews, Muslims, and Christians in Medieval Spain* (New York: G. Braziller in association with the Jewish Museum, 1992), pictured on p. 10; its provenance is less certain than that of Berengaria's pillow.

50. See above, note 8.

51. See above, note 8; images of the doors are found in *El Jardín Musulmán.*

52. For Ibn Saʿīd, see above, note 11; Muḥammad Ibn Dāniyāl (1249 or 50–1310 or 11), *Three Shadow Plays*, edited by the late Paul Kahle; with a critical apparatus by Derek Hopwood (Cambridge, England: Trustees of the "E.J.W. Gibb Memorial," 1992), and *Thalāṯh masraḥīyāt Arabīyah muththilāt fī al-qurūn al-wuṣṭā* [microform] (Baghdād: Maṭbaʿat al-Iʿtimād, 1948). See also *Les comédiens de la rue (Théâtre d'ombres)*, trans., René R. Khawam (Paris: L'Esprit des Péninsules, 1997).

53. For the troubadour *vidas* and *razos*, key publications are: Jean Boutière and A.-H. Schutz, *Biographies des troubadours [textes provençaux des XIIIe et XIVe siècles]* (Toulouse, E. Privat [distributed in the United States by Ohio State University, Columbus, 1950 [c. 1949]), followed by Camille Chabaneau, *Les biographies des troubadours en langue provençale: publiées inté-*

gralement pour la première fois avec une introduction et des notes (Genève: Slatkine Reprints; Marseille: Laffitte Reprints, 1975) and Margarita Egan, trans., *The Vidas of the Troubadours* (New York: Garland Pub., 1984); see also Elizabeth Wilson Poe, *From Poetry to Prose in Old Provençal: the emergence of the Vidas, the Razos, and the Razos de Trobar* (Birmingham, Ala.: Summa Publications, 1984). An eloquent reminder of the primarily performative function of troubadour lyric comes in María R. Menocal's *Shards of Love: exile and the origins of the lyric* (Durham: Duke University Press, 1994). Scholarship has traditionally been quite cautious about asserting a performative function for the *razos*; recently, however, Elizabeth Aubrey, "La *razo* trouvée, chantée, écrite et enseignée chez les troubadours," in *Toulouse à la croisée des cultures: actes du Ve Congrès international de l'Association internationale d'études occitanes, Toulouse, 19-24 août 1996*, ed., Jacques Gourc et François Pic (Pau: Association internatiole d'Études Occitanes, 1998), pp. 297–306, has argued forcefully for the *razos* having formed an integral part of the performance of troubadour songs before 13th- and 14th-century audiences.

III

BEYOND THE FRAME: CONSIDERING THE OBJECT

The Aesthetics of Aggregation: Persian Anthologies of the Fifteenth Century

DAVID J. ROXBURGH

Despite the early appearance and continuous presence of anthologies (*dīwān, safīna, majmūʿa, jung*),[1] throughout the history of the Islamic book and their often stunning semantic and semiotic breadth, which one might think would make them irresistible objects of study, they still stand on the margins of scholarship. The anthologies fall between the cracks having not been studied in detail either by historians of literature or of art, although images from their pages are frequently used to illustrate publications. In the absence of a scholarly discourse about the anthology it is only possible to imagine how literary historians would study them by discerning patterns of analysis of other texts. Were the literary historian to study the anthology, he would perhaps examine it as a literary practice of collection, selection, and edition and thus as a way of organizing and containing particular groups of literature and knowledge and ultimately as a symptom of larger trends in literate society (e.g., the impulse to make canons through processes of classification and as some expression of taste).[2] But since their investigations have rarely attended to "materialist philology" or to the artifactual properties of books,[3] like the historian favoring instead the analysis and interpretation of a book's content, it is unlikely that the texts as a gathering or the generic juxtapositions that they produce would form a central subject of inquiry. The anthology is just there, a useful and convenient assembly of texts awaiting analysis independently of each other. Until quite recently Western medieval miscellanies suffered a similar methodological fate and general neglect.[4]

The art historian is similarly blinded by the visual categories and taxonomic hierarchies that they have produced. In studying the arts of the book, weight is given to painting and to the changing relationship of painting as illustration to the accompanying text. Gradually, painting in the book is understood to acquire a measure of autonomy, valued by its contemporary viewer as painting and not solely illustration,[5] a change signaled by the amount of space between the image and its relevant text, which were often separated from each other by a number of pages; by the expansion of the painting to fill the page; and by the layers of meanings in the painting that goes beyond the strictly textual requirements of visualizing an event and the story's main actors. Most of these developments had occurred by the late fourteenth century.[6]

The general category of book painting has been refined through the identification and description of visual idioms geared to specific textual genres (scientific, historical, epic, poetic)[7] and might now accommodate some of the forms of images found in anthologies. Auxiliary aspects of the book's visual and material properties, however, still tend to be sidelined in favor of attending to the reader's movement between text and image, the privileged phenomenon of textual and visual experience. This emphasis and the hierarchy produced by it relegate the book's auxiliary visual elements to alternate, usually functional, categories. The binding contains and protects the textblock. Illumination marks transitions in the text's structure. Any non-narrative paintings or drawings are classified as decorative, added to augment the book's value and proclaim its status as a luxury object to the reader in a culture where ownership of fine books signaled high social status and prestige. It is clear that this functional formula fails to provide a holistic account for the book as object. Painting is analyzed separately from the book, which is its context, and although the painting's immediate context is sometimes addressed through word-image analysis, the book's materiality and full visual range are not.[8]

This set of functional classifications is especially critical for the anthology because of the impact it has had on the nature of its study. Some anthologies employ such a diverse range of visual idioms as to appear inchoate, heterogeneous, as if replete with images on holiday.

Visual genres match textual genres although the signifying power of the former is qualified by a schema in which storytelling pictures are given emphasis. Thus, word-image analysis can be a self-selecting process that closes off an analysis of visual phenomena for which there would appear to be no text. In analyzing relations between texts of different genres and their accompanying images we can get lost in the labyrinth of success, of how well the image does its job of illustration.

What I have chosen to do here is to study those aspects of the book that would be classified as non-narrative/decorative (as opposed to the category of narrative painting), and to explain how they may have operated. In producing images for texts that often appear to be unillustratable, what choices are made? But before I return to this objective some additional explanation about my chosen line of inquiry is necessary. Word and image analysis (nascent in the fields of Islamic literature and art) tends to fall subject to recurring frameworks of analysis. At the foundation of these frameworks lie two dictums: Horace's *Ut pictura poesis*, and Gregory's statement that "pictures are the books of the illiterate." The former produced a mass of literature on the relationship between poetry and painting, given expression through such phrases as "the sister arts" or "correspondence of the arts," and it served as a pole around which questions of aesthetics and the study of *ekphrasis* figured prominently.[9]

Gregory's statement opened up questions of literacy and legibility in both the textual and visual media, of the communicative function of word and image in which they were implicitly posited as exclusive, as two systems that functioned reciprocally as a supplement one to the other, addressing the different capacities of the reader/viewer. It was only through semiotics that these initial, defining problems could be circumvented or reassessed.[10] I have chosen not to pursue the subjects of literacy and sign theory, largely because the crucial research remains to be undertaken for the historical context of fifteenth-century Iran. But I also avoid them because my main concerns are a holistic analysis of the anthology, and a visual analysis of non-narrativizing images for which a semiotics of word and image is not productive. Rather, I focus on experiential dimensions of the anthology and the decoding of its visual contents.

To initiate an investigation of these questions about the anthology, I will begin with examples made in Iran during the fifteenth century, mainly for Iskandar Sultan, a Timurid prince and governor of Shiraz, and through them I will focus on a set of interrelated themes.[11] But first some words of caution. By focusing on the fifteenth century I do not mean to suggest that the concept of the anthology was developed at that time. Among the earliest dated examples is Ibn Sina's *Dānish-nāma-yi ʿalāʾī* (a compendium of philosophy [logic, metaphysics, physics, geometry, astronomy, arithmetic, and music]) completed by 1041 (and edited by his student Juzjani). It represents one example of the digest or encyclopedia devoted to a particular theme, discipline, or branch of knowledge. A cursory examination of cultural production in various metropolitan centers under the Timurids in the early fifteenth century, however, suggests an emphasis on the compilation of anthologies, perhaps as an attempt to come to terms with a cultural past by collection and codification,[12] and thereby to write the Timurids into Perso-Islamicate cultural history. One good example is the Timurid Prince Baysunghur's order that Amir Khusraw Dihlawi's poetry be collected and made into a *dīwān*. Baysunghur ultimately abandoned the project when 2,000 lines were found beyond the 20,000 lines that he had already gathered.[13]

By the early years of the fifteenth century the anthology and the realization of the book's aesthetic potential placed a particular set of problems before the book designer. To give a collection of often disparate texts some degree of coherence called for the development of structural and formal solutions that would adequately unite texts and images. The absence of an index demanded the creation of visual prompts inside the manuscript to mark off separate sections, formats for the text on the page, the use of captions and rubrics, and tables of contents (*fihrist*).[14] Changes in aesthetics and developments in techniques and materials ultimately transformed the book: it was no longer a gathering of single sheets stitched into a textblock and bound between protective leather covers. Each page became an aggregate of bits and pieces of calligraphed, gold flecked, tinted, colored, painted, and illuminated paper glued together to form a constructed page. It may be that the design problems posed by the anthology, its aggregate of texts and images, and the solutions found to answer them led to the transformation of the conception of the book.

Iskandar Sultan's Anthologies

Iskandar Sultan (1384–1415) governed the city of Shiraz in southern Iran until 1414. His uncle Shahrukh b. Timur, fearful of his expansionist policies, autonomy, and strong likelihood of sedition, was forced to march on Shiraz, setting out for the city in October 1413. Dawlatshah Samarqandi gives the following account of the events in his *Tadhkirat al-shuʿarā* (Biography of Poets, 1487): "In the end Iskandar Sultan was taken prisoner by Shahrukh and, through the machinations of Gawhar-shad [Shahrukh's wife], Shahrukh gave his approval for both the prince's eyes, which were the envy of the black-eyed houris, to be stripped of the garb of sight, like the eyes of the narcissus. That occurred on Friday, July 20, 1414."[15] Iskandar Sultan was incarcerated in Herat and languished in prison until his death in 1415. During his tenure as governor of Shiraz, numerous manuscripts were made for his library, twelve of those that still exist contain dedications to him, and based on formal and stylistic features an additional six have been attributed to his patronage.[16]

Many of these dedicated and attributed manuscripts are anthologies. Among them are two, one in the British Library (dated 1410–11),[17] and a second in the Topkapı Palace Museum Library (dated 1413–14).[18] The London Anthology is closely related to another one in Lisbon (dated 1411):[19] they share a small format—prime examples of the *vade mecum* —and are fat volumes ranging from four to five hundred folios, mainly of poetry. Because of these numerous similarities I will not discuss the Lisbon Anthology. The Istanbul Anthology is larger in format but shorter, running to some thirty folios in all. Characteristic of all these examples is their wide range of textual genres and topics. Comprised mainly of poetry, the London Anthology also offered the reader texts on astronomy, astrology, and medicine, and shorter treatises dealing with prosody, religious observance, Islamic law, and, in one, a dictionary. Priscilla Soucek has commented on their didactic tone and suggested that the London and Lisbon anthologies may have been made "to provide a member of the Timurid family with a basic introduction to Iranian Islamic culture."[20] These portable anthologies gave Iskandar Sultan access to abridgements of poetic texts—perhaps highlights of favorite works—with the shorter treatises functioning as reference works.

A recent analysis of the London Anthology focused on the problems presented by the organization of its disparate texts:[21] the *Khamsa* (Quintet) of Nizami; three episodes from Firdawsi's *Shāhnāma* (Book of Kings: Siyawush and Sudaba, Bizhan and Manizha, Bizhan's rescue by Rustam); an episode from Khwaju Kirmani's *Humāy u Humāyūn*; qasidas in praise of the Prophet Muhammad and the Shiʿite imams; a treatise on the law of religious observances by Abu Hanifa; a treatise on the computation of the calendar and the use of the astrolabe with tables of conjunctions of the planets; and a treatise on astrology. The manuscript opens with a double-page illumination, illuminated frames that contain medallions bearing Iskandar Sultan's titles. The double-page is essentially an ex libris.

One page (fol. 28a), the conclusion of the *Makhzan al-asrār* (first *mathnawī* of Nizami's *Khamsa*), shows the major division between text (*matn*) and margin (*ḥashīyyat*) that runs throughout the anthology (Plate 1). The poetic text of Nizami is written in the *matn*, arranged in four columns, with each new subdivision in the *Khamsa* marked by an illuminated heading (*ʿunwān*), a broad rectangular band placed at the top of the *matn*. Boxes of gold *thuluth* sometimes found in the center field of the *matn* offer pious exhortations or serve as rubrics to describe the general content of the adjacent text. At the conclusion of the *Makhzan al-asrār* comes the colophon, the leftover space filled by a repeat geometric design and symmetrically opposed floral motifs. A small, rotated square contains the name of ʿAli, son-in-law of the Prophet Muhammad and first Shiʿite imam, repeated four times in gold over a lapis lazuli ground. The margins are signaled not only by the gold rulings that divide them from the *matn* but also by their diagonally oriented script. Small triangles of illumination at top and bottom, along the gutter of the folio, and the thumbpiece on the middle of the outer side add emphasis to the diagonal script and fill in the spaces that remain when the text has to shift direction in order to be read from a single position. The triangles and thumbpieces exhibit an extraordinary diversity of subject and motif. Thus, it is clear that, like any other Islamic book, illumination in the anthology serves to mark beginnings and endings and at the same time lend both formal and structural coherence to the manuscript and its parts. Illumination also increases the sense of continuity across the manuscript's pages.

The anthology contains numerous illustrations to its poetic texts, and it is these very paintings that are discussed over and over in the scholarship, mainly because some of the compositions were repeated in manuscripts of the later fifteenth century.[22] Compositional prototypes, all from Nizami's *Khamsa*, that were later imitated include "Shirin Looking at the Portrait of Khusraw Watched by Shapur";[23] "Nushaba Recognizing Iskandar by his Portrait";[24] and "Layli and Majnun Fainting at their Meeting."[25] Others, like the story of ʿAli and the Christian monk who was converted to Islam when ʿAli saved him from falling to his death, set in qasidas in praise of the Prophet Muhammad and the imams,[26] were never repeated. In a fairly straightforward way, each painting draws on the subject matter of its relevant text and depicts that text's dramatis personae at a specific moment; they deal with causes and effects. The narrative elements of poetry are emphasized.

But how are non-narrative texts handled in the London anthology? An "Abridged Text on the Science of Astronomy" (fol. 340b) is introduced by an illuminated *ʿunwān* with the margin given over to illumination and a small diagram in gold and black ink outlining planetary orbits. Pages from the middle section of an unabridged treatise on astrology (fols. 409b–410a; Plates 2 and 2A) similarly contain a variety of diagrams and charts and representations of constellations and signs of the zodiac. These prose texts run continuously across the page and are placed in the *matn*. What is curious, however, is that the page is still structured to accommodate a marginal text although one is not required. Instead of expanding the prose to fill the paper sheet, the illumination is designed to suggest a marginal text that is not there—thumbpieces and triangles are executed at the top and bottom, although there was really no need for them. Legibility and coherence do not seem adequately to explain the illumination's composition. The design of the page and the illumination in particular invert our anticipation of their prime function as we have come to understand them from the normative practices of this and other manuscripts. Our visual experience of the page is in conflict with our knowledge of a practice that we expect to see again.

More visual conundrums crop up as we leaf through the same unabridged treatise on astrology. One page comprises eight designs for elaborate bookbinding components (Plate 3), including scalloped oval medallions, cusped finials, and corner pieces, executed in black and gold with wash, the ensemble drawn on the page's *matn* and enclosed by a double ruling. Three of the components are filled with designs including arabesques, split palmettes, and sprays of flowers. The remaining five contain two parrots symmetrically arranged and surrounded by flowers, a monkey and a tree, an eagle attacking waterfowl set over a *waqwāq* design (composed of monkey, lion, simurgh, and fox heads), two qilins (a mythical beast serving apotropaic function), and a simurgh and dragon in combat. The page is an aggregate, providing options for bookbinding designs.[27] Comparable compositions are found in the same manuscript and in others made for Iskandar Sultan.[28] A second example in the London Anthology (fol. 543b) comprises two triangular shapes with rectangular panels above and below them in the *matn*. The cusped borders invoke the cornerpieces of bookbindings and contain a lion fighting a simurgh above and a series of birds below.

The group of designs is governed by a functional class, components of a binding, and also, therefore, a specific context. Yet, one may ask why the group of designs appears at the conclusion of a treatise on astrology, and indeed in the London Anthology? Like many designs and drawings in the anthology, the image does not perform a narrative or illustrative function. It might be explained as registering a break between texts for the reader, like a full-page illumination. The correlation, however, between structure (textual sequence) and such narrative-free images is not limited to places of textual beginning or ending. That is, the anthology's texts are not only bracketed by such visual events, but also contain them as a series of visual interpolations. One example of an image embedded in a text appears in the section on astrology (fols. 372b–542b). The center field of fol. 539a depicts the signs Cancer and Leo (corresponding to the relevant text), but the marginal drawing depicts Majnun in the desert joined by animals. A similar combination of astrological illustration and marginal poetic/visual narrative occurs on fol. 538b. This marginal "illustration" to the narrative of *Laylī u Majnūn* appears approximately 401 folios after the Anthology's section on *Laylī u Majnūn*. A component of Nizami's *Khamsa* occupies fols. 90b–138a, and is illustrated by three paintings (including "Majnun in the Desert with the Animals"). On fol.

539a the division between margin and text is shown by contrasting visual idioms in much the same way that textual genres can be contrasted between these two spaces of the page.

Some images in Iskandar Sultan's anthologies do directly illustrate narrative texts or function as diagrams to technical treatises, as the preceding examples have amply demonstrated. Somewhat more perplexing, and perhaps more characteristic of his books, is their unprecedented variety of visual types and subjects, which challenge any attempt to categorize them. They not only collapse categories like narrative illustration, but also straddle visual genres and structural contexts; as we have seen, they confront our expectations with surprise. One could propose that pages like the eight bookbinding components offered the reader a pleasant respite from the act of reading. This is undoubtedly one function. To limit its interpretation to a vague form of aesthetic pleasure or ornament—and to place it in the category of the decorative—would only shortchange the image.

One of the most intriguing aspects of the aggregate depiction of bookbinding components in Iskandar Sultan's London Anthology is its affinity with many of the composite pages of an album commonly known as the "Baysunghur Album."[29] The majority of the Baysunghur Album's folios are completed drawings, sketches, and preparatory designs, the traces of an artistic process of production in which designs for execution in diverse media (e.g., bindings, manuscript paintings, textiles, furniture, metalwork, and wall paintings) were made. Comparison between pages in the album and anthology suggests that Iskandar Sultan's manuscript is a visual conceit, a rendering in ink of a collection of designs pasted onto an album page, arranged according to the functional context of bookbinding. But the anthology dates from twenty years before the earliest extant album of drawings. At present, it is impossible to argue which came first: Iskandar Sultan's anthology page might be a representation of what had become an established procedure—album pages assembled from drawings—or it might have given impetus to this practice through the sheer force of its pictorial invention. Whichever the case, pages in album and anthology become allegories of the design process and offer the viewer a series of visual choices.

This referencing of the book's process of production is but one dimension of the self-reflexive nature of images in Iskandar Sultan's Anthology. It is clear that the anthologizing process was mirrored by the development of a visual program that includes illumination, narrative illustration, diagrams, charts, and designs or narratives in the margins. The depiction of the bookbinding components alludes to the binding that contains the book; it makes the book a subject of representation by bringing the book's binding into the manuscript's pages. This reflexive movement is also found in the treatment of illumination, for example, the pages of prose that were framed by illuminated *ḥashīyyat*, where a space dedicated to marginal text becomes a field for illumination which in its design produces features associated with text but one that is absent from the margin in this example.

The second anthology made for Iskandar Sultan, now in Istanbul, does not appear to have been completed. It was salvaged and, after some years in storage, bound into a Timurid-period album. The date and provenance of the Istanbul Anthology are based on information provided by a single text copied on one of its folios (fol. 159a) dated Tuesday, 21 June, 1413. The scribe states that he copied it in Isfahan. The documentation provides a rough period for the execution of the anthology with a *terminus ante quem* of October 1413 when Iskandar Sultan was removed from power.

Although this anthology awaits comprehensive study, its general textual contents have been summarized as "a description of the beneficent and detrimental properties of foodstuffs, a historical listing of the rulers of the earth, geographical works, descriptions of games, calendrical systems, commentaries on omens and auguries, a brief history of Timur's family emphasizing Iskandar Sultan, and a collection of Aristotelian aphorisms."[30] Among the geographical works is a map of the Timurid world of the Balkhi school (fols. 141b–142a). Standard cartographic techniques are used to signify water (silver, now blackened through oxidization) and mountains, with cities located by gold dots and labeled. The seven climes are drawn in thin red lines.[31] A single-page text on anatomy (fol. 139a) is copied in a continuous text of *nastaʿlīq* script, divided into two parts by colored ink headings.[32] At its center, standing on the lower edge of the page, is a human skeleton, represented in schematic form, the text forced to run around the bones. Where appropriate and useful other texts in the Istanbul Anthology are accompanied by charts and gridded diagrams, especially in those sections that cover genealogy and astronomy.

Following the "Synoptic Account of the House of Timur" (fol. 159a) comes a page of "Amuletic Designs for Ornamental Stones" (fol. 159b).[33] It is a page of human and animal figures rendered in a monochrome palette of black ink and faintly colored washes that recalls the long-established conventions used in scientific manuscripts to depict the signs of the zodiac as anthropomorphized constellation diagrams. This page faces a single-page drawing (fol. 160a) devoid of text, depicting a mass of swirling clouds inhabited by angels. The movement between texts and images found in the London Anthology is dramatized in the Istanbul example by a rapid page-to-page change in subject, sudden shocks of changes in subject matter and in literary and visual style.

After a page that combines gridded boxes and diagrams with excerpts from the epistolography of the famous vizier Rashid al-Din Muhammad Watwat, we come across one devoted to the poetry of ʿAttar, Nizami, and Firdawsi (fol. 161b). Three headings copied across the top of the page each introduce two columns of poetry: "The Dervish who Fell in Love with the Shahzada" by ʿAttar; "The Fable of the Hunter, Dog, and Fox" by Nizami; and "Rustam Conquers the Div Akhwan" by Firdawsi. These were moralizing tales directed to the reader. Here we see a massive reduction of text, pared down to the single story or anecdote, a textual sequence excerpted from the longer literary work. The single page is a micrographic example of the anthologizing behavior that takes the principle of abridgment to infinity. As if to enhance legibility, but certainly to augment the pleasure of the text, small ink-wash monochromatic illustrations are provided to represent the central action of each poem. Monochrome drawing replaces polychrome painting in the portion of the anthology that deals with narrative. It is almost a visual signal to the reader, as if the apprehension of the text were insufficient. Text reduction requires visual reduction; polychrome is reduced to monochrome.

A final example from the Istanbul Anthology is an awesome invention that encapsulates some of these observations. The illuminated painting (fol. 164a)—for it is done throughout in two golds, one with a warm, the other a cool tone, outlined in black ink—offers two halves of an imaginary binding (Plate 4).[34] The upper half is a landscape inhabited by real and fantastic animals. A dragon settles into a rocky outcrop; a lion and cloud bixie at center fight off two simurghs; qilins gambol across the landscape; antelope run wild; and numerous species of flying and flightless birds pepper the lush landscape filled with numerous species of flowering plants, leafy shrubs, and gnarled trees. The entire surface is rendered in minutely inked detail for the eyes.

Below is a nearly aniconic bookbinding design, based on a large geometric medallion and a series of borders separated by thin strips of pearl roundels. Split-palmettes and arabesques sprout plump creatures, bird-bodied and dragon-headed, almost entirely concealed by the vegetation. Blue pigment augments the gold and black. Like many of the preceding examples, the illuminated painting is a technical hybrid, a rendering in gold of what might more often have been executed in leather or pigment. It is self-referential in that it hints at the bookbinding and the book as a material, physical artifact, and it moves illumination away from its standard content and expected function. The page is to be wondered at and has nothing to do with the textual context that it inhabits.

Iskandar Sultan's anthologies are engaged in a conceptual process of visual anthologizing, a series of visual events, subjects, modes, and manners. They promote, or reinforce, a habit of looking that did not require reading, a cultural method with obvious relevance to the wider study of Persianate visual culture. Thus, the anthologies offered Iskandar Sultan, as well as other readers, a range of visual idioms that equaled the textual genres in variety and complexity; reading and looking demanded of him a series of shifts in perceptive and cognitive engagement. But in order for the visual puns, these subtle games and inventions, to be discerned the book's constituent parts—page structure, illumination, drawing, painting, binding—could only attain legibility through comparison to normative practices, and this assumed a fair degree of visual literacy on the part of the viewer because the visual events are in fact a series of extremely subtle mutations and hybrids. They move along axes and position themselves at points between poles: text and image (narrative/non-narrative, diagrammatic/schematic) register degrees of co-dependence and interdependence. Representational techniques and media have the same effect: illumination can make the manuscript's structure legible or the medium can be transformed into something akin to painting; drawing, a graphic system used mainly for diagrams in manuscripts and thought of mainly as the medium of preparatory design, can become an autonomous system of depiction. Things visual exhibit an extraordinarily permeable quality.

Ibrahim Sultan's *Shāhnāma*

Under the governorship of Ibrahim Sultan (1394–1435), son of Shahrukh and grandson of Timur, bookmaking in Shiraz continued long after Iskandar Sultan's demise. But did the experiments in bookmaking in Shiraz continue? If so, did they extend now to the non-anthologistic text?

Key among the manuscripts produced under Ibrahim Sultan's patronage is a *Shāhnāma* of Firdawsi;[35] Ibrahim Sultan is named in the ex libris on fol. 12a. Although key aspects of this manuscript's production remain undocumented, for it has no colophon, it is generally agreed that the manuscript was made in Shiraz and probably around the years 1430–35. It contains a fairly extensive program of illumination as well as some forty-seven illustrations to the *Shāhnāma* and three double-page paintings in the prefatory pages depicting the royal themes of the courtly gathering, hunt, and battle. Eleanor Sims suggested that it is Ibrahim Sultan who is depicted in the three double-page paintings.[36] If this is the case, the portrayals create a kind of mytho-historical conflation in painted form of royal prerogatives and courtly practices past and present. Ibrahim Sultan is shown in the prefatory text to the *Shāhnāma* as prefiguring the ancient kings of Iran whose acts will be depicted in the main text; he prefigures them only insofar as he precedes them in the text's order as a proleptic representation.

The implied genealogy of rulership signaled by the double-page paintings and their specific placement in the manuscript is entirely consistent with Timurid dynastic pretensions and strategies.[37] Indeed, the genealogy of rule implied by these double-page paintings (in relationship to what will come later in the body of the text) finds its immediate textual analog in the *Shāhnāma*'s prefatory pages. Here the introductory text alternates prose and charts, the latter diagramming in gridded format the names of key rulers of the past along with tidbits of biographical information. The paintings seem to have a narrative freedom from the text, they do not serve a specific illustrative role, for an instant destabilizing the expected relationship between text and image until the connection between living and dead kings is ascertained.

But it is the manuscript's illustrative program in the body of the text and not the curious images that accompany the preface that has garnered the greatest amount of scholarly attention. Here we find not only the three double-page paintings and the gridded charts which list rulers, but also four drawings in ink and gold,[38] which point to other orders of meaning beyond the relatively straightforward one of narrative illustration. Two examples include a drawing in black ink on ivory paper depicting a man riding the back of a lion holding snakes while a crowd watches and a man, perhaps fearful, clings to the leafy fronds in the upper reaches of a palm tree (fol. 6b). The gold and ink drawing depicts a landscape occupied by animals, a lion and humped ox set at the center as if on the brink of combat (fol. 3a).[39] Like the drawings in Iskandar Sultan's anthologies, their presence in Ibrahim Sultan's *Shāhnāma* suggests a degree of autonomy for drawing as well as the habit of gauging images whose narratives—if they exist—are not to be found in the immediate textual context of the book.

The handling of the prefatory section to Ibrahim Sultan's *Shāhnāma*, with its combination of gridded charts, diagrams, and non-narrative double-page paintings, and drawings (in ink or gold and ink) continue a practice of bookmaking first discernable in Shiraz under Iskandar Sultan's governorship. Thus, experiments in anthologies have been applied to the non-anthologistic book, albeit to its prefatory section, allowing it to contain a broader range of visual genres and systems of representation as well as variously configured word-image relationships. The visual adjunct to the preface does nothing less than to re-define the textual connection between preface and text.

The *Ṣad Kalima* of ʿAli b. Abu Talib

The manuscript of ʿAli's *Ṣad Kalima* (One Hundred Sayings) is executed entirely in *découpage* (*qaṭʿi*) calligraphy, making it one of the earliest extant examples of its kind, with a wide variety of scripts employed (including the "six scripts," *nastaʿlīq*, and *taʿlīq*).[40] The manuscript does not contain an ex libris or any mention of its place of production. The only internal documentation appears in a colophon on fol. 20a: "The book was completed with God the great's assistance under the hand of the poor, wretched, broken, weak, emaciated, sinful—who yearns for his God, beloved of the poor and the humble—the servant Muḥammad b. Sayyidī Aḥmad b. ʿAlī al-Ṣūfī al-Marāghī in the year 876 [20 June 1471 to 7 June 1472]." The text is organized in two parts (fols. 1b–12a and 12b–20a), both arranged in alternating lines of Arabic with interlinear Persian. In each part different types of scripts are used.

One man is named in the introductory and concluding passages, Muhammad b. Muhammad ʿAbd al-Jalil al-Rashid al-Katib al-Watwat/ Mawlana Jalal al-Din al-ʿAdil (fols. 1b and 12a, respectively). He is identifiable as Rashid al-Din Muhammad b. Muhammad b. ʿAbd al-Jalil al-ʿUmari (known as Watwat), who died in 1182–3.[41] During his life he served as chief secretary to the Khwarizmshah Atsiz and his successor Il-Arslan. Among his literary works are bilingual collections of his correspondence in Persian and Arabic, and his famous collection of one hundred sayings attributed to ʿAli, first collected by al-Jahiz. In Watwat's translation of the *Ṣad Kalima*, each saying/aphorism is given in Arabic and is followed by an Arabic paraphrase, a Persian commentary, and a poetic Persian gloss.

In the *Ṣad Kalima* different methods are used to differentiate Arabic from Persian. If their separation into discrete lines of writing—as opposed to a continuous, uninterrupted flow of text across the page—were not enough, Persian texts are cut out from white paper to stand apart from the Arabic texts cut out from colored papers. These are fairly standard structural and visual techniques used to signal the text's discursive and linguistic differences. But what about the manuscript's other aesthetic values?

A limited program of illumination—there are no *ʿunwāns* and no ex libris—in the form of interlinear small gold rosettes studded with blue spots and the standard seam ruling composed of gold and black bands project an initial sense of austerity. There is little contrast of color or material for the eye to gauge; all seems quiet. Tuning in again, however, the eye is treated to a subtle range of color contrasts and harmonies effected by a range of tinted papers: pink, pale yellow, mustard, ivory, light pink, white, pale gray, brown, and blue. These colored papers are used not only for the *découpage* calligraphy but also for the surfaces over which the text is glued. If that were not enough, the pages are not unitary, single sheets but are composed of bands of different papers, each band contrasting cutout calligraphy with ground, and ground juxtaposed against ground as a set of horizontal stripes down the page's vertical axis. The aggregate sheets are in turn framed by paper margins that are also produced through a process of assemblage. After the text pages were produced, an ample margin was added around them by laying strips of paper along the outer edges of upper and lower sides of the text bearing sheet and gluing them in place. The margins also employ different colors of paper, derived from the same source as the *découpage* and their supports.

The manuscript's twenty folios are a technical tour de force, not only for their *découpage*, showing the paper-cutter's skill in a gamut of scripts and in positive and negative cutout work,[42] but also in the careful orchestration of color harmonies within a narrow range. The entire manuscript is an aggregate of paper strips and cutout letters that makes a virtue of limited materials—colored papers—, and methods—cutting and gluing. This conceit of economy, even austerity, is perhaps most forcefully stated by the manuscript's endpapers, a grid of leftover squares and rectangles, glued together and laminated into a patchwork.

A comparison may be drawn between the *Ṣad Kalima* and a *Dīwān* of poems by Sultan Husayn Mirza, the last ruler of the Timurid dynasty, that was produced in Herat, ca. 1490.[43] The *Dīwān* contains ghazals composed by Sultan Husayn Mirza under the *takhallus* "Husayni" and in Turki, a poetry collection faintly praised by Babur because it used only one meter from beginning to end. This *Dīwān* is done in colored *découpage* contrasted against colored grounds but it uses *nastaʿlīq* throughout, by then the pre-eminent script employed for poetry. Calligraphy is interspersed with elaborate and equally minute illumination containing phrases that refer to the Timurid poet and ruler such as "also by him" and "God make his rule eternal."

The major point that I want to make here is one of aesthetic difference: the contrast between visual excess and austerity and a distinction in textual content through the type of script.[44] Still, both books—one an anthology of poetry and the other of wise sayings—make their point primarily through technique and not by representing something in the text: the material is material, the paper is paper. The fact of beautiful writing, constantly flickering between image and idea, is enhanced by the properties of material and color. Media are not used to portray referents of things other than themselves—the only illusory quality is that the *découpage* calligraphy escapes our grasp by a seamless execution.

The two *découpage* anthologies also seem to be the apotheosis of the examples made in the early years of the century. Now the anthology achieves full "aggregateness" as it transforms the aesthetics of aggregation by manipulating pieces of colored papers. The stable, single sheet has been dispensed with in favor of the assembled page of variously treated and processed surfaces. These examples pinpoint the understudied issue of the phenomenon of holding, scrutinizing, of visually taking in the book's words and images where the difference between what it contains and what it is made of can be elided in its apprehension as artifact.

Conclusion

I have attempted to examine some of the ways that the anthologies' broad range of images may have functioned. The viewer's literacy has not been examined, nor has the visual intelligence of the "non-narrative" elements of the anthology been explained in anything other than general terms as augmenting the book's value and the pleasure of reading.[45] Such a function for paintings was asserted in the older preface to the *Shāhnāma* where Rudaki's Persian translation of the *Kalīla wa Dimna* is mentioned: "Then the Chinese added images to it so that the seeing and the reading of it should please everybody."[46] In order to figure out potential meanings or significations for the curious illuminated paintings, marginal illumination, and drawings in the fifteenth-century anthologies I needed to contrast them with what I termed normative practice, the expected structural and formal behavior of various techniques and manners of working (our categories of painting, illumination, drawing, writing, binding).[47] Alternate meanings became possible only when images transgressed, running against the viewer's "horizon of expectations," a phrase used by Todorov it in his study of genre.[48] In fact, it is precisely this dynamic process that unveils the genre, giving it a sharper focus, a more definite form than it ever had before, only before it shades off into becoming something else, or "A new genre is always the transformation of an earlier one, or of several: by inversion, by displacement, by combination."[49] Gauging differences between actual experience and expectation in the anthologies of Iskandar Sultan was critical for the image to acquire legibility. The complex images resonated with those visual memories accrued from the experience of using books.

By these means, the book's properties as artifact and the experience of using it became a subject of representation. In the examples studied here it was achieved not through some mimetic form—the literal representation of a figure holding a book, implying the sense of hearing through the actions of speaking and listening[50]—but through non-mimetic means that invoked the enactment of reading/seeing. The reader's experience of the book was dramatized through representational means—the figuring of the book's physical and textual dimensions in visual terms—and later, only through the materiality of the medium, of colored paper. The reader was in the book in a double sense.

Notes

1. The *dīwān* is perhaps the simplest term to define; it is a collection of poetry by a single writer. *Safīna* is a name given to a type of boat, apropos the *safīna* we may surmise because of its format (oblong and bound on the cover's short side). *Safīna*s contain collections of poetry of a particular genre (mainly ghazals and *rubā'ī*s) by one or several poets. The last two commonly used terms, *majmū'a* and *jung*, refer not to a format or technique of binding but to a catholic gathering of texts that can encompass poetry and prose, and subjects as wide-ranging as astronomy, mathematics, epic poetry, history, anatomy, geography, genealogy, and biography. *Jung* was another term derived from boat terminology.
2. The only "anthologizing" text that has garnered sustained interest thus far in scholarship about the Islamic book is the *inshā'* (lit. composition; epistolography), collections of correspondence and other forms of texts gathered into a single volume. Literary historians have focused on unitary works of prose and poetry by single individuals.
3. Nichols and Wenzel used the phrase to refer to the codicological features of medieval Western miscellanies. See Stephen G. Nichols and Siegfried Wenzel, eds., *The Whole Book: Cultural Perspectives on the Medieval Miscellany* (Ann Arbor: The University of Michigan Press, 1996), pp. 1–6. "Materialist philology" is defined in ibid., p. 2.
4. The essays in Nichols and Wenzel, eds., *The Whole Book*, mark the turn in the study of the medieval miscellany. Wenzel notes the problematic aspect of the term "miscellany" and how it suggests "an arbitrary principle of organization for the manuscripts in which there may be a perfectly clear organizing principle" (ibid., p. 3). The term miscellany has been used to describe the Persian manuscripts studied in this paper. I use the term anthology, which has a neutral aspect, except that in current English it has the sense of a compilation of selected published texts, and thus is not wholly appropriate to the pre-modern context. I avoid compendium because its primary meanings involve a process of abridgement, a sense that is not always appropriate to the Persian anthologies.
5. Three essays that provide overviews of changes in relationship of image to text in the period spanning the fourteenth and sixteenth centuries are Lisa Golombek, "Toward a Classification of Islamic Painting," in *Islamic Art in the Metropolitan Museum of Art*, ed. Richard Ettinghausen (New York: Metropolitan Museum of Art, 1982), pp. 23–34; Marie Swietochowski, "The Development of Traditions of Book Illustration in Pre-Safavid Iran," *Iranian Studies* 7 (1974): 49–71; and Sheila S. Blair, "The Development of the Illustrated Book in Iran," *Muqarnas* 10 (1992): 266–74.

6. Two well-known manuscripts help to demonstrate the potential options for the image in the book at the turn of the fifteenth century. Paintings in the 1396 manuscript of the *Three Mathnawis* by Khwaju Kirmani (London British Library, Add. 18113, copied in Baghdad by Mir ʿAli b. Ilyas al-Tabrizi al-Bawarchi with one painting signed by Junayd Naqqash al-Sultani) offer evidence of several features that would predominate thereafter: a shift to a vertical format, a reduced rate of illustration in poetic manuscripts, and dense congregations of visual information in paintings. In the *Three Mathnawis*, text and image are tightly integrated, coordinated to establish a tempo throughout the manuscript, the relevant text is drastically reduced to a few verses inserted into the painting in a cursory verbal introduction to the painting's panoramic field. The *Dīwān* of Sultan Ahmad, dated to ca. 1400–5 (Washington, D.C., Freer Gallery of Art, nos. 32.20–32.37), reverses the spatial and conceptual relationships between text and image found in the *Three Mathnawis*. The *Dīwān's* images of landscapes populated with people, animals, and angels are not only placed in the margins, and thus enframe the text, but the visual content is related to poetry at the level of metaphor and not as the visual figuration of actors and events in the poetry. The marginal drawings in ink and wash have been interpreted as symbolizing the human soul's search for God through the representation of birds, invoking ʿAttar's *Manṭiq al-ṭayr* (Conversation of Birds). It was an interpretation of the marginal drawings advanced by Deborah E. Klimburg-Salter, "A Sufi Theme in Persian Painting: The Diwan of Sultan Ahmad Galair in the Freer Gallery of Art," *Kunst des Orients* 11 (1976–77): 43–84.

   For details about the *Three Mathnawis*, see Norah M. Titley, *Miniatures from Persian Manuscripts* (London: British Museum Publications Limited, 1978), cat. no. 251. Paintings from the manuscript are frequently illustrated. See Thomas W. Lentz and Glenn D. Lowry, *Timur and the Princely Vision: Persian Art and Culture in the Fifteenth Century* (Los Angeles and Washington, D.C.: Los Angeles County Museum of Art and Arthur M. Sackler Gallery, Smithsonian Institution, 1989), pp. 54–55; and Ivan Stchoukine, *Les peintures des manuscrits Tîmûrides* (Paris: Librairie Orientaliste Paul Geuthner, 1954), pls. 4–8. For a summary of the marginal drawings and illustrations in the *Dīwān* of Sultan Ahmad, see Esin Atıl, *The Brush of the Masters: Drawings from Iran and India* (Washington, D.C.: Freer Gallery of Art, Smithsonian Institution, 1978), pp. 14–27.

7. Lentz and Lowry identified these categories of illustrative idiom. They attribute the Timurids with the codification of the idioms, noting that in some instances conventions had already been long established (e.g., images for scientific texts). See Lentz and Lowry, *Timur and the Princely Vision*, chap. 3, esp. p. 166. An earlier study that pursued similar questions but to

different effect is by Richard Ettinghausen, "The Categorization of Persian Painting," in *Studies in Judaism and Islam*, ed. Shelomo Morag (Jerusalem: Magnes Press, 1981), pp. 55–63.

8. It is worth mentioning at this point that the genesis of the ontological paradox of the painting in the book—phrased ultimately as a somewhat confounding choice between painting or illustration—stems from the history of exhibition and collecting practices. Suffice it to say that from the inception of the study of the Islamic arts of the books, and of Persian painting in particular, paintings were removed from books and exhibited on the gallery wall.

9. The implications of Horace's dictum were also noted by Peter Wagner, "Introduction: Ekphrasis, Iconotexts, and Intermediality—the State(s) of the Art(s)," in *Icons, Texts, Iconotexts: Essays on Ekphrasis and Intermediality*, ed. Peter Wagner (Berlin and New York: Walter de Gruyter, 1996), pp. 1–40, esp. pp. 5–6. Wagner offers other translations of Horace's simile (ibid., p. 5, n. 10).

10. Wagner notes the semiotic turn and dates it to the late 1980's but notes the delay. He writes: "Is there no room in ekphrasis, we may ask with Stephen Bann, 'for the modern conviction... that a good proportion of what is experienced in looking at a work of art simply cannot be expressed in verbal terms?' If poststructuralism has taught us anything it is the knowledge that making meaning depends on the fickle nature of the sign, which is subject to personal and social determinants. When, it may be asked, will this undeniable fact be recognized and considered by our more reluctant confrères who are writing on visual poetics and the relation of verbal and visual art?" (ibid., p. 7). It is a point well taken but lacking from Wagner's references is Michael Camille's 1985 article, "The Book of Signs: Writing and Visual Difference in Gothic Manuscript Illumination," *Word & Image* 1 (1985): 133–48. Camille applies the very semiotic concepts to the study of his material whose absence Wagner laments.

11. This essay is a part of a larger study of the anthology in the fifteenth century. Missing here are some critical examples, especially a cluster of *safīna*s made at the middle of the century, not considered due to constraints of length.

12. As suggested by Paul E. Losensky, *Welcoming Fighānī: Imitation and Poetic Individuality in the Safavid-Mughal Ghazal* (Costa Mesa, Calif.: Mazda, 1998), chap. 4, esp. pp. 145–47.

13. The anecdote appears in Dawlatshah Samarqandi, *Tadhkirat al-shuʿarā*, ed. Muḥammad ʿAbbāsī (Tehran: Bārānī, 1337), p. 267.

14. For an illustration of a fifteenth-century *fihrist*, see Yuri A. Petrosyan et al,

Pages of Perfection: Islamic Paintings and Calligraphy from the Russian Academy of Sciences, St. Petersburg (Lugano and Milan: ARCH Foundation and Electa, 1995), p. 182, cat. no. 29. The section titles are written in small circles stacked in a gridded format. The manuscript is a *Kulliyāt* of Saʿdi, dated 1425, and probably copied in Shiraz.

15. Trans. in Wheeler M. Thackston, *A Century of Princes: Sources on Timurid History and Art* (Cambridge, Mass.: Aga Khan Program for Islamic Architecture, 1989), p. 31.
16. A complete list of dedicated and attributed manuscripts is available in an essay by Priscilla P. Soucek, "The Manuscripts of Iskandar Sultan: Structure and Content," in *Timurid Art and Culture: Iran and Central Asia in the Fifteenth Century*, ed. Lisa Golombek and Maria E. Subtelny, Supplements to Muqarnas 6 (Leiden, New York, and Cologne: E. J. Brill, 1992), pp. 116–31; app. 1, p. 128.
17. London, British Library, Add. 27261. 543 fols., 181 x 125 mm. For further information, see Titley, *Miniatures from Persian Manuscripts*, cat. no. 98.
18. Istanbul, Topkapı Palace Library, B. 411, fols. 138a–166a. 480 x 364 mm.
19. Lisbon, Gulbenkian Foundation, L. A. 161 (vols. 1 and 2). For a description of its contents, see Soucek, "Manuscripts of Iskandar Sultan," app. 2.
20. Ibid., p. 128. The articulation may require some rewording, after all Iskandar Sultan was 26 when the manuscript was made, although that would not diminish the texts' everlasting didactic value.
21. Ibid.
22. Sequences of interrelated paintings and compositional types are shown in Lentz and Lowry, *Timur and the Princely Vision*, app. 3.
23. Add. 27261, fol. 38a. For color illustration, see ibid., p. 116, fig. 35.
24. Add. 27261, fol. 225b. For illustration, see ibid., p. 378, no. 4a.
25. Add. 27261, fol. 131b. For illustration, see ibid., p. 378, no. 5a.
26. Add. 27261, fol. 305b. For color illustration, see Norah M. Titley, *Persian Miniature Painting and Its Influence on the Art of Turkey and India* (Austin: University of Texas Press, 1983), pl. 4, p. 52.
27. Jessica Rawson noted the relationship of the designs to those found in extant bookbindings and she compares them to diagrams of bookbinding components from a nearly contemporary manuscript, an anthology of poetry made in Yazd, 1407 (Istanbul, Topkapı Palace Library, H. 796). For illustrations, see Jessica Rawson, *Chinese Ornament: The Lotus and the Dragon* (London: The British Museum, 1984), fig. 142. For the binding, see Basil Gray, ed., *Arts of the Book in Central Asia: 14th–16th Centuries* (Paris: Unesco, 1979), figs. 32–33.

28. Additional manuscripts include a birth chart (horoscope) made for Iskandar Sultan (London, Wellcome Institute Library, ms. Persian 474) and dated 1411 at Shiraz. In addition to its double-page painting depicting the chart, the manuscript contains ink wash drawings, one a depiction of a binding composed of a central medallion containing a simurgh and four corner pieces containing waterfowl, all birds set over cloud bands and florals. For an analysis of the birth chart and a summary of its contents, see Fateme Keshavarz, "The Horoscope of Iskandar Sultan," *Journal of the Royal Asiatic Society* 2 (1984): 197–208. A second manuscript is an astrological prose text dated 1411–12 (Istanbul, Istanbul University Library, F. 1418). The division between *matn* and *ḥashīyyat* is used and it combines a painting with frequent ink drawings depicting constellations and signs of the zodiac. For illustrations and analysis, see Zeren Akalay, "An Illustrated Astrological Work of the Period of Iskandar Sultan," in *Akten des VII. Internationalen Kongress für Iranische Kunst und Archäologie* (Berlin, 1979), pp. 418–25.
29. Istanbul, Topkapı Palace Library, H. 2152, 98 fols., 680 x 500 mm. Assembled in Herat before ca. 1447.
30. Lentz and Lowry, *Timur and the Princely Vision*, p. 157, n. 112.
31. For an illustration, see ibid., p. 150, fig. 50.
32. For an illustration, see ibid., p. 149, fig. 49.
33. For an illustration, see ibid., p. 148, fig. 48.
34. The split between upper and lower designs reflects the practice of placing figural subjects, generally animals in landscapes, on the upper and lower covers of bindings (worked in leather), and non-figural designs on their doublures, often executed in filigree from paper or leather and using polychrome. Although common, this distinction was not absolute.
35. Oxford, Bodleian Library, Add. 176. 468 fols., 287 x 195 mm.
36. Eleanor Sims, "The Illustrated Manuscripts of Firdausī's *Shāhnāma* Commissioned by Princes of the House of Tīmūr," *Ars Orientalis* 22 (1992): 43–68; 46. A fourth double-page composition appears within the body of the text proper, fols. 239b–240a.
37. It is one shown most clearly through the sponsorship of historical writing by Timurid ruler Shahrukh and also fostered by princes like Ibrahim Sultan and Baysunghur. See John Woods, "The Rise of Timurid Historiography," *Journal of Near Eastern Studies* 46, 2 (April, 1987): 81–108.
38. The drawings appear on fols. 2b, 3a, 6b, and 7a.
39. For an illustration, see Basil Gray, *Persian Painting* (Geneva: Skira, 1961), p. 100.
40. Istanbul, Museum of Turkish and Islamic Art, no. 2474. 20 fols., 458 x 334

mm. A note on the endpaper names the manuscript as a *Majmaʿ al-khuṭūṭ*. I thank Dr. Şule Aksoy for bringing this extraordinary manuscript to my attention in the summer of 1997.

41. For the author, see *Encyclopaedia of Islam*, 2nd ed., s. v. "Rashīd al-Dīn Muḥammad b. Muḥammad b. ʿAbd al-Djalīl al-ʿUmarī" (F. C. de Blois).

42. Two forms of *découpage* are used. In the first (positive), letters are cut out of a sheet of paper and the cutout letters glued onto a support. In the second (negative), the single sheet has the letters removed and the sheet is taken and glued over a support, the color of the underlying support showing through the spaces cut out of the upper sheet.

43. The manuscript is in Istanbul, Museum of Turkish and Islamic Art, no. 1926. Several pages from the manuscript are now dispersed. For illustrations, see Lentz and Lowry, *Timur and the Princely Vision*, pp. 268–70.

44. By this time it had become standard practice to reserve the "six scripts" for the Koran and *nastaʿlīq* for works of poetry and prose.

45. Lentz and Lowry described Iskandar Sultan's anthologies as "richly ornamented objects, not simply texts to be read" (Lentz and Lowry, *Timur and the Princely Vision*, p. 118).

46. Trans. in V. Minorsky, "The Older Preface to the Shāh-Nāma," in *Studi Orientalistici in Onore di Giorgio Levi della Vida*, 2 vols. (Rome, 1956), 1: 159–79; 168.

47. Each has a terminological equivalent in Persian technical literature.

48. Tzvetan Todorov, *Genres in Discourse*, trans. Catherine Porter (Cambridge: Cambridge University Press, 1990), p. 18 and p. 14. Todorov may have taken the term from Husserl's phenomenology of perception.

49. Ibid., p. 15.

50. Pictorial examples in the Islamic tradition abound of a single figure gazing at an open book, or a figure holding an open book before a companion figure. For a discussion of the depiction of the book in the medieval West, see Michael Camille, "Visual Signs of the Sacred Page: Books in the Bible Moralisée," *Word & Image* 5, 1 (January, 1989): 111–30.

The Sound of the Image/ The Image of the Sound: Narrativity in Persian Art of the 17th Century

SUSSAN BABAIE

In negotiating the boundary between texts and images, Persian art of the Safavid period (1501–1722) can profitably yield strategies for understanding the ways in which the image-text boundary blurs in practice.[1] The recognition of an intimate link between the written and the visual in Islamic arts in general has somewhat shielded the negotiation from collapsing into an embattled discourse between the text and the image.[2] Yet attempts to devise interpretive rather than illustrative approaches to Persian painting and its literary component have remained confined to the case of the composite art of the illustrated manuscript. The highly original style of Persian painting is inherently dependent upon the corpus of classical poetic texts that inform its conceptualization and were in fact its *raison d'être*.[3]

The shift in late 16th-century Persian painting from manuscript illustration to single-sheet painting has problematized our normative art historical approaches.[4] Single-sheet painting, presumably intended for an album, often consists of a pasted assemblage of artfully written and framed poetic passages surrounding a pictorial composition mainly of repeating figural types unrelated to known narrative constructs (Plate 1). The difficulty in assigning a "story-line" and the apparent disjunction of the text and the image have led us to commonly describe the image and transcribe the text as discrete realms of meaning. Moreover, lacking the aura of the lofty ideals of a classical text, conventionalized in form and devoid of an explicit narrative, meaning in these works appears to have degenerated into representations of trivial states of elegance or curiosity.

The work of Massumeh Farhad has demonstrated the possibility of a different reading of these images.[5] She argues that the idealized and standardized themes and subjects depicted in these paintings and drawings were intended to satisfy the tastes of a rising cultural elite that competed through acts of patronage with the traditional royal patrons of the illustrated manuscripts. Accordingly, these works relied on "implied rather than explicit action," suggesting "space and time duration beyond their borders" which encouraged the participation of the viewer in constructing his own "stories in picture" or they could be construed as poems in pictures.[6]

Expanding on Farhad's findings, this study suggests another approach to the "reading" of single-sheet paintings. It takes its cue from the evidence of an emergent representational mode in Persian art of the Safavid period in which the textual and the pictorial are not simply juxtaposed but rather fused to create persuasive narrative linkages. It shall argue that meaning in such works of art operated in a mental world of shared literary and pictorial allusions that had become both performative and democratized.[7] A reconstruction of the particulars of culturally and socially distinctive circumstances of their production and consumption will elucidate the ways in which such paintings came to activate imagination. My aim is not so much to extract the meaning of these works as to illustrate possible scenarios in which the artist manufactured "meanings" comparable in aesthetic and social function to those conceived by the poet.

It scarcely needs repeating that epigraphy or the visual evidence of the text occupies a supreme position in, and is an integral part of, the arts in the Islamic world. In its Persian variant, the arts of the Safavid period signal a substantive change in the interface between the text and the image.[8] In both architecture and the portable arts, a more potent interweaving of thematic and conceptual threads between the textual and the visual occasion the gradual emergence of the image not as an auxiliary to the text but as an equally potent carrier of the intended message. The imagery may be conveyed through the function of the building (as in a cistern), the shape of an object (as in an inkwell), or the figural scenes represented in conjunction with the text.[9]

A brief consideration of a Safavid wine bowl, dated 1620–21, in the Victoria and Albert Museum serves to illustrate the point.[10] Decorated only on the outside, a sequence of three bands articulates the surface. An epigraphic frieze at the top and a band of scrolling floral and vegetal ornaments at the bottom support a wide ribbon of cusped cartouches. Lively representations of animals, individually or in pairs, occupy the inner and outer spaces of the cartouches. The poetic passage weaves together mystical allusions to wine and an invocation to ʿAlī, the first Shiʿite Imam, as *saqī-yi kawsar*, the cup-bearer of the Paradise River, to conjure up a mental image of the bowl itself. The animal scenes amidst vegetation may be seen as an evocation of the *bādīya*. Meaning "wilderness," the term itself is also the name of this type of wine bowl. As wilderness, *bādīya* is often associated with Majnūn's mystical journey and by association draws onto ʿAlī's role as the guide to the wanderer in his search for the love of God.[11]

The complex layering of meanings in this example threatens to entangle the modern viewer into imprudent "over-reading." Notwithstanding the multiplicity of meanings that may be conveyed, it is precisely this entanglement of the text (the poem and the implied linguistic sign) and the image (including both the shape of the bowl and what is represented on it) that signals the more robust participation of the image in constructing the meaning here. The image, in other words, enhances the words as much as the words enhance the image.

In comparison to this Safavid object, the epigraphic and representational components in metalwork from the earlier period in Iran, for example, tend to be handled more literally, often investing the text with the primary task of facilitating the interpretation.[12] The distinction of this wine bowl and other text-enriched works from the Safavid period is in that the pictorial and linguistic signs are pulled together more tightly, both figuratively, because the two signs are integral to the object, and metaphorically, because the meanings are interwoven. Admittedly, the bowl without its poetic inscription would not engender the same complex of meanings. But if we posit an integrated text-image mentality, which, as I shall argue, underlined the cultural fabric of this period, the image begins to function like a poem and speaks with the same eloquence as the text.

Such eloquence may be deduced from the reading of single-sheet paintings and drawings.

An album page at the Metropolitan Museum of Art illustrates the parameters of the problem that prompts this study and elucidates the potential eloquence of the imagery. The page is composed of a collage of three pieces within a decorated border: the figure of an old man, that of a youth, and a single written line (Plate 1).[13] The two figures, delicately drawn and tinted, are dateable to the second quarter of the 17th century and bear the signature of Riżā ʿAbbāsī, the celebrated artist of the late 16th and early 17th centuries.[14] As is the case in the composition of many album pages, the two drawings and the text have been chosen as samples of venerable handiwork by the brush and the pen.

The assembly of such pieces for an album page is ordinarily a post-production by a person other than the artist and the calligrapher. When the album is preserved, the interrelation of the pieces may be deduced from written and visual elements that unify the whole and are internal, and integral, to the entire album.[15] But when the album sheet is detached, as is the case here and in the majority of single-sheet paintings and drawings from the Safavid period, the perceived absence of a literary armature, comparable to a classical text in an illustrated manuscript, has precluded readings of the text and image as a coherent whole. Furthermore, such figures as the youth or the old man, depicted in similar poses, costumes, expressions, and props, were produced in multitudes and have often survived without an accompanying text or one that may be relevant.

Farhad's "implied story," persuasive as it is, is not so easy to access when the majority of single-sheet paintings and drawings are devoid of either any text or a relevant one. And since where there is a text, it is pasted and not perceived as "original" to the image, we have tended to ignore its import.[16] The line of text in "The Old Man and the Youth" is a poetic fragment which, when translated literally, reads: "your green line that is a beautiful mark." There are several ways to translate and interpret the poem. For example, *khaṭ* may be taken to mean *ṭarīqa* or path in a mystical sense and if taken with *āya* in its reference to the verses of the Koran, the line assumes a mystical dimension.[17] Alternately, *khaṭ* as "writing," taken with the word *āya* as verse in general, renders a pun on the poetic fragment itself. However these two terms may be interpreted, the verse's primary meaning is embedded in the "green line," a poetic convention that alludes through the imagery of new grass to the signs of an adolescent boy's first beard.[18]

The juxtaposition of the two figures in these poses and expressions may not require a text label to elucidate the erotic yearnings of the old man for the youth. Such an "implied story" may also govern the formulation of other similarly juxtaposed figures. In this page the two figures appear to be by the same hand and perhaps intended by the artist as a group. But the deliberate selection and collation of the images is further evident in a similar page in the Bibliothèque Nationale in which the two drawings are by different artists and the poems surrounding the images are from the epic of the *Shāhnāma*, with an import which, at first glance, appears unrelated.[19]

There are, however, other possible interpretations for the pairing. Not only could the yearning portrayed in these pages be of a mystical rather than carnal nature, but the two could also represent abstract ideas such as the arrogance of youth and the wisdom of old age. Whatever the meaning, in the "Old Man and the Youth," the very selection of these images, cut and pasted together with this particular calligraphic sample, indicates intimate familiarity on the part of the collector with at least one possible meaning of the otherwise stock figures.

Although this may confirm Farhad's suggestion that such images could have been used and collected for a variety of purposes, the inherent ambiguity of the single figures and their actions cautions against generalizations. The assumption that, for instance, all single figures of an elegantly attired standing youth, of which dozens are extant, invite the homoerotic yearning of an implied old man leaning on a stick and wistfully looking into space, a visual trope which also exists in multiple examples, may appear ludicrous at first. Yet it could be tentatively argued that as in the Paris and New York pages, discreet images of such figures in fact conjured up an assembled "scene" with a primary meaning that was fixed and transparent to its contemporary viewer.

As collages, these scenes could have been "composed" by any number of people who may or may not even have been contemporaries of the original artistic milieu of these works. Yet enough 17th-century evidence of the shared precepts exists to justify its attribution to this particular milieu. The "Young Portuguese," dated 1634, in the Detroit Institute of Arts, is not a patchwork, like the previous two examples, and bears an inscription on the right side of the image itself with an exact date, the name of the patron, and Riżā ʿAbbāsī's signature (Plate 2).[20] I shall have more to say about the significance of the precise nature of the inscription. For now, our focus is on the image and the accompanying poetic text. A young man clad in European costume leans against pillows, holds a bottle under one arm, and offers a cup of drink to a lap dog. One of the pillows, around which the youth wraps his right arm, is decorated with an embroidered image of a middle-aged man holding his knees and looking up at the young man. The implied meaning seems at first to be clear; the young man, leisurely posed, beautifully attired, and playfully presented, appears to be the object of his elder's desire.[21] Ignoring the text for the moment, we are so distanced by time and culture from the world of meanings to which these figures allude that our reading of the image may stop at this conclusion.

But the inscription on this page indicates that the image could awaken other possible meanings in the mind of its contemporary viewer. The text reads in part: "Love compels me to run bare-foot and -headed in that alley [of desire] like [those] foreign slaves (*ghulāmān-i farangī*)."[22] The poetic "I" in the distich appears to be the elder figure who ponders, not his desire after a youthful foreign boy, but his state of love which can compel him to pursue his desire looking like the foreign boy. Although neither figure is disheveled, as the "bare-foot-and-head" implies, could the languorous boy, whose foreignness is made explicit by his costume and his tenderness towards a dog (something a Muslim would not have done), be an idealized visualization of the elder in his rapture?[23] Sheila Canby has read the text differently and has suggested a few other possible interpretations. Foremost in her analysis is that the youth is the object of the old man's desire. She speculates that the elder may be the patron or even possibly the artist, and interprets the youth as an idealized depiction of the beloved. Alternatively, the youth could be a European patron whose inability to understand the verse would render the poem's content a satirical statement on his high opinion of himself.[24]

For the purposes of the argument here, it hardly matters which one of the possible readings of the text-image we may choose. And the text too, like the one-liner in the "Youth and the Old Man," may oscillate in expression of intent between the mystical and the carnal. What remains constant is the expression of some homoerotic liaison in both the text and the image. In complexity, the textured weaving of the visual signs in this painting, as well as the two assembled drawings in "The Youth and the Old Man," are comparable to that of the wine bowl, and signal a shared penchant for intricate webs of meanings. But whereas in the wine bowl, the text and image are coordinated to operate in cohesion, in this painting the image appears to precede the text, and the poem, explicit as it is, is incapable of supplanting the other meanings inherent to the picture. More significantly, however, is the fact that the image plants clues capable of conjuring up a range of complimentary non-visual readings analogous to the eloquence we ordinarily attribute to poetry in Persian culture.

In our assessment of the dialectic of word and image in Islamic culture, the word has generally held the loftier position. This is justifiable for the very fact that the scriptural, the spoken or written word, and the art of the calligrapher have always been regarded as the bearers of mysteries too profound to visualize effectively. In Islamic culture, the visual tends to stumble in that "protracted struggle for dominance between pictorial and linguistic signs" that W. J. T. Mitchell has suggested to be the story in part of the history of any culture.[25] Persian arts of the Safavid period indicate a normalizing of the balance between the linguistic and the pictorial in which the pictorial begins to assume some of the proprietary rights of the linguistic. The propensity for subtly inter-related webs of meaning in the visual domain and their potential for generating diverse and original meanings, presupposes circumstances in which the work of art could legitimately perform "ventriloquism."

An oft-quoted anecdote by a poet about Sādiqī Beg, the famed painter, royal librarian, poet, and author of the reign of the Safavid Shah ʿAbbās I (1587–1629), helps us to thread together a backdrop against which this new propensity appears particularly cogent.

> I wrote a qasidah in praise of Sadiqi and went to recite it in a coffee house. The qasidah had not yet come to an end, when [Sadiqi] seized it from me and said, "I don't have the patience to listen to more than this!" Getting up after a moment, he tossed

> down five tomans bound in a cloth, along with pieces of paper on which he had executed black-line drawings. He gave them to me and said: "Merchants buy each page of my work for three tomans. They take them to Hindustan. Don't sell them any cheaper!" Then he excused himself several times and went out.[26]

This passage has served scholars in the elucidation of two points: as evidence for the emergence of new markets for the artist's work and for the increased mobility of the artist, his freedom from the confines of the royal workshop.[27] The anecdote records an encounter that took place in Isfahan, the city in central Iran that became the capital of the Safavid dynasty from 1590–91 until their demise in 1722. The works of art that we have discussed—the wine bowl, the drawings, and the painting—all belong to the same context in terms of production, consumption and chronology (i.e., first half of the 17th century) .[28]

Recent scholarship has considered many facets of the cultural milieu of 17th-century Isfahan.[29] As the center of the political and economic life of the Safavid empire, Isfahan became a cosmopolitan metropolis, the site of exchange for people and of goods and services from as close as the borders of the state to as far as England and China. Although not the sole urban venue for cultural activity in Safavid Iran, both European and Persian sources abundantly testify to the vitality and primacy of Isfahan as the place where Safavid culture was manufactured and from where it emanated. Beginning in the 17th century, and at a rate hitherto unmatched, artists begin to work, show, and sell independently of the confines of the royal workshops, the traditional source of support for painters.[30] Denizens of Isfahan—ranging from government functionaries, lesser nobility, and wealthy physicians and merchants, to poets and artists themselves—vie with the shah and the court for the prestige and edification which the commission and collecting of works of art could afford.[31]

Seventeenth-century Isfahan also sets a scene of encounter, for ideas and for art, markedly different from the past. The court and royal workshops, mosques and cloisters, bazaars, and private houses were the traditional places of gathering of the "intelligentsia." A notable addition in this period is the coffeehouse.[32] Public spaces—from the vast main city square, the *Maidān-i Naqsh-i Jahān*, with its varied functions, to the verdant and recreational *Chahār Bāgh* promenade, to the interior liveliness of numerous coffeehouses—were integral features of the urban renewal of Isfahan in her transformation into a capital city. European travelers vividly describe the coffeehouses as large, airy spaces with a water basin at the center of rows of seats where people gathered to meet and to seek entertainment.[33] Poets, professional storytellers, magicians, and even the clergy participated in both providing and enjoying the entertainment. Could artists' work have also been a regular feature of the "show"? The anecdote about Sādiqī Beg points in this direction. Additionally, Safavid biographical literature is peppered with references to the erotic liaisons of the poets and artists with the young boys who worked in the coffeehouses of Isfahan. In this light, the homoerotic themes of so many of the single-sheet paintings and drawings may in fact reflect the atmosphere of such "café culture."[34]

We can further probe the story about Sādiqī Beg for another sort of evidence. The way in which the artist cavalierly pulls some drawings from his coat pocket indicates more than his readiness to sell his works where there is a market. The exchange was of favors as well as of merchandise; the accolades showered on the artist by the poet prompted a response that could not only be measured quantitatively but also qualitatively. Sādiqī Beg's warning "not to sell them any cheaper" than the going price subtly evaluates his works as an equivalent in kind of the poet's panegyric. He hands over drawings on paper for a poem on paper, which he impatiently seizes out of the poet's hands. His air of arrogance notwithstanding, Sādiqī Beg's attitude with regard to the worth of a drawing is also evident in his claim, made in one of his literary works, that representational arts and painting (*fann-i taṣvīr va naqqāshī*) are the most difficult among all the arts.[35]

Extolling painting was not limited to a discourse on technical dexterity. Qāżī Aḥmad, historian of the late 16th century and author of *Gulistān-i hunar*, the celebrated treatise on Safavid calligraphers and painters, reiterates a 16th-century theory of two *qalams*, which elevates the brush of the painter to the level of the pen of the calligrapher.[36] Much scholarly wisdom has been devoted to the significance of the *qalam* (reed pen) and of writing as prime instruments for the transmission of the divine words.[37] The talisman of the written word, its divine inspiration, stems from the attribution of the invention of the pen to God and of the kufic script, the first Arabic writing style in which the Koran was recorded, to ʿAlī, the son-in-law of the prophet.[38] By virtue of its function as a mediator for the divine word and its association with the most venerated member of the prophet's family, the skill of writing invested the draftsman with a loftier spiritual and moral character than that which might be claimed by practitioners of the other arts. Relying on this well-established tradition in Islamic culture, and on the intense Shiʿite sentiments of his audience, Qāżī Aḥmad extends the mystical and magical properties of the reed pen to the brush by adding that ʿAlī himself had used the brush to decorate his writings with illuminations. By analogy, then, he equates the powers of the calligrapher with those of the painter.

Qāżī Aḥmad's theory and his entire treatise needs more contextualized analysis than is possible here.[39] And the two-pen paradigm was already creating a stir in the 16th-century writings of his contemporaries. Nevertheless, the practical effect of this elevation of the status of the brush and the painter finds its strongest echoes in the changed artistic landscape of late 16th- and 17th-century Iran. Paintings and drawings on loose leaves, signed or bearing an attribution to the artist, conceptually resemble the signed sample writings of the great calligraphers and appear with a frequency comparable to calligraphy but hitherto unknown for painting.

Good writing skills were moreover seen as evidence of a purity of soul and virtuosity of intellect capable of insights into complex mysteries which poetry could explore. Many calligraphers were noted poets and many poets crafted good writing.[40] Although calligraphers were not alone among artists and craftsmen to have composed poetry, nor was this a new phenomenon of the Safavid period, the painters' creative faculties were now explicitly associated with divinely guided inspirations emanating from ʿAlī, the axis of holiness.[41] These painters are perceived as "wizards of art," who could, through the brush, "ascend the throne of talent." The equation of the brush and the pen implicitly draws analogies between the painter's creativity and that of the poet. This is not to say that in the late 16th- and 17th-century Iran the distinctions were blurred. Rather, the painter's brush was recognized for its potential for rendering profound meanings analogous to what words alone had, until now, been thought to purvey.

The recognition of visual eloquence had a practical side effect. Signing paintings and drawings may have been occasioned by the broadening of the market or the heightened atmosphere of connoisseurship among the new patrons. But it also signals a latent confidence on the part of the painter. The repetition of standardized motifs and themes, so unflatteringly perceived in modern scholarship as the sign of the degeneration of meaning in Persian painting, may instead be interpreted as a logical extension of this confidence. As Farhad has demonstrated, while it may be true that the images are repeated, they also constitute a range of new genres of images. Invention, rather than convention, should be the operative concept here.

In the quest for crafting a distinctive cultural universe, a spirit of innovation underlined the Safavid ethos, as it did also that of the contemporary Ottoman and Mughal worlds in their early modern age.[42] In literary terms, the new style, generally known as *sabk-i Hindī*, characterized a poetic output that valued creative departures from tradition, and placed a high premium on novel images and styles. A similar creative fusion of traditional modes and new styles informs the visual world of the Safavids.[43] Many of the figural motifs in the loose sheets of painting and drawing appear at first to have been lifted out of the compositions that graced earlier illustrated manuscripts. But once removed from the context of the whole manuscript, the loose sheets are aggrandized as the main visual sign, in endlessly variegated combinations of narrative motifs, props, and settings, and the painter's work in single-sheet paintings and drawings signals a preoccupation in visual terms with that spirit of invention sought by the poets in this period. The painter quotes from and elaborates on his own work, his teacher's, or a recognized master's in the same vein as does the poet.

The analogy between the poet and the painter manifests itself also in the microcosm of the Persian artist's marks on the work of art which began to appear with greater frequency, and specificity of content, from late 16th century onwards. What shall concern us, however, is not the taxonomy of the signature, or the basic facts of date, place, and sitter, but the notations about how the painting or drawing was made.[44] In paintings and drawings from this period, it is not uncommon to find inscriptions that specify the place of a work's execution. To note that the work was done in the painter's house, at the court, or the house of a physician or high-ranking government official says much about the mobility of the artist and the broadening of his market.[45] But to name the person for whom the work was made and to add the exact day of the month and the year, which also occurs repeatedly, signals the importance of the timing of the work's execution.

In a humorous rendition of a pilgrim in Mashhad, now in the Freer Gallery of Art, for example, the artist notes that he drew this work in the "company of friends" and especially for a certain Mīrzā Khwājigī.[46] In style, the drawing exhibits the kind of spontaneity that may be associated with a quick dash of the brush to capture a fleeting moment. Other drawings with no hint of the presence of the subject, are accompanied with notes indicating that they were made in some alley or shop.[47] Whatever the particular circumstances surrounding each case, these works share with more elaborately finished drawings and paintings the implied presence of observers, be they sons, friends, colleagues, or patrons.[48] It has already been observed that, in the wake of diminishing royal patronage, economic factors necessitated the replacement of the costly and time-consuming practices of manuscript illustration for the more affordable single or paired figures, simply drawn or tinted. In light of the analogies I have drawn here between the painter and the poet, it may also be possible to read in the single-sheet works allusions to practices which were common in this period among poets.

Although not unique in the larger context of poetry, two points are particularly relevant in this consideration of the visual arts: one is the notion of creative imitation, the other is the ability to compose extemporaneously.[49] Biographies of poets (*tazkara*) of the 17th century are replete with praises especially reserved for the poet who eloquently imitated the masters and injected new meanings into established conventions. Another category of special praise is for the poet who could compose in the presence of others without premeditation. In one example, the poet is Khwāja Ghīyās, the most famous textile designer of the time.[50] Sādiqī Beg, author of this biography, notes that the artist could compose hundreds of verses in a row with such ease that the audience did not realize they were the product of improvisation.[51] Naṣrābādī, whose *Tazkara* is among the richest of our sources on these multitalented practitioners of the arts, recalls the poetic dexterity of a certain Sarājā, whom he portrays mainly as a painter, but who nonetheless composed poetry imitating both the old and the new styles and furthermore was able to do so extemporaneously.[52]

These references pertain to poetry but might they not also indicate similar evaluations of and circumstances for the painter's art? A motif such as the old man leaning on a stick derives from a well-known figural type popularized by the great Persian master Bihzād.[53] Lifted out of its narrative context of an illustrated manuscript, the later Safavid artist relies on the master's license to invent infinite variations on both the formal and the iconographic bearing of the motif. Alone or in unison with other such equally novel forms, pictures can be improvised to assemble non-verbal clues capable of conjuring up a wide range of mental images comparable to those of poetry. His status now exalted and the powers of his brush sanctioned, the artist is enabled to produce with confidence and spontaneity before an audience and for a specific occasion. Although there is no equivalent for the painter of the evidence we have for the poet's display of his craft, in the atmosphere of democratized access to the arts, the artist, one imagines, joins the literati and the cultured in performing in the arena of the public space provided by the coffeehouses. Like poetry of the time, the repetitions in form, a characteristic of these single-sheet paintings and drawings, may be seen as recitations, in silence, of novel twists in the use of established idioms.

Reassembling the threads woven in this study helps to forge a picture that, far from contradicting what others have formulated, enhances, I should hope, our understanding of the social and aesthetic function of these single-sheet paintings and drawings. Altogether the evidence suggests an integrative experience of these works which occasioned a complex sensory engagement of the receptor, one in which the image is not only seen but is also made audible by virtue of its potential for engendering diverse linguistic responses. Our cultural distance may necessitate a systematic reading of the texts in order to read the images. But we should not lose sight of the fact that, when isolated, the picture too can speak. Released from the literary demands of a classical text, the detached image facilitated access to a body of interwoven textual and visual material which could be [re-]produced for and transmitted to a broader audience.

An informed audience could, moreover, re-imagine the shared precepts through any of the sensory or mental cues provided by the work of art even without the text.

Notes

1. In *Iconology: Image, Text, Ideology* (Chicago and London: University of Chicago Press, 1987), p. 154, W.J.T. Mitchell advocates such attempts as one remedy to disentangle the text-image border skirmishes. His theoretical framework underlies my thinking in this essay. The list of studies devoted to the text-and-image problem is too long for this space; for further bibliographies see Mitchell, *Iconology*, and ibidem, *Picture Theory: Essays on Verbal and Visual Representation* (Chicago: University of Chicago Press, 1994).
2. For a brilliant and expansive discussion of the subject in Islamic art in general, see Oleg Grabar, *The Mediation of Ornament* (Princeton: Princeton University Press, 1992).
3. Even so, in Persian studies, the illustrative and the literary have remained disjointed in most analyses of Persian manuscripts. For an integrated and interpretive study see the monumental work of Marianna Shreve Simpson, *Sultan Ibrahim Mirza's* Haft Awrang. *A Princely Manuscript from Sixteenth-Century Iran*, Freer Gallery of Art, Smithsonian Institution, Washington, D.C. (New Haven and London: Yale University Press, 1997). See also Oleg Grabar and Sheila Blair, *Epic Images and Contemporary History: The Illustrations of the Great Mongol Shahnama* (Chicago: University of Chicago Press, 1980); and Robert Hillenbrand, "The Iconography of the *Shāhnāma-yi Shāhī*" in *Safavid Persia. The History and Politics of an Islamic Society*, ed. Charles Melville (London and New York: I.B. Tauris, 1996), pp. 53–78.
4. Lisa Golombek, "Toward a Classification of Islamic Painting," in *Islamic Art in the Metropolitan Museum of Art*, ed. Richard Ettinghausen (New York: The Museum, 1972), pp. 23–34, summarizes the different characteristics of Persian painting into an illustrative mode, as in manuscript painting, and an aesthetic mode, as in single-sheet paintings. In the latter mode, painting is not intended to edify or communicate a lofty idea but to visually enchant. Golombek's attempt to make sense out of these paintings, however, has not prevented much thinly disguised dismissals of single-sheet paintings as frivolities in paint.
5. Massumeh Farhad, "Safavid single page painting, 1629–1666" (Ph.D. diss.,

Harvard University, 1987), successfully lifts the art historical curse on these later Persian paintings.

6. Farhad, "Safavid single page painting," p. 267. See also pp. 217–268 for a discussion of the figural types and themes and their meaning. In an unpublished paper delivered at the Institute of Fine Arts, NYU, in 1996, she further suggested that such images could be seen as poems in pictures. My analysis below parallels this idea and attempts to show how the images may have behaved like linguistic signs.
7. Marianna Shreve Simpson has persuasively argued for an interface between the pictorial programs on medieval Islamic objects and a literary corpus that was accessible to the patrons and users of such objects. The objects in her study however are not embellished with texts. Rather they evoke a literary world that existed outside their visual domain; see "Narrative Allusion and Metaphor in the Decoration of Medieval Islamic Objects," in *Pictorial Narrative in Antiquity and the Middle Ages*, ed. Herbert L. Kessler and Marianna Shreve Simpson (Washington, D.C.: National Gallery of Art, 1985), pp. 131–149.
8. Sussan Babaie, "Epigraphy iv. Safavid and Later Inscriptions," *Encyclopaedia Iranica* VIII, pp. 498–504. Among the changes, one of the most significant is that Persian poetry and pious Shiʿite texts replace with greater frequency the Arabic inscriptions favored in the previous era. This reflects not only the Shiʿite militancy of the Safavid dynasty but also a systematic Persianization of the state apparatus and its culture.
9. Several examples are discussed in Babaie, "Epigraphy."
10. The bowl, of cast and raised copper, is published and analyzed by Souren Melikian-Chirvani, *Islamic Metalwork from the Iranian World, 8–18th centuries* (London: Her Majesty's Stationery Office, 1982), pp. 329–330. He considers this bowl's decoration to be radically different from the late 16th- and early 17th-century Iranian metalwork. This may be so, but as we shall see its aesthetic is not exceptional in the artistic milieu of the period.
11. Majnūn's journey stands as a mystical metaphor for man's spiritual journey through life; *Encyclopaedia of Islam*, new ed., s.v. "Madjnūn Laylā."
12. For examples and a discussion of the Timurid (15th c.) objects see, Linda Komaroff, *The Golden Disk of Heaven. Metalwork of Timurid Iran* (Costa Mesa, CA and New York: Mazda, 1992), esp. pp. 60–66.
13. Published in Marie Lukens Swietochowski and Sussan Babaie, *Persian Drawings in the Metropolitan Museum of Art* (New York: The Museum, 1989), pp. 74–75.
14. Sheila R. Canby, *The Rebellious Reformer; The Drawings and Paintings of Riza-yi ʿAbbasi of Isfahan* (London: Azimuth Editions, 1996), p. 209, has

rejected this attribution on stylistic grounds but the point does not affect my reading of the page.

15. On such albums and the production of albums in general, see S. C. Welch, A. Schimmel, M. L. Swietochowski, and W. M. Thackston, *The Emperor's Album: Images of Mughal India* (New York: Metropolitan Museum of Art, 1987) and David Roxburgh, "'Our Works Point to Us': Album Making, Collecting, and Art (1427–1565) under the Timurids and Safavids" (Ph.D. diss., University of Pennsylvania, 1996).

16. I have been guilty of the same sin in my essay on the "The Old Man and the Youth" in Swietochowski and Babaie, *Persian Drawings*, p. 74. At the time, I argued for the scene to represent a homosexual liaison by comparing this painting with similar examples. To further justify my "reading" I had linked the image to one with a similar iconography from a manuscript illustration where the text and image were not assembled as in these single-sheet works. Canby's separation of the two images as "Page Walking Looking Back" and "Old Man Leaning on a Long Stick" implies a reading of each as discrete pieces even though the two drawings are in fact on identical paper and with identical signs of wear; see *The Rebellious Reformer*, p. 209.

17. For Islamic mysticism in general see, Annemarie Schimmel, *Mystical Dimensions of Islam* (Chapel Hill, N.C.: University of North Carolina Press, 1975); for the mystical path and fraternal unions of piety in Safavid Iran see, Kathryn Babayan, *Mystics, Monarchs and Messiahs: The Spiritual Landscape of the Qizilbash in Early Modern Iran*, forthcoming.

18. Dick Davis, trans. and intro. *Borrowed Ware: Medieval Persian Epigrams* (Washington, D.C.: Mage, 1997), p. 21.

19. Bibliothèque Nationale, Paris, MS. Suppl. Pers. 1171, folio 29a. For an illustration of the full page see Ivan Stchoukine, *Les Peintures des Manuscrits de Shah ʿAbbas Ier à la Fin des Safavis* (Paris: P. Guenthner, 1964), plate xxxiv. Canby, *The Rebellious Reformer*, p. 90, distinguishes the style of the two drawings as works of different artists: the old man, by Riżā and the youth by Sādiqī Beg (more on him later), both dateable to the first quarter of the 17th century.

20. Published as an authentic work of the artist by Canby, *The Rebellious Reformer*, pp. 174–176, and cat. 128.

21. A similar image-within-the-image conceit is found in another painting by the artist; in this case the theme is of heterosexual love. See Canby, *The Rebellious Reformer*, p. 166.

22. Canby's reading and translation of the distich, "Bare from head to toe, my passion pursues a foreigner [*farangī*] in that empire of youths [*ghulams*]," is mistaken; *The Rebellious Reformer*, p. 200.

23. Allusions to *farangī* and foreignness, a novel feature in the arts of 17th-century Iran, are also found in the contemporary Persian poetry; for examples see, Muḥammad Ṭāhir Naṣrābṣdī, *Tazkara-yi Naṣrābādī*, ed. Vaḥīd Dastgirdī (Tehran: Kitābfurūshī-i Furūghī, 1361/1982), pp. 111, 133, 300, 368, 384. The European presence in Safavid Iran in this period and its impact on the arts have been extensively studied. What remains to be seen is the ways in which such "otherness" may have been sublimated in the arts and literature of this period.
24. Canby, *The Rebellious Reformer*, p. 176.
25. Mitchell, *Iconology*, p. 43.
26. Naṣrābādī, *Tazkara-yi Naṣrābādī*, pp. 39–40. Naṣrābādī quotes Mullā Ghurūrī whom he considered to be a respectable poet and a reliable source. Translation is by Anthony Welch, *Artists for the Shah: Late Sixteenth-Century Painting at the Imperial Court of Iran* (New Haven and London: Yale University Press, 1976), pp. 186–187.
27. Farhad, "Safavid single page painting," p. 255–256; Anthony Welch, "Painting and Patronage under Shah ʿAbbas I," in "Studies on Isfahan," pt. 2, *Iranian Studies* 7, nos. 3–4 (1974), pp. 458–507, esp. pp. 489–490.
28. The evidence of a shift in emphasis dictates my focus on this period and place but, as is true in all historical changes, transformations had begun earlier in the 16th century and continue to affect the following periods. For the Safavid transformations see, R. M. Savory, "The Safavid Administrative System," in Peter Jackson and Laurence Lockhart, eds., *The Cambridge History of Iran* vol. 6, *The Timurid and Safavid Periods* (Cambridge: Cambridge University Press, 1986), pp. 351–369, and Kathryn Babayan, "The Waning of the Qizilbash: The Spiritual and the Temporal in Seventeenth Century Iran" (Ph.D. diss., Princeton University, 1993). Sussan Babaie, "Safavid Palaces at Isfahan: Continuity and Change (1590–1666)," (Ph.D. diss., New York University, 1994) discusses the changes as pertain to palace architecture.
29. The literature is vast and still growing. Jackson and Lockhart, eds., *The Cambridge History of Iran* vol. 6, *The Timurid and Safavid Periods* surveys various facets of Safavid Isfahan. Recent "Safavid Roundtables" have yielded two volumes of articles on a wide range of subjects: Jean Calmard, ed., *Études Safavides* (Paris, 1993) and Melville, ed., *Safavid Persia* Institut Français de Recherches en Iran and Tehran: (London and New York: I. B. Taurus & Co., 1996). A third volume edited by Andrew Newman is forthcoming.
30. The altered circumstances of patronage, from royal to a broader clientele, for the arts in the 17th century has been noted and discussed in a negative light

by Anthony Welch, *Shah ʿAbbas and the Arts of Isfahan* (New York: The Asia Society, 1973), pp. 19–21, and as a positive factor in Farhad, "Safavid single page painting," pp. 251 ff. For royal workshop system in Safavid Iran, see M. S. Simpson, "The Making of Manuscripts and the Workings of the *Kitab-Khana* in Safavid Iran," in *The Artist's Workshop*, ed. Peter M. Lukehart (Washington, D.C.: National Gallery of Art, 1993), pp. 105–121.

31. On the cultural role of a newly-empowered class in Isfahan, see Sussan Babaie, Kathryn Babayan, Ina Baghdiantz-McCabe, and Massumeh Farhad, *Slaves of the Shah: New Elites of Safavid Iran* (London and New York: I. B. Tauris, forthcoming 2002).
32. The coffeehouses were included in Shah ʿAbbās' initial plan for the city; see R. D. McChesney, "Four Sources on Shah ʿAbbās' Building of Isfahan," in *Muqarnas* 5 (1988), pp. 109 and 113. An informative study on the coffeehouses is Rudi Matthee, "Coffee in Safavid Iran: Commerce and Consumption," in *Journal of the Economic and Social History of the Orient* XXXVII (1994), pp. 1–32.
33. See Matthee for references and the relevant passages from these sources; "Coffee in Safavid Iran," pp. 20–22.
34. Coffeehouse scene is described by European travelers and alluded to in Persian sources. For a European description, see Jean Baptise Tavernier, *Les Six Voyages du Jean Baptise Tavernier*, vol. 2, p. 132 (Amsterdam, 1679), 2 Vols. For the richest Persian source on the subject see, Naṣrābādī, *Tazkara*, pp. 48, 108, 143, and 388 among other places. Explicit representations of eroticism and homosexual love in particular are found in 17th-century Safavid painting in different media: on paper, on walls, and in lacquer. The preoccupation with and the celebration of homoeroticism, also evident in the contemporary poetry, needs elucidation.
35. This statement is found in his biography of a poet-painter-nobleman in his *Majmaʿ al-khavāṣ*, translated into Persian with introduction by A. R. Khayyāmpūr, (Tabriz: Chāpkhānah-i Akhtar-i Shumāl, 1948), p. 73. Sādiqī Beg's literary output is as varied and important as his paintings. An accomplished poet as well, he composed a romance and compiled several anthologies of his own poems. His *Qānūn al-ṣuvar-i naqqāshī*, a versified treatise on techniques of painting and his biographies of poets, *Majmaʿ al-khavāṣ*, in Chaqhatay Turkish are among the most important of his literary works. The latter publication also includes the treatise in Persian. For the treatise's English translation see, S. C. Welch and M. B. Dickson, *The Houghton Shah Nama* (Cambridge, Mass.: Published for the Fogg Art Museum, Harvard University, by Harvard University Press, 1981). Welch, *Artists for the Shah*, pp. 41–99, gives a detailed biography of the artist and a list of his literary

works, and discusses his art.

36. Qāżī Aḥmad, *Gulistān-i hunar*, ed. Aḥmad Suhailī Khwānsārī (Tehran: Kitābkhānah-i Manūchihrī, 1366/1987; 3rd ed.), pp. 8–10 on the two *qalams*. Also see idem. *Calligraphers and Painters: A Treatise by Qadi Ahmad, Son of Mir-Munshi*, trans. V. Minorsky (Washington, D.C.: Freer Gallery of Art, 1959).

37. See Annemarie Schimmel, *Calligraphy and Islamic Culture* (New York: New York University Press, 1984) for a mine of information on the practical and mystical aspects of writing; see also Grabar, *The Mediation of Ornament*, pp. 47–118.

38. Qāżī Aḥmad, *Gulistān-i hunar*, pp. 8–15 and 128–129 on the brush-pen comparison and the significance of Imam ʿAlī.

39. Minorsky's notes in *Calligraphers and Painters* and scattered references to the treatise remain unsatisfactory. Forthcoming articles by David Roxburgh, "The Pen of Depiction: Drawings of 15th and 16th Century Iran," *Harvard University Art Museums Bulletin* (Spring 2000) and by Yves Porter, "From the 'Theory of the Two Qalams' to the 'Seven Principles of Painting': Theory, Terminology, and Practice in Persian Classical Painting," in *Muqarnas* 17 (2000) shall significantly advance our understanding of Persian painting. For the problematic nature of the treatise as a historical document see, Massumeh Farhad and Marianna Shreve Simpson, "Sources for the Study of Safavid Painting and Patronage, or Méfiez-vous de Qazi Ahmad," in *Muqarnas* 10 (1993), pp. 286–291.

40. Examples abound in the biographies of poets and calligraphers. For calligraphers who also wrote poetry see, among others, Naṣrābādī, *Tazkara*, pp. 206–212; and p. 141, and p. 344 for poets who wrote well.

41. References to artists and artisans who also composed good poetry are numerous. For a few examples see, Naṣrābādī, *Tazkara*, p. 138 (architect-poet), p. 141 (painter-calligrapher-carver-poet), pp. 294, 296, 377 (painter-poets), p. 382 (potter-poet); and Sādiqī Beg, *Majmaʿ al-khavāṣ*, pp. 92, 97, 254 (painter-poets), and p. 239 (papermaker-illuminator-poet).

42. Gülru Necipoğlu, *The Topkapı Scroll—Geometry and Ornament in Islamic Architecture* (Santa Monica, CA: Getty Center for the History of Art and the Humanities, 1995), pp. 217–223, concludes her brilliant study of the sign systems in Timurid architecture with a general analysis of the aesthetic changes in the early modern empires. The phenomenon of innovation in Safavid literary criticism is explored by Paul Losensky, *Welcoming Fighānī: Imitation and Poetic Individuality in the Safavid-Mughal* Ghazal (Costa Mesa, CA: Mazda, 1998) esp. chapter 5, pp. 193 ff.

43. The artistic dimensions in the Safavid age await systematic analyses. My

preliminary attempt to venture in this direction was presented in a paper at the conference, "Inscription as Art in the World of Islam," Hofstra University, April, 1996.

44. For an interesting example of the artist's notations in this period see, Massumeh Farhad, "An Artist's Impression: Muʿin Musavvir's *Tiger Attacking A Youth*," in *Muqarnas* 9 (1992), pp. 116–123. In this same article Farhad notes, however, that inscriptions on Safavid paintings and drawings of the 17th century tend to offer standardized basic facts. As we shall see, more can be extracted from these apparently formulaic bits of information.

45. Farhad in "Safavid single page painting," and Canby in *The Rebellious Reformer*, among others, have dealt extensively with this issue.

46. The drawing is attributed to Riżā ʿAbbāsī and published most recently by Canby, *The Rebellious Reformer*, pp. 56 and 183, cat. 26.

47. Such specifications are found on two drawings signed by Muʿin Musavvir. The subjects, a woman and a couple, could hardly be actual portraits. Farhad, "Safavid single page painting," pp. 326–327.

48. The "Young Portuguese," discussed above, is one such example in which, however, the name of the patron has been erased. Others may be found in Farhad, "Safavid single page painting," pp. 323–333, and Canby, *The Rebellious Reformer*, p. 195, cat. 94.

49. Losensky, *Welcoming Fighānī*, pp. 100–114, discusses varieties of intertextuality in the poetry of this period.

50. Sādiqī Beg, *Majmaʿ al-khavāṣ*, p. 187.

51. An added imagery here is the analogy between the weaving technique and poetry; see J. W. Clinton, "Image and Metaphor: Textiles in Persian Poetry," in C. Bier, ed., *Woven from the Soul, Spun from the Heart: Textile Arts of Safavid and Qajar Iran, 16th–19th Centuries* (Washington, D.C.: Textile Museum, 1987), pp. 7–11.

52. Naṣrābādī's *Tazkara*, p. 139.

53. For two examples among many, see Thomas W. Lenz and Glenn D. Lowry, *Timur and the Princely Vision: Persian Art and Culture in the Fifteenth Century* (Washington, D.C. and Los Angeles: Los Angeles County Museum of Art, 1989), p. 283, cat. no. 140 and p. 289, cat. no. 147.